See You at the Hall

See You at the
Hall

*Boston's Golden Era of
Irish Music and Dance*

Susan Gedutis
with a foreword by Mick Moloney

NORTHEASTERN UNIVERSITY PRESS
Boston

Published by University Press of New England
Hanover and London

NORTHEASTERN UNIVERSITY PRESS

Published by University Press of New England,
One Court Street, Lebanon, NH 03766
www.upne.com

First Northeastern University Press/UPNE paperback edition 2005

Printed in the United States of America   5   4   3   2   1

ISBNs for the paperback edition:
ISBN-13: 9781555536404
ISBN-10: 1-55553-640-9

Library of Congress Cataloging-in-Publication Data
Gedutis, Susan
See you at the hall : Boston's golden era of Irish music and dance /
Susan Gedutis ; with a foreword by Mick Moloney.
p.   cm.
Includes bibliographical references (p.   ), discography (p.   ), and index.
ISBN 1-55553-610-7 (cloth : alk. paper)
1. Irish-Americans—Massachusetts—Boston—Music—20th century—History and
criticism. 2. Dance music—Massachusetts—Boston—20th century—History and
criticism. 3. Dance music—Ireland—20th century—History and criticism.
4. Dance halls—Massachusetts—Boston. I. Title.
ML3554G44 2004
781.62'9162074461—dc22   2004001099

Dedicated to the Memory of Leonard Sealey
May 7, 1923–August 5, 2003
Educator, author, inventor, artist, and inspiration.
Thank you, Leonard.

Acknowledgments

I feel very fortunate to have been so warmly welcomed into the kitchens and sitting rooms of the people I interviewed for this book. Every visit yielded a new friend, and without exception I left positively glowing from people's openness and generosity. None of this history has previously been written down in book form, and this volume very literally would not have been possible without the help of all whose stories make it up. In particular, I thank Joe Derrane for piquing my interest in Dudley Street, and Frank Storer for first telling me to write the book. Many thanks also to Frank, as well as Paddy Noonan, Mickey Connolly, Janice Kleinbauer, Larry Reynolds, Joe and Karin Joyce, Michael Cummings, Dick Senier, and Terry Landers for the generous loan of photos. Reviewers Thomas O'Connor, Boston College university historian, and Michael Quinlin of the Boston Irish Tourism Association provided critical insight that helped to shape the final manuscript. I extend very special thanks to Michael and Noreen Cummings. Despite the fact that Mike was homebound with Lou Gehrig's disease, he was clear-thinking and eager to help me.

I am deeply grateful to a long list of people whose help and support ensured both my short-term and long-term sanity. Initial support and encouragement for the project came from my mentor and advisor at Tufts University, Dr. Tomie Hahn. Senior Editor John Weingartner first championed the book at Northeastern University Press, and his successor, Robert Gormley, ushered the manuscript to production with wisdom and warmth. Production Director Ann Twombly expertly managed its journey to finished product, and David Reich copyedited the book with clarity and precision. I thank also Dr. Jane Bernstein, of Tufts University, for her vision; Beth Sweeney of the Irish Music Archives of the John J. Burns Library at Boston College; Nancy Sealey, whose kindness, love, and understanding seem to know no bounds; Dana Slawsky, lifelong friend and an editor and a half (and, of course, Mark Wixted for brilliant contributions at critical moments); Debbie Cavalier for unerring support and flexibility; Maureen Hurley for getting me through the second draft; Lorna Flanagan for proving once and for all that the Liths can hold their own among the Irish, by poring through five hundred pages of interviews to research the catalog of musicians found in the appendix; Jil McMahon for her willingness to help; Deb Maher for input and help with research; Paul Mulvaney for giving me the tunes and the flute, and first telling me about Dudley Street; Dan Reidy for dogged determination and wisecracks disguised as research assistance; Peg Reidy's sharp eyes and beef stew (I'm not sure which I appreciate more); and friends and family who patiently accepted yet another rain check. Through it all, Stephen Lindsay was my rock. His love, patience, and support exceed all logical expectations.

Finally, I send deep gratitude in advance to that person out there whom I forgot to thank—I know you're out there. I owe you one. See you at the bar.

Contents

Illustrations

Foreword

The phenomenon of Irish dance halls in America began in the early twentieth century with the ballroom dancing craze that swept the United States. By this stage there were more than three million Irish-born immigrants in America; there were many million more descendants of the great waves of Irish men and women who left Ireland to build a new life across the Atlantic in the decades after the famine. A great number of these immigrants had settled in urban America and established the communities that gained such a secure foothold in all walks of American life by the end of the nineteenth century. By then the Irish in America had moved from being a marginal group, discriminated against and feared by an Anglo-Protestant establishment, to a position of relative security in American social, economic, and political life. When the dance hall craze hit urban America, the Irish were willing and able participants.

For the next half century the Irish dance hall in urban America became a very important social institution for the immigrant Irish. It was here that the newly arrived immigrant was introduced to the community. In the dance halls friendships were made, networks were established between native born and immigrant, courtships took place, and future marriage partners were met.

Social dancing meant many things to the new immigrants and to young Americans of Irish ancestry. Most important, it represented an opportunity for a very American statement of personal liberation whereby young people could select their own life partners without the kind of Old World social strictures previously imposed by family and community. This development was quite revolutionary when viewed in the context of a deeply conservative post-famine Irish society in which arranged marriages had been the norm for great numbers of rural people for decades.

In America young immigrants could defiantly assert their right to choose their own partners in romance and marriage and they did so freely. However, many chose to do so within the confines of the dance hall, where one was of course sure to meet potential partners from a similar cultural background. So, in addition to furthering the cause of individual liberation, the dance hall was also an institution that encouraged social and cultural continuity in the Irish and Irish-American community.

Nobody has conducted a detailed study of this seminal chapter in the story of twentieth-century Irish America until now. Susan Gedutis has written a wonderfully engaging, highly intensive study of the Irish dance hall scene in one city famed for its Irish immigrant and ethnic population. It is a richly detailed historical ethnography of the Irish dance halls on Dudley Street in the Roxbury area of Boston, a scene that flourished in the late 1940s and throughout the 1950s, at the tail end of the era of Irish-American dance halls. Much of her study is based on primary research that she meticulously carried out with musicians who played through the Dudley Street Irish dance hall era, as well as with a wide range of the men and women who danced in these ballrooms—places such as the Hibernian, the Intercolonial, the Dudley Street Opera House, the Rose Croix, and Winslow Hall. She tells the story of the bands that played the native and hybrid dance music in the Boston area, ensembles with colorful names like Dan Sullivan's Shamrock Band, O'Leary's Irish Minstrels, Mattie Tuohey's Irish Minstrels, and Johnny Powell's Irish Band. The very mention of these names evokes deep nostalgia for thousands of people in the Boston area who spent countless enjoyable hours listening and dancing to their music. Gedutis furnishes information on the various kinds of group and couple dances that were popular and on the music and how it was learned, selected, and performed in the dance halls—as well as at other social occasions such as weddings and "kitchen rackets."

The Dudley Street dance hall scene emerges as a study in the negotiation between tradition and modernity, between the cultural norms of the Old World and those of the new world, where hybrid, acculturated values and ideas often displaced the immigrant culture—but never entirely. The study is placed deftly in a sociohistorical context that examines changes in immigration patterns, demographics, and social tastes. This beautifully written book is a major contribution to the study and understanding of Irish-American urban culture at a pivotal era of transition and change.

MICK MOLONEY

New York, September 2003

Preface

In October 1999, I attended a lecture in Watertown, Massachusetts, by the legendary Boston accordion player Joe Derrane. Derrane ignited my imagination with colorful stories of Dudley Street, the locus of a great era of Irish music in Boston in the first half of the twentieth century. He spoke of Irish dance halls so packed you could hardly move. He spoke of widows, waltzes, and weddings, and gigs so plentiful that he made more money playing accordion than he did as a shipping and receiving clerk in Boston's leather district. He spoke of accordions, fiddles, and flutes but also saxophones, drum sets, and trumpets—instruments that nowadays could get you sent packing from any "traditional" Irish session. I was transfixed. It was as if I, a saxophone player who'd just recently taken up the traditional Irish flute, had just discovered that my favorite old chair was a priceless antique. The seeds were planted.

I had heard people reminisce about the Dudley Street dance halls since I had begun to play the Irish flute a year before, but I had never encountered any detailed history of the era—because there is no such thing. Memories of Dudley Street are not written down but rather stay vividly in the minds of the senior generation of musicians in Boston.

To research this book, I spoke with both Irish nationals and Irish-Americans. Boston and its environs are so chock-full of Irish and Irish-American people that a casual mention of the book to my bus driver once turned my morning commute into a spontaneous and fruitful interview. I even discovered that the security guard in the research department of the

Boston Public Library had regularly danced at the Hibernian Hall, one of the largest and most popular of the Dudley Street dance halls. The further I got into the book, the more important it became to have my notebook handy at all times.

The content of this book was developed from interviews. My deepest regret is the underrepresentation in this book of those musicians who have passed on. Influential musicians such as Gene Preston, Billy Caples, Tom Senier, and Jimmy Kelly were talented, beloved characters on the postwar dance hall scene, and we can take solace in knowing that they are happily playing their flutes, accordions, and banjos in the Big Dance Hall in the Sky. These musicians gave much to the Boston Irish music scene, and while I don't tell their stories in the same depth as those of their still-active contemporaries, their contributions are no less vital. (The catalog of musicians at the end of this book honors musicians who were part of Boston's Irish traditional music scene from the 1930s through the 1960s.)

It isn't just musicians who have kept Irish music alive in Boston for fifty years. Music has set the tempo for Irish social life, from public political rallies and parades to private housewarming "kitchen rackets." Those who "made" Irish music were nannies for wealthy Boston Brahmins and machine operators at the rubber mill. They brought you your fish chowder. They climbed the light poles to replace the bulbs. They built the plasterboard ranch houses and curvy suburban streets that envelop Boston like the batter on a sausage roll.

Three thousand miles, a thousand people, a thousand experiences, yet one thing is constant: all remember the Dudley Street dance hall days as a heyday for the Irish in Boston. While waves of immigration have brought superior musicians to and from Boston for years, and Irish traditional music has come into and gone out of vogue, the people who share their stories here have kept the flame burning steadily all along. They are the reason Irish music—in all its forms—prospers in Boston today. The people I interviewed for this book were generous with their knowledge, their time, and their memories. It is my honor to present their stories.

Note: Some names in this book have been changed to honor the privacy of the persons involved.

The Band Played On

Matt Casey formed a social club that beat the town for style
And hired for a meeting place a hall
When payday came around each week they greased the floor with wax
And danced with noise and vigor at the ball.
Each Saturday you'd see them dressed up in Sunday clothes;
Each lad would have his sweetheart by his side.
When Casey led the first grand march they all would fall in line,
Behind the man who was her joy and pride—for

Chorus
Casey would waltz with a strawberry blonde and the band played on
He'd glide across the floor with the girl he ador'd and the band played on
But his brain was so loaded it nearly exploded
The poor girl would shake with alarm.
He married the girl with the strawberry curls
And the band played on.

Such kissing in the corner and such whisp'ring in the hall
And telling tales of love behind the stairs.
As Casey was the favorite and he that ran the hall,
Of kissing and lovemaking did his share.
At twelve o'clock exactly they all would fall in line
Then march down to the dining hall and eat.
But Casey would not join them although everything was fine
But he stayed upstairs and exercised his feet

Chorus

Now when the dance was over and the band played "Home, Sweet Home"
They played a tune at Casey's own request.
He thanked them very kindly for the favors they had shown,
Then he'd waltz once with the girl that he loved best.
Most all the friends were married that Casey used to know
And Casey too has taken him a wife.
The blonde he used to waltz and glide with on the ballroom floor
Is happy Mrs. Casey now for life.

Chorus

—John F. Palmer, 1895

Introduction

Next Stop: Dudley Station

Thursday night, Boston, 1949. Evelyn Degan rushes home from the John Hancock Insurance Company's building in the heart of Boston's Back Bay, where she has worked as an insurance clerk since she came out from Ireland a year before. As quickly as she can, she pins her hair back, changes into her dancing dress, and meets her cousin Annie Haley. They board the trolley from Somerville for the hourlong journey to Roxbury's Dudley Square, eight miles away on the other side of the city. It's the highlight of their week and a warm-up for the weekend—"maid's night out," as it's called. Evelyn isn't a maid, and neither is Annie, but a lot of the girls coming out from Ireland these days are, and anyway, the Intercolonial Hall will be packed to the rafters.

From the Dudley Street station, it's just a short walk to the Intercolonial, the largest dance hall in the square. Evelyn and Annie arrive just before eight o'clock. The doorman winks as he takes their fifty-cent admission fee, and they fly up the two flights of a wide staircase that climbs to a large hall. There, women in lipstick and crinoline petticoats sit like truffles on the long benches along one side of the hall. Men with Brylcreem in their hair, wearing crisply pressed jackets, ties, and trousers stand in small groups on the other.

Onstage, Johnny Powell's band starts the first waltz, "The Snowy Breasted Pearl," at eight o'clock sharp. A young man, fortified by a draught from the barroom downstairs, takes the first bold steps across the wooden expanse to ask a girl to dance. Another follows his lead, and another, and another. Within a half hour, Evelyn finds herself caught in the flow of hundreds of couples gliding across the floor. Above, a crystal ball slowly spins, shedding spots of dim light that gently propel the wave of dancers counterclockwise around the room. By eleven o'clock, you either must dance or get out of the way. If you stand still, you'll be bowled over by the passing waves of dancers.

On the stage at the front of the hall, a band of ten or more musicians is playing a set of jigs, with a young accordion player, elbows and hair flying, sitting front and center. He's only about nineteen years old, a young lad to be leading the tunes onstage. Around him sit another accordion player, a few fiddlers, a saxophone, a banjo, a piano, and a drummer keeping time on a woodblock and snare. Around ten o'clock, the accordion player nods imperceptibly to the pianist, and the band tears into the Siege of Ennis, a popular group dance that, when timed right, always gets the floor shaking.

In the 1940s and 1950s, Dudley Square on a Saturday night was like the heart of any Irish city. Thousands of Irish and Irish-American people from miles around would take the "el"—the elevated trolley—to the dance halls that dotted the crossroads of Winslow, Dudley, and Warren Streets: the Intercolonial, the Hibernian, Winslow Hall, the Dudley Street Opera House, and the Rose Croix. At the dance halls, you could find couples spinning across the floor to a fox-trot, reel, set dance, waltz, schottische, or highland fling, while off to the side, lovers met, old friends reunited, and businessmen cut deals.

Three thousand miles from home, Irish immigrants sought familiar faces, or at least people with familiar values, accents, and worldviews. For the newly arrived from Ireland, it was a critical first stop. You might meet someone who'd give you a dance. You might meet someone who could give you a job. If you visited the dance halls a few weeks in a row, you were *bound* to meet someone from your hometown.

It didn't matter what time of year it was; in the evening, the streets of Dudley Square were always packed. On the sidewalks, at the train station, in pubs like the Emerald Café, Pat Lynch's, Greeley's Roxbury Grille, or Joe McPherson's Greenville Café, young men and women congregated on their way to the dance halls, while a few straggler musicians rushed by on their way to the halls from wedding gigs. Over the click-clack of high heels on pavement, the careful listener could pick out accents from all over Ireland—the singsong rhythm of Cork, the flat tones of Tipperary, the country inflections of Galway and Kerry, the Donegal people who always sounded as though they were asking a question even if they were telling you a tale. Above it all, the lively lilt of an accordion would spring out of a third-floor window. A saxophone, fiddle, guitar, and drums played an Irish jig or reel amid laughter and the shuffle of hundreds of dancing feet.

For the thousands of young Irish people who flooded Boston in the years following World War II—not to mention the American-born Irish whose parents had immigrated a generation before—Dudley Square was where it all happened. It was an Ireland within America. Many called it "the American capital of Galway." Three thousand miles away from Ireland, in a part of the Boston metropolitan area known as Roxbury, it was the center of the city's Irish cultural life.

The dance halls were filled with music Wednesday through Sunday evenings, for nearly three decades. Thursday and Saturday were the big nights, when thousands of Irish and Irish-Americans crowded into the five ballrooms in this four-block area known as Dudley Square, or "Dudley Street." Boston's dance hall era reached its height well after the golden eras of Irish dance music in New York and Chicago had passed, earlier in the century. But a huge postwar influx of Irish immigrants into Boston brought Irish music from the firesides of isolated homes and parish-sponsored céilí dance halls in rural Ireland directly to the ballrooms of urban Roxbury, a predominantly Irish neighborhood during the first part of the twentieth century.

Many familiar with the Dudley Square area today are shocked to hear that Irish traditional music—an instrumental dance music—thrived in Roxbury, now a black and Latino neighborhood. Roxbury underwent a complete change from white to black in the 1950s and 1960s. With the change, it seemed that city government, in tandem with the financial and real estate industries, had completely abandoned the area, leaving new residents to fend for themselves. It was not long before Dudley Square was making national headlines for its sky-high crime rates, extreme poverty, and advanced deterioration. Today, Dudley Square residents are struggling to renew and rebuild the area into a thriving, vital community with colorful cultural celebrations, music, and dance of its own.

Dudley Square at its former height also was home to a number of Irish and Canadian bars, and was one of New England's largest shopping districts, second only to downtown Boston. Nearby were Ferdinand's Blue Store, which sold furniture, Blair's Market, Hovey's, Dutton's, and Thom McCann, as well as the Rivoli Theater, the fire station, the Boston Edison Electric Company, and the office of the local draft board—a too-familiar sight as America moved from World War II into the Korean War. Also close by was the Waldorf, a popular after-hours café, located directly under the Winslow Hall, where you could get the city's best apple pie and ice cream before the trolley ride home. Just around the corner from Dudley Station was the O'Byrne DeWitt record shop and travel agency, where you could book travel to Ireland, purchase Irish, classical, or popular recordings, buy an accordion, saxophone, or drum set, and take music lessons.

Today, ask any member of the older generation of Irish Bostonians about Dudley Square, and you will hear them wax nostalgic: "Those were great days. Great days." Dudley Square was just a short trolley ride from Irish communities in South Boston and Dorchester, but many young women also traveled on foot, by bus, and on the el for more than two hours from stately homes in wealthy suburbs such as Cambridge, Newton, and Belmont, where so many were employed in domestic service after World War II. What brought them to Dudley Square in such numbers? Why has there been nothing like it before or since?

First and foremost, most new immigrants who came to America in the 1940s and 1950s were unmarried. Alone, unattached, and young, they sought entertainment, and in the postwar boom they had money to spend. Most new arrivals found work easily. Long gone were the bad old days when the Irish had been forced to live together in tight quarters in waterfront shantytowns; by this era, they were drawn together by choice—by a longing for each other, and a longing for home. And home, for anyone of Irish descent, inevitably included music and dance.

It is not surprising that Irish music had such a hold on Boston crowds. Boston was a popular destination at which to disembark on the eight-day ocean voyage from Cobh Harbor in county Cork. The Irish had been coming to Boston nearly since the city was founded, in the seventeenth century, and by the mid-1950s, the city's Irish community was very large. Immigration laws at the time required that new immigrants be sponsored by a friend or relative in the United States who could guarantee that they would have a job and a place to live, so that they would not become a burden on the state. There seemed to be no shortage of sponsors, however; the Irish in Boston always looked after their own.

By the time the Boston-born Irish-American John Fitzgerald Kennedy began his ascent from local politician to become the first Catholic U.S. president, the Boston Irish had enjoyed nearly six decades of political leadership in the city. With the launching of a major urban redevelopment project and city government as green as the almighty dollar, there were plenty of jobs for young Irish men and women. For those in whom Irish blood ran thick, postwar Boston was an ideal place to be.

Ironically, in the 1940s, just as Irish music reached its height of popularity in Boston, the same music was being swept into a corner in Ireland in favor of more "modern" American and English sounds. But in Boston the music served as a source of pride, an up-tempo representation of who the Irish were, where they were from, and what they were to become. In fact, one young New York businessman, Justus O'Byrne DeWitt, foresaw such a burgeoning market for Irish music in Boston that he relocated his business there, establishing the headquarters of Copley Records, a record company devoted entirely to Irish music. Long after wartime shellac shortages had put an end to ethnic record markets elsewhere, Copley Records was making and selling hundreds of records by Irish musicians specifically for an Irish audience.

What Is Irish Music?

The phrase *Irish music* means as many things to as many people as you'd care to ask about it. There is the pure traditional instrumental music: plaintive airs, and lively reels and jigs for dancing, which you might hear today in any Irish pub where musicians gather to play Irish tunes in what is referred to as a "session." The same traditional jigs and reels are also played by the more structured céilí (pronounced KAY-lee) dance hall bands— larger ensembles made up of instruments such as accordion, flute, fiddle, whistle, drum set, banjo, and piano. There is also vocal music such as the centuries-old Irish Gaelic ballads, some of which are still sung by contemporary balladeers, including Christy Moore, Sean Tyrell, Mary Black, Delores Keane, and Sinéad O'Connor. There are pub songs that have been popularized by folksingers like the Clancy Brothers and ballad bands such as the Dubliners and the Furey Brothers. There is the nostalgic balladry of the Irish tenor, who might sing songs from a list of Irish-American favorites such as "Danny Boy," "Did Your Mother Come from Ireland?" "Kathleen Mavourneen," and "I'll Take You Home Again, Kathleen."

The Irish musical tradition is a tree with many limbs, but each limb comes from a single trunk, one that has changed and evolved over time. Musical

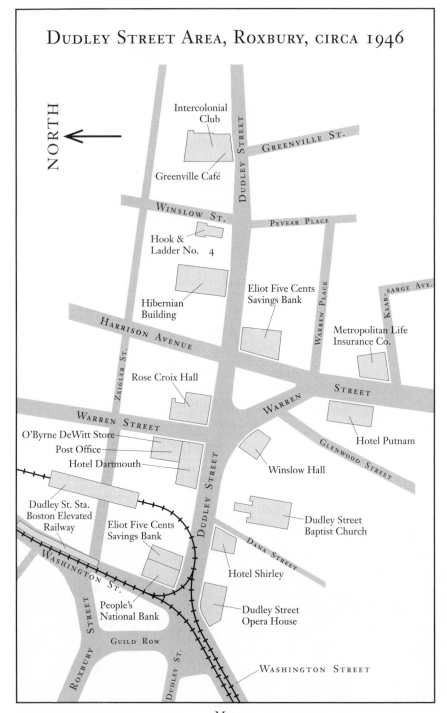

Map

change is a peculiar animal; a change of music can change a people, but just as often, evolving tastes enforce change on what might seem to be a stable musical tradition. If musicians want to survive, they must adapt. The Irish musical tradition as we know it today survived hundreds of years of invasions in its homeland, famines and disease that wiped out a third of Ireland's population, massive emigration that shipped its music all over the world, and the twentieth-century American cultural invasion of Ireland, which is still going on today. Irish music has adapted to each of the challenges it has faced, maintaining roots that are somehow characteristically Irish but also absorbing and transforming the best of the new influences.

One significant influence on Irish music has been its displacement to New World settings such as Boston's dance halls. Irish dance halls existed in Boston from as early as the 1850s, and as the Irish reached the height of their cultural influence in Boston in the postwar era, so did the Dudley Street dance halls. The rise and fall of the dance halls during this period traces the rise and fall of the Irish influence on the city at large. The Dudley Street golden era started after World War II, peaked in the mid-1950s, and slowly faded until it died completely in the mid-1960s. Reduced immigration, urban social upheaval, and a shift in neighborhood demographics capped a heyday of dance hall music in Boston.

Since then, Irish music has moved from the big ballrooms to smaller venues. Today, nearly forty years since the last dance hall closed, one can hear live Irish traditional music seven nights a week at concert halls, parties, clubs, and pubs throughout Boston. The city, which still boasts a large Irish population, is known both locally and in Ireland for one of the liveliest Irish music scenes in the United States. However, very little has been written about how the Boston Irish musical tradition began, took root, and changed over time.

This work aims to fill that void by exploring a single period in a larger history that spans four centuries—through the eyes of those who lived it. This twenty-year period is particularly important to the story of the Irish in America because it was a time of cultural transition. It was a bridge from the Old World to the New, on musical, historical, and social levels. After Dudley Street, dance was no longer the primary outlet for Irish traditional music in America, Roxbury was no longer Irish, and the Boston Irish community continued its ascent up the social ladder and out to the suburbs, while Ireland itself began to make its own transition from a rural to an increasingly industrial society.

The stories of those who wore out their shoes dancing on Dudley Street during this memorable era provide a missing link in Boston's Irish history. With a few exceptions, they were not politicians, nor were they poverty-stricken famine victims. Rather, they were the beating heart of Boston's city infrastructure: they read meters for the gas company, lodged deposits at the bank, repaired telephone wiring, typed legal documents, managed finances at Boston's Metropolitan Transit Authority. And for almost all of them, the dance halls were at the center of their lives.

They are living witness to the ways in which music was, and still is, woven into the fabric of the Irish-American experience both on and off the dance hall floor: the excitement of the kitchen racket house party; the delight of meeting an old friend in a new land; the wonder a musician felt when he discovered a new musical style via a borrowed recording; the camaraderie that developed late at night while two friends bickered over the right way to play the turn of "The Blackbird." These encounters were an inextricable part of the dance hall era. And when the dance halls shut down, when Irish music was no longer all the rage, when the young Irish married and bought houses in the suburbs, the musicians kept on playing.

From Shanties to Three-Deckers

Boston as an Irish Destination

Countless Irish songs and tales recount the heartache of immigrants who left their country never to return or see their families again. For many early Irish immigrants, these stories were true to life, but by the 1950s most Irish immigrants were finding work not long after they arrived in America, and many returned home for regular visits.

By the twentieth century, Boston was already an Irish city, a well-deserved victory, hard won over several centuries of anti-Irish oppression. In the 1630s, Boston had been a budding nation's Anglo-Saxon stronghold, a place where fear and hatred of Catholicism were particularly acute. The 1636 arrival of the Irish vessel *St. Patrick* in Boston Harbor ignited riots in the city among those who feared a "papist invasion."[1] For more than three centuries in Boston, the Irish were fiercely hated for their Catholic beliefs and ostracized from mainstream American life. An advertisement placed by a wealthy Brookline couple in the *Boston Evening Transcript* in 1868 typifies the prevalent anti-Irish sentiment:

> WANTED—A good, reliable woman to take the care of a boy two years old, in a small family in Brookline. No washing or ironing will be required, but good recommendations as to character and capacity demanded. Positively no Irish need apply.[2]

Boston Yankees looked to Protestant England as a source of cultural enrichment and refinement; to many of them Irish Catholics were barbaric and inferior. Arriving on Boston's shores without special skills or trades, the Irish historically had to take the bottom-of-the-barrel jobs that other

Bostonians would not. Lacking means to earn an adequate income, the Irish were consigned to lives in slum apartments in the cellars of converted warehouses and buildings along Broad Street, South Cove, Fort Hill, and other Boston waterfront areas.[3]

This anti-Irish, anti-Catholic attitude persisted for more than two hundred years, but it didn't stop the Irish from coming; things were far worse under centuries of oppressive British rule in Ireland. To add to the suffering, the failure of the Irish potato crops starting in the 1820s led to decades of widespread famine and disease in Ireland. By 1851, the population of Ireland had dropped by about two million, half from emigration and half from starvation and disease. From 1820 to 1920, some 4.7 million Irish emigrated to the United States,[4] and by 1890, the Irish-born population of the United States had reached 1.8 million. In 1880, more than seventy thousand of those Irish-born people were living in Boston.[5]

The first-generation immigrants settled and had families, and by the end of the 1920s, the second-generation Irish population of the United States exceeded three million. But still, at the turn of the century, anti-Irish, anti-Catholic sentiment pervaded. An Irish surname alone was enough to secure season tickets on the bread line, recalls Roxbury native Joanne McDermott:

> My grandfather was born in 1875 in Galway, and he was married here in Cambridge in 1904. He came over at the turn of the century, when there was shame attached to being Irish. My grandfather Richardson, who lived in Roxbury, worked for the Boston Fire Department as a wire inspector. He wore a suit to work, which was a big deal for that time. I remember him saying to me as a kid, "Well it's a good thing my name isn't Murphy or O'Brien, or I wouldn't have my job." I didn't know what he meant. But as I got older, I realized what he was saying: "If I had an Irish name, the city of Boston wouldn't have hired me." The city wasn't full of Irish politicians when he was a boy, like it is now. Things changed for the Irish when the Irish politicians really made it big: Lomasney, Curley, McCormack, John B. Hynes.

At the turn of the century, Boston's ethnic political wards were headed by ward bosses. Frequently getting their start as successful business owners in their communities, ward bosses were at the top rung of a sophisticated hierarchy of ward committees, captains, lieutenants, and the legions of volunteers eager for the reward that supporting a ward boss inevitably won. While John F. Fitzgerald graduated from North End ward boss to U.S. senator in 1894, and Patrick Kennedy took power as ward boss in East Boston, "Pea Jacket" Maguire was settling comfortably into the role of boss of Roxbury's Ward 17—only to be unseated by political upstart James Michael Curley.

While the 1920s were not easy in Boston, the city's Irish community enjoyed rising social status as James Michael Curley wrested power from Boston's blue-blooded Brahmin ruling class. Like ward bosses all over the city, Curley curried favor among his constituents through backdoor favors and the outright provision of letters of credit for coal, groceries, and other necessities, not the least of which might be a well-placed phone call to ensure an escape from tangles with the law. For the Irish, jobs were often assured by this old ward-politics system of patronage: the old neighborhood boys were first in line for municipal jobs and contracts. For Roxbury native Frank Devin, politics was part of growing up Irish-American in Boston:

> In those days if you needed a job, you went to see a politician because there were no jobs around. You either worked at Edison, the gas company, or the state or the city. You had to get friendly with the politicians. In Roxbury we ran campaigns of all kinds. I've been in politics all my life. As a kid, I'd be the drummer going up and down Winthrop Street for James Michael Curley. And as I got older, I worked on campaigns. Everybody used to do it.

Political organizations grew up around ward bosses to support their careers. In Roxbury, the famous Tammany Club was formed to garner support for Curley's emerging political career. He was elected mayor in 1913 and would continue to serve in the city as mayor, governor, and congressman (sometimes from a jail cell) in a career that spanned three decades.

The Old Neighborhood: Roxbury

Roxbury, the center of Boston's Irish community in the first half of the twentieth century, had been a close-knit Irish neighborhood for nearly a century by 1940. One of Boston's oldest neighborhoods, it was also a center of commerce and a major train and bus hub.

Founded by colonists from England in 1630, the town of Roxbury was originally connected to Boston by Washington Street, which ran along the narrow strip of land that anchored Boston to the mainland. Massive landfill, built up over two centuries, further connected the town to Boston. Originally called "Rocksberry" for its unique outcroppings of pudding stone, it was a rich source of farmland, lumber, and stone. Roxbury was settled almost immediately after its founding. The streets of Dudley Square today—Washington, Dudley, Centre, Roxbury, and Warren Streets—were laid out in 1632.

In 1840, poor Irish immigrants built shanties along Roxbury's tidal flats, and in that same year, an anti-Irish Catholic riot led to the killing of an Irish immigrant on Dudley Street. Around that same time, St. Patrick's Church was founded on the corner of Hampden and Dudley Streets.

In the later years of the nineteenth century, the old farms of Roxbury were subdivided for housing, and Roxbury became a suburb. The establishment of electric trolley service in 1887 drew people in large numbers to Roxbury's newly built row houses, three-deckers, and single-family homes.[6] Right from its earliest days, Dudley Square was a bustling center of commerce and a major transportation center, where kids would cling to the backs of streetcars to save a nickel and hope their mothers didn't catch them.

By the middle of the twentieth century, the Dudley Square area had become a very tightly knit community of Boston's Irish-American working class, who lived in relative peace alongside Canadians, a small Jewish community on Blue Hill Avenue in the Grove Hall area, and a small Italian community in the George Street area. Said the Roxbury native Ann Devin, "Everybody was thick as thieves in Roxbury."

By that time, the Irish in Roxbury were mostly second- and third-generation American. There were few Irish-born people living in Dudley Square, other than those who had come out to live with distant relatives. But even third-generation immigrants still considered themselves Irish, though most of their houses had only an Irish-born grandparent living in. Most new immigrants lived in other parts of Boston, including Somerville, Dorchester, and South Boston. Joanne McDermott, raised in Roxbury in the 1940s and 1950s, recalls a cohesive community entirely based around the parish, as it had been in Roxbury for several generations:

To us, St. Patrick's parish was a village and Dudley Street was Main Street. St. Patrick's Church was on Dudley Street, and our

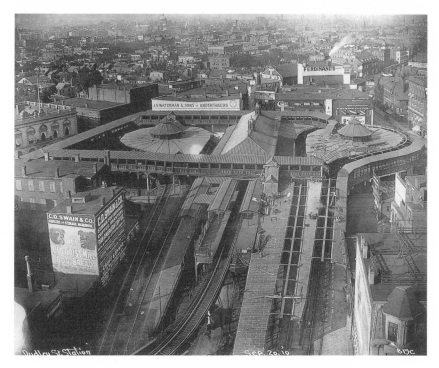

Dudley Street Station, 1910. Its sign pictured in the center toward the back, Ferdinand's Blue Store was a Dudley Street fixture until well into the 1950s. (Courtesy of the Boston Public Library, Print Department.)

whole social life revolved around the church. We knew everybody. I felt safe there. It was a very tight community.

Everyone that you knew was either Irish Catholic or at least belonged to the parish. There was no competition economically; we were all in the same boat. We weren't desperately poor, but nobody was really rich, either. Everybody pulled together. It wasn't so much Irish pride. With us, it was just a close-knit community. We loved each other, we trusted each other. It probably was like that in Ireland too. And maybe part of it was that they brought it over with them.

At that time, in stark contrast to its later reputation, Roxbury was considered safe. Women thought nothing of walking the streets after the dances at 1:00 A.M. People knew all the cops on the beat, and theft was rare.

A wallet or handbag left behind in the dance hall was likely to still be there the following week—cash and all.

The area's safety was due in part to the fact that the economic landscape was relatively flat; there was little social stratification within the Roxbury Irish community. Frank "Deacon" Devin, who grew up in a typical Irish-American Roxbury home, describes the local scene this way:

> Everybody lived in a million houses in Roxbury. Everybody rented except a few of the people on the outskirts. Something came up that was bigger or better, so you moved. We were five boys and three girls, and my father was a conductor for the Boston el. His route was from Dudley Street to Blue Hill Ave., which is now Grove Hall.
>
> You worked as soon as you could walk. I mean, everybody sold papers, but I was working at the ballpark selling peanuts when I was eight to ten years old. We did all kinds of jobs; it wasn't just me. I worked in longshoring for a while. Then I worked at a bookbinding company, grinding things off the backs of books. Some lousy jobs. I worked on the railroad; we worked in the post office at Christmas, like a lot of kids used to do. The happiest moments of our lives, I guarantee you this, we spent in Roxbury. We were poor but never knew it.

The Irish in Boston navigated the city by Catholic parishes. According to Dick Senier, flutist and the son of a prominent Boston accordionist, Tom Senier:

> There were thirteen parishes in Dorchester alone and another seven in South Boston. You never said you were from Dorchester or Roxbury without saying the parish. There was a sort of hierarchy in our parents' eyes. If you were going out with a girl from St. Gregory's in the Lower Mills section of Dorchester or St. Brendan's near Neponset Circle, you would get a nice reaction. But, if you were to say St. Patrick's in Roxbury or St. Augustine's in South Boston, it would be quite different.[7]

Roxbury's St. Patrick's (founded in 1840) and Mission (1878) churches served as the spiritual and social centers for the neighborhood's Irish Catholics. Frank "Deacon" Devin's life was integrated into parish life, but not just for the religion, as he tells it:

Getting to church was a good walk for me. At one time I used to walk from Woodville Street, which was seven or eight blocks. But everybody did. There were five or six masses at St. Patrick's Church, and they were all jammed every Sunday. We guys hung out on the corner of Dudley and Blue Hill Ave., directly across from St. Patrick's. Well, after mass fifty people would be there, fifty guys joshing. When I started to go to high school in 1942, the corner became a focal point in my social groupings.

Getting There: The El

With its southern terminus at Dudley Station, a spaghettied system of clanking trolleys and rumbling buses could get you to Dudley Street from just about anywhere. People would hop the el, or elevated railway, to Dudley Street from all over the Boston area, including neighborhoods in Jamaica Plain, Brookline, South Boston, Dorchester, Milton, Canton, Somerville, Cambridge, Everett, East Boston—anywhere the Irish worked or lived.

Located at the center of metropolitan Boston and designed by the architect A. W. Longfellow, Dudley Station opened in 1901 as the southern terminus of the privately run Boston Elevated Railway (BERY). Even when the railway went into public ownership and was renamed the Metropolitan Transit Authority in 1947, it was still just the el to the locals.[8]

According to Frank Devin, "Everything revolved around the el. At that time, you negotiated your way either by the parish you lived in or the line you lived on." And from the station, it was just steps to any of the five major dance halls that dotted Dudley Square.

The accordionist Joe Derrane, a Mission Hill native and the most renowned musician that the Dudley Street dance hall scene produced, believes that the el may have been the key reason that the dance halls were attended by such a large number of people. At the time, he points out:

Nobody had cars. Without [the el], the place never would have had the impact it did. From Dudley Street, you could go into town, pick up the Blue Line, go from East Boston, Somerville, Everett, wherever. It was right on Dudley Street. This is the wonderful thing. You walked no more than two or three hundred yards, and you had your choice of any one of five ballrooms going every Saturday night.

Once Dudley Street's reputation started to build, many also came from New Hampshire, from Massachusetts cities such as Worcester and Springfield, and from Connecticut and Rhode Island. Sensing that there was a similar market for dance among the large Irish community in Worcester, Derrane once attempted to start a dance hall there. His efforts failed, however, because of the pull of Dudley Square. Derrane recounts, "I ran it for four weeks; then I gave up because they were standing outside to get the bus to head out to a meeting point where they'd all pile into three or four cars and drive in to Dudley Street. It was a mecca."

Roxbury was far from the green, green grass of home, but it was very much a home away from home for the Irish who lived, worked, and played there. No matter how much ironing the woman of the house gave you for how little pay, and no matter how far the road works gang on Washington Street was from the old bog road, there was always something doing on Dudley Street.

The 1920s

My Father's Band

Unlike previous immigrant generations, Irish people who came to Boston after 1920 did not live in the musty basements of Boston's waterfront warehouse buildings. They lived in apartments in bright three-decker houses in areas such as Dorchester, South Boston, Roxbury, West Roxbury, and Jamaica Plain. After two centuries of poverty and anti-Irish sentiment, the first decades of the twentieth century ushered in a time of prosperity during which the Boston Irish began to express themselves as a thriving, fully integrated ethnic group—and the dance halls were one of the more colorful musical expressions of their ethnicity.

The dance halls first opened in Roxbury before World War II, setting the stage for times to come. Performers in the prewar dance halls were the parents, teachers, and mentors of the musicians who performed on Dudley Street during its heyday from the 1940s to 1960s. The earlier performers had arrived in America in the 1920s with fresh memories of fierce British rule and the uprising that led to Ireland's independence. Many had themselves served in the Irish Republican Army. Rebel blood still boiled in their veins, and they taught their children the songs of emancipation and patriotism that they brought with them. To fully understand what happened in the Dudley Street dance halls after World War II, it is helpful to step back a generation to the 1920s and 1930s and explore the roots of Boston's rich Irish musical tradition.

To Freedom's Fair Shore

While America enjoyed economic prosperity in the Roaring Twenties, the political situation in Ireland was dire. Starting with the 1916 Rising in Dublin, Ireland threw itself into the turmoil of the five-year War of Independence. Finally, in 1921, the Anglo-Irish Treaty was signed, signaling the war's end but instigating the Civil War, which was fought over how the newly independent country should be ruled. Civil War violence continued until a ceasefire was declared in 1923.

The Civil War had divided families and neighborhoods, and to make matters worse, it left the nation burdened with war debt. Ireland's economy was highly dependent on agriculture, and a major slump in agricultural prices from 1920 to 1927 exacted a heavy toll on the economy. Because the country lacked an industrial base to take up the slack, unemployment soared. Under these conditions, emigration became increasingly attractive; an average of 33,000 people per year left Ireland from 1921 to 1931.[1]

According to U.S. Census data, more than seventy thousand Irish-born people were living in the Boston area in the 1920s, and American-born Irish outnumbered Irish-born by three to one. However, that didn't make it much easier for new arrivals.[2] Accordion player Jack Martin's father, who was born in Ireland not long after the famine, had witnessed the brutish patrols of the mercenary Black and Tan police brought in from England to end the civil unrest that followed Irish independence. Fed up with English subjugation that seemed solely designed to humiliate and terrorize the Irishman on his own turf, Jack's father came to America. As Jack tells it,

> When my father come out here as a kid, at seventeen years old—which was a very common thing in those days—you left home never to go back and never to see Mom and Dad again. You left, and that was it.
>
> My father came over here in 1925 and got a job. In those days you had to be sponsored. My Uncle Ed sponsored my father and my Uncle Pat. He had to have so much money in the bank to accept these two boys coming from Ireland so they wouldn't be a burden on the state. My uncle, he had their butts out the door the next day looking for a job, and that was it.

My mother was only about fourteen when my aunt brought her over, sponsored her. When she got here, she got a job working for a family, and that's what she did until she met my father and they got married in '29. That was the era. People were poor; a lot of them didn't have jobs.

Among the older generations in Boston, the stories are strikingly similar. Most of the Irish who settled in Irish neighborhoods like Fields Corner in Dorchester and Mission Hill in Roxbury came from rural areas in Ireland, where an elementary education was all that was needed to keep the farm afloat. Often arriving in Boston with little more than the equivalent of an eighth-grade education, most had to do whatever they could to get by—sweep the discarded peanuts and popcorn from the grandstands at Boston's Fenway Park, shovel coal into the flaming furnaces that provided heat and power to the city's numerous hospitals, repair steam lines in the city's asbestos-laden subway system—and forever dread the inevitable awkward telegram from Ireland telling them that someone at home had gone to God, and the only thing to do is keep feeding one's children their porridge. Many men left extreme hardship at home, only to have large families and then die young in America.

The hardships suffered by early Irish immigrants are legendary—but it wasn't all bad in the twentieth century, and at least there were jobs to go to. By the 1920s, Boston had become a truly Irish city. While work life was hard, social life was thriving. Several Irish dance halls catered to the large population of first- and second-generation Irish-Americans, as well as the growing numbers of newly arrived Irish-born people, eager for entertainment and community that celebrated this new land but also reminded them of home. The Irish dance hall band arose to fulfill that demand, playing a combination of Irish and Irish-American selections. In Boston the bands bore distinctly Irish names such as the Emerald Isle Orchestra, Dan Sullivan's Shamrock Band, and O'Leary's Irish Minstrels. These bands performed in dance halls that dotted the Dudley Street area, including Deacon Hall, between Northampton and Dover Streets in Roxbury, the Hibernian Hall, Winslow Hall, and the Dudley Street Opera House.

While some large bands were able to build a following by playing exclusively Irish music, most bands mixed popular Irish forms such as reels and two-steps with American waltzes and fox-trots. This mixed repertoire was in demand at their typical venues: Irish weddings, dance halls, parties, and concerts. Bands also performed Irish-style songs made popular by vaudeville and Tin Pan Alley composers, including such favorites as "When Irish Eyes Are Smiling," "My Wild Irish Rose," "Danny Boy," "Daisy, Daisy," and "Did Your Mother Come from Ireland?"[3] On the traditional side of their repertoire, Irish-American dance hall bands drew from the same collection of dance tunes played in Ireland at the time. However, American audiences, some ethnically mixed, might also request couple dances such as strathspeys, waltzes, barn dances, and schottisches, as well as show tunes and light classical music.

The 1920s and 1930s were times of great demand for musicians. While monies earned performing in a dance hall were not enough to support a family, the "four or five bucks a night" certainly helped during the Depression of the 1930s,[4] according to the Irish accordionist Gene Kelly (in an interview with the musician and historian Mick Moloney). As the Irish began to operate as a successful cultural unit in the United States, Irish music flourished, not just in the dance halls but also through the new technologies of radio and recorded music.

Radio and Records

Starting in the 1920s, radio transformed Irish music in Ireland, bringing to a national audience regional styles, repertoire, and tunes once known only locally. The radio also introduced Irish ears to new sounds and musical styles popular in the United States and in England.

Meanwhile, the boom economy of the 1920s in America meant disposable income to purchase records and an increased interest in music. A new invention, the windup gramophone, became omnipresent in households in both America and Ireland. It seemed that every Irish household, no matter how poor, had a gramophone and a collection of 78 rpm records of Irish music, which was being recorded almost exclusively in America at the time.

Recording companies in New York, Chicago, and Boston catered to the thriving dance scene in American cities by producing hundreds of recordings destined for Irish ethnic markets. In New York City, a number of recording companies specializing in Irish music emerged, including Emerald, M & C New Republic Record Company, Keltic Records, and the Gaelic Phonograph Record Company. As the market grew, Columbia and Victor stepped up production of Irish music, as well. This decade saw the rise of the most definitive recorded musicians, including fiddlers Michael Coleman, James Morrison, and Paddy Killoran.

Musicians and bands that were recorded or that appeared frequently on radio were afforded special status, becoming legends in their own cities. In Boston, bands like Dan Sullivan's Shamrock Band, Terry O'Toole's Irish Echoes, and O'Leary's Irish Minstrels made weekly radio appearances, and Joe O'Leary, leader of the Irish Minstrels, hosted an Irish music program on WEEI, using the show to promote his band and sell recordings.

Dan Sullivan's Shamrock Band

Dan Sullivan's Shamrock Band was one of the first dance hall bands in Boston, employing numerous musicians for weddings as well as dances. The band was popular locally and internationally for its recordings produced during the 1920s and 1930s. Sullivan's was one of the few Boston bands to play almost exclusively Irish selections during that era.

Dan Sullivan was the namesake of his father, a fiddler and flutist profiled by Francis O'Neill in *Irish Minstrels and Musicians*. Sullivan Sr. came to America in the late 1800s, after having spent some twenty years in London. He brought with him a vast repertoire of Irish airs as well as classical concertos. There can be little doubt that the young Sullivan was inspired by the musical talent of his father and his father's friends, brothers William and Michael Hanafin, of Callinaferry, Miltown, county Kerry.[5]

The young Dan Sullivan began playing piano in his teens, and when he finished school, he took a job at the Steinway Piano Corporation in Boston. In the mid-1920s he formed Dan Sullivan's Shamrock Band, which became an instant hit. Only a couple of months later, Sullivan was traveling with his band to New York in a rented bus to record the band's first record. The band also appeared regularly at Boston's Deacon Hall and on weekly radio broadcasts on WNAC 1230 AM for a few years in the early 1930s.

During the band's career, Sullivan made recordings for three record labels. On recordings from around 1926, the lineup included Sullivan on piano, his father's friend Michael Hanafin on fiddle, Daniel Murphy of county Kerry on pipes and flute, Tom Ryan of Tipperary on fiddle, and

Daniel Moroney of Caherciveen, county Kerry, on pipes and flute. Over the years, band members left and were replaced by others, including a line-up of some of Boston's best musicians: Tom Senier of Clifden, county Galway, on accordion, Owen Frain of Roosky, county Sligo, on flute, Niall Nolan on banjo, Gene Preston of Sligo on flute, Martin Mullins of Galway on fiddle, Connie Hanafin on accordion, Dominic Doyle on pipes, Murty Rabbitte, flute and piccolo, and Larry Griffin, vocals. Tunes recorded by the band were to remain popular in the dance halls even after the war. They included "The Varsouviana," "Johnny, Will You Marry Me?" (the air of which was played for highland flings), and "Lanigan's Ball."

Dan Sullivan had a unique style of accompaniment that increased the harmonic complexity of the band's tunes. While most Irish tunes include only two or three chords—and the piano accompaniment on many early Irish recordings is often criticized as insensitive and incorrect by modern musicians—Sullivan used more sophisticated chord progressions and an active right hand, playing the melody along with the rest of the band, un-like most accompanists of the time.

The mainstay of Sullivan's band was Mike Hanafin, brother of William "Bill" Hanafin. Michael Hanafin was born in Ireland in 1880. He emi-grated to America from Kerry around the turn of the century and made his name in the dance halls and Prohibition-era speakeasies, becoming an im-portant influence on the Boston scene until his death in 1970.

Gene Frain, a pianist, flutist, and piper whose father, Owen, played with the Sullivan band, has early childhood memories of Hanafin's speakeasy, not far from downtown Boston in Central Square, Cambridge. Recalls Frain:

> I would jump a streetcar with my father, down to Central Square. Where Mike was, there was always music. There was a saying years ago—you buy a barroom, put Mike in it, and Mike would draw the Irish from everyplace. He was a nice guy to talk to. En-tertaining, as well. He played the tin whistle; he'd play the violin. When he got a real good crowd going, he'd sell the place and move right to a new joint. He had a good thing going.

Gifted both as musicians and as step dancers, the Hanafin family's con-tributions to Irish music and dance in the city are recognized so widely that the Boston branch of the international Irish musician's association, Comhaltas Ceoltóirí Éireann, is called the Hanafin-Cooley Branch, partly in their name.

Myles O'Malley, the Tin Whistle King

Another important Boston musician of this time was Myles O'Malley (1910–2000), dubbed the Tin Whistle King. He was born in Everett, Massachusetts, to Irish natives Michael and Mary O'Malley, and grew up in a mixed Italian and Irish neighborhood in South Everett. In an interview with Mick Moloney in 1984, Myles said he grew up in quite the Irish household, entertaining "all the colleens and the greenhorns" who gathered at the house Thursday and Sunday evenings for Irish jigs and reels. The music was supplied by his father, Myles, and two brothers.

Mike O'Malley ensured that his sons learned music from the age of five, watching over their practice sessions with a stern eye. In his teens, Myles discovered the saxophone. Swept away by the new modern sounds of Benny Goodman, Artie Shaw, and the Dorsey brothers, he practiced the sax to the detriment of all else, including his schoolwork. He graduated from high school in 1928 and moved easily into the Truman Carew Big Band, a Boston band with whom he performed six nights a week for two years.

Along the way, he also started playing a whistle brought to him by a friend from Ireland. Because the fingerings were similar to the fingerings for saxophone, he mastered the instrument quickly. For a St. Patrick's night broadcast in 1931, band leader Carew wrote an arrangement intended to feature the budding whistle player.

Feature him, it did. The large Boston Irish population was just crying out for sounds of home, and soon O'Malley was performing on whistle for short commercial broadcasts on a regular basis. It was after one of these broadcasts on WNAC that he got a call from New York. Someone from a new recording company, Decca, had picked up the broadcast on sister station WEAF in New York, via the Yankee Network. Eager to build up their ethnic catalog in what was proving to be a booming market for ethnic recordings, the Decca representative invited O'Malley to come to New York. He went expecting an interview and an audition on whistle, nothing more. But the Decca representatives heard him play and moved fast, putting him into the studio the next day with an accompanist from Columbia Records who had performed on other Irish recordings.

Over his career, O'Malley recorded well-known tunes that are still played by nearly every Irish musician, from beginner to advanced: "Off to California," "Connaught Man's Rambles," "Sweeps" (also known as "Sweet's

Hornpipe"), "Swallow's Tail," "Well Dance the Keil," "The Londonderry Horn," "Quarrelsome Piper," "Shandon Bells," "Kildare Fancy," and "Off She Goes." While he never made a huge amount of money from his recordings, the annual royalties certainly helped ease the sting of the Depression.

O'Malley went on to make another record with his Decca Recording Orchestra, comprising Clary Walsh on saxophone, Johnny Connors and Joe Glennon on piano, brothers Jack and Joe Fahey (who had a band of their own at the time with their brother fiddler, Johnny, known as the Fahey Brothers' Emerald Gems), and Dr. John "Tut" Connolly on drums.

Somewhere along the way, O'Malley acquired the nickname "The Tin Whistle King," but he kept his skills well polished on both instruments, the Irish whistle and the big band saxophone. While many musicians lost work during the Depression, he maintained a steady income until 1938 with his fifteen-minute commercial broadcasts on whistle.

O'Malley's music manuscripts, which reside at the Irish Music Archives in the Burns Library at Boston College, attest to the diversity of his band's repertoire: Irish favorites like "The Old Bog Road" and "Where the River Shannon Flows" sit beside quintessential American tunes like "Take Me Out to the Ball Game" and "I'm Forever Blowing Bubbles."

Emerald Isle Orchestra

The Emerald Isle Orchestra was fronted by Tom Senier, one of the enduring characters of the prewar generation of musicians. Tom Senier was born in Galway town in 1895, and moved to Clifden. He was the son of a weaver; his father founded the Streamstown Woollen Mill. Like his contemporary Owen Frain, Tom Senier ran away from home at sixteen and joined the British Army, fighting with the Irish regiment known as the Connaught Rangers. He had an eleven-year military career, serving in India and Mesopotamia during World War I. He had been an adept fiddle and mandolin player until a gunshot to his left hand left it functional but without feeling. He took up the Irish button accordion then, a ten-keyed accordion that was played primarily with the right hand.

He was discharged from the army as a sergeant major following a bayonet wound to his back, and returned to Ireland to recover. He lived in Clif-

*Tom Senier was an influential accordion player in Boston
from the 1930s until he passed away in 1977.*
(From the library of Richard Senier.)

den with his wife long enough to have two sons and move with his family
to veterans' housing in Killester, Dublin, taking a job at the British Min-
istry of Pensions amid the furor of the budding Irish Civil War. After the
birth of two more children in Dublin, Senier sought opportunity in America and emigrated to Boston on a British passport in 1926. He traveled on
his own, but having settled in with work and after joining Dan Sullivan's
Shamrock Band, he sent for his family.

Senier taught his young sons to play music at an early age, and soon the
halls of his large ten-room home on Whiting Street in Roxbury rang out
with the sounds of Irish music, both from his own sons and from the constant stream of stray musicians referred to the generous Seniers by cousins
and friends back in Ireland. The house became the scene of regular house
parties. Guests paid twenty-five cents at the door to enter and dance, socialize, or have a beer at the bar Senier had had installed in the basement.

By 1938, Tom Senier had started his own band, the Emerald Isle Orchestra, and with it, a regularly scheduled dance at Winslow Hall on Dud-

ley Street. The major band at that time in Boston was O'Leary's Irish Minstrels, which performed mostly popular modern selections. Senier was always disappointed he had never been invited to join the band, but the band
played from sheet music charts, and he was trained traditionally. Though
he had never learned to read music, he could learn any tune by ear.

So while O'Leary's Irish Minstrels' union musicians played arrangements
of modern and some Irish tunes at private events and at the Hibernian Hall,
Senier's Emerald Isle Orchestra held court first at Deacon Hall and later at
Winslow Hall. Before World War II, Senier's bands included a revolving
lineup of musicians, depending on who was available, and the band often
expanded onstage, depending on who was sitting in. The basic instrumentation was accordion, piano, drums, and a horn. That, of course, always included Tom himself on the "'cordeen," with a revolving cast of others: Jack
Storer or Danny Cullity, accordion; perhaps Billy Higgins, Johnny Connors, or Joe Glennon on piano; "Tut" Connolly, Dick Hanaway, Leo
Tracey, or Dutchie Deiss on drums; Chris Murphy or Mike and Joe Fahey
on banjo; Johnny Fahey, Pat Carey, or Pat Connolly on fiddle; perhaps a
whistle player such as Murty Rabbitte, or a horn or clarinet player that may
be either Clary Walsh or Joe Elwood.

Tom Senier was a great promoter, and his dances at the Winslow Hall
were very popular until the war years, when many of the musicians and the
patrons went off to fight, and fellow musician Matty Toohy drew dancers
away to the band that he had started at the Dudley Street Opera House.
Senier remained very active in the Boston Irish music scene until he passed
away, at age eighty-two, most likely of a stroke, en route to a playing en-
gagement at the Irish Social Club in West Roxbury.

O'Leary's Irish Minstrels

Perhaps the most influential band in the prewar era was O'Leary's Irish
Minstrels, led by Joe O'Leary, a fiddler from Maine. Featuring Jerry
O'Brien on accordion, backed by a full brass section, the band fully catered
to its crowd by interspersing popular big band hits of the day with Irish
waltzes and dance tunes.

O'Leary's Irish Minstrels made recordings on the Columbia label.

*Jerry O'Brien (left) played with O'Leary's Irish Minstrels
and taught a whole generation of young accordion players.*
(From the library of Paddy Noonan.)

O'Leary also ran a live Irish radio show in Boston, which aired on WEEI 590 AM and featured the band's live in-studio performances. The show was so successful that by 1930 O'Leary had given up his daytime job and was playing music full-time.[6]

One enduring musician from O'Leary's band was Jerry O'Brien (1899–1968), who was very influential on the next generation of accordion players. Born Jeremiah Patrick O'Brien in Kinsale, county Cork, he was in Ireland to witness the days of the 1916 Easter Rising and the War for Independence that followed. As a teacher of Gaelic, he was sought out by the Black and Tans, but was smuggled out of Ireland in 1920 to avoid being hanged.

O'Brien soon found himself in Boston with his brother Timmy, working as a butler in Beverly Farms, a town near Gloucester, Massachusetts. During this time, he taught himself to play the melodeon. He also was a deft step dancer, winning a cup at the 1936 New York Feis, an annual competition of Irish dance. O'Brien met his wife, Mary Egan, at a house party, or "kitchen racket," in Norwood in 1932. Soon with a young family, they relocated closer to the city, to Dorchester, and Jerry secured work as a welder at the Quincy shipyard.[7]

During the Depression years of the 1930s, Irish immigration slowed to a trickle, and business at the dance halls began to slow down considerably. However, as tight as money was, bad times hadn't gotten in the way of dance and music in Ireland, and they certainly wouldn't get in the way in America. When things got tight, it was out of the dance halls and into the kitchens.

3

The 1930s

*If You're Irish, Never Mind the Parlor.
Come into the Kitchen!*

The inflated U.S. stock market crashed in October 1929, ushering in the worst economic collapse in the history of the United States. Without money to attend dance halls, the Boston Irish turned to house parties, commonly called kitchen rackets, for their entertainment. Weekend after weekend, Irish-born "greenhorns" and first-generation "narrowbacks" alike crowded into small city apartments to dance and socialize.

The kitchen was the center of activity, the place where musicians would play for the enjoyment of dancers. The recipe for a kitchen racket: find a fiddle or accordion player, clear away the furniture, secure all breakable objects, and strike up a tune. Soon streetcars full of people—adults and children alike—would arrive on the doorsteps of whichever three-decker had the music. House parties were just a part of being Irish and living in Boston, and there was no occasion too sacred for a party—a "hooley," as it was called. The accordion player Joe Derrane recalls the kitchen rackets of the 1930s and 1940s as a lively scene:

> People in those days didn't have a lot of money, so they hosted parties at their house, whether it be a wedding, christening, or other event. They would bring in a musician, maybe a few if they could, to play music. The music and dancing would happen in the kitchen, where there was linoleum. The old ladies would sit in the parlor, as we called it in those days, with their tea and maybe some

Irish bread, ham, or potato salad, and the men would stay near the bathroom, because the beer was kept there, in the bathtub. The dancers would go into the kitchen, where you could clear away furniture and dance. People would dance sets and waltzes, and maybe someone would sing a few songs.

I remember once playing in Mission Hill, in Roxbury. It was a small house, and in order to fit everyone into the kitchen, they set me up playing on the fire escape, with the accordion playing in through the window. At a place in West Roxbury, there were too many who wanted to dance one night, and they kept moving me from one corner to another. They decided they wanted to do set dancing. Once they start swinging around in the kitchen, you're fair game. Then they took away my chair and set me on the counter to play. I almost got knocked off it twice, so finally, I got disgusted with it, took off my shoes and socks, spun around on the counter, and put my feet in the sink and played the rest of the night. For safety![1]

Kitchen rackets were Derrane's musical proving ground. His teacher, Jerry O'Brien, nurtured Derrane's musical career by taking him along to the parties. Derrane, who was just fourteen or fifteen at the time, recalls, "I would listen and play along; then, when he needed a break, I'd play tunes, and he would give me pointers."[2]

Kitchen rackets were many musicians' introduction to Irish music and dance. For one such musician, the accordion player Jack Martin, the 1930s kitchen rackets are bright memories:

My mother was from Cork, my father was from Galway, and I used to go with them when I was a little bitty guy to South Boston to these kitchen rackets. During the Depression, people had no money. They had peanuts: nothing. A lot of people didn't have jobs. So you go to some place, they'd put on a pot of tea, and my mother would make an Irish bread and bring it over, and somebody else'd do the same thing.

Everything got moved out of the kitchen! And up they'd come with an accordion or a flute, and they'd sit down and play jigs and reels. There'd be two or three musicians, sometimes there'd be half a house full of them, and they'd be up there dancing and

In this "kitchen racket breakdown," as the dance was sometimes called,
John Ryan of Canada plays a tune (on fiddle) while Jack Storer (left)
and Johnny Ahern dance in Johnny Connors's kitchen.
(From the library of Frank Storer.)

stomping away—and they were really, really hard-stepping it! It's
a wonder they didn't come down through the floor.

Jeez, sometimes you'd go to these places and there'd be forty or
fifty people in a little bloody apartment! And of course, everybody
hangs in the kitchen, you know, and the teapot'd be flying, and the
old Irish ladies from Galway would be sitting there with their
shawls—"schmokin'" a pipe. Those times a lot of us didn't have
cars. You'd be over there 'til the wee hours of the morning, and
the only way to get back and forth was by streetcar.

Kitchen rackets had their roots in Ireland, according to one Irish native, Nora McGillicuddy, who immigrated to the United States from Moycullen village in county Galway:

> We used to have kitchen rackets in our own house in Ireland. That's where we learned to dance. You learned, or you'd be left sitting down all night.
>
> For the kitchen parties, my aunt Peg used to play the accordion. You'd be dancing in the kitchen all night, and eating and drinking. Well, we wouldn't drink, but the guys might have a few drinks. But that was the thing to do. . . . You see, you had no TV or anything, and we didn't have a radio in our house until maybe a year before I left Ireland. But it was nice . . . it was all fun. Nice clean fun.
>
> It was always in the kitchen. You'd be dancing so much in the kitchen, my father'd be always afraid—we had a dresser of dishes—he'd be afraid that they'd break the dishes, swinging around. Your shoes'd be all dust from the floor, you know, because they only had the cement floor. But boy, you'd dance no matter what kind of a floor it was when you had the music!

Dance is a centuries-old tradition in Irish culture, dating from before people started writing about the country. Though very little was written about dance in early and medieval Ireland, scattered historical accounts indicate that twelfth-century Norman invaders brought French carol and round dance forms with them to Ireland. Historians generally agree that these imported dances constituted the roots of the early Irish group dance forms that flourished over the next three centuries. While there are few formal accounts of dance from the fifteenth and sixteenth centuries, passing observations such as one made in 1681 by an English traveler, Thomas Dinley, underline the growing popularity of group dance forms. The Irish, Dinley wrote, "are at this day much addicted . . . to dance after their countrey [sic] fashions, the long dance one after another of all conditions, master, mrs, servants."[3]

By the mid-seventeenth century, Ireland had developed dance forms of its own, though many of these were abandoned in favor of new French dances taught by traveling dance masters in the eighteenth century. By 1780, the English geographer Arthur Young observed that dancing was "very general among poor people, almost universal in every cabin. Dancing masters of their own rank travel through the country from cabin to cabin, with a piper or blind fiddler; and the pay is sixpence a quarter."[4]

At a house party, Paddy Cronin on fiddle is accompanied by Johnny Connors (left, facing piano) and Cronin's brother Mike (on chanter).
(From the library of Frank Storer.)

With that addiction to dancing came an addiction likewise to music, an addiction that was long lasting. For Connie McEleney, who grew up in Donegal in the 1940s, music had been a part of daily life in Ireland. Mc-Eleney says that evenings often consisted of friendly visits, known as céilí, from neighbors who stopped in for music and conversation. "You didn't have television and radio, and you didn't have electricity. You just sat around the fire and sang songs," he recalls.

Seamus Mulligan, the radio host of "A Feast of Irish Music" on WATD 95.9 FM, also recalls the parties at home in Ireland:

> Because there was no canned entertainment, you had to have
> these house parties. You had to manufacture your own. And every
> child in Ireland always had a "party piece"—a song, or poem, or

dance. And people would have parties in rotation, in different homes every weekend. So you would go to this house this night, and another house the following week. That was the only form of entertainment that they had.

But Ireland's house parties were to come to an end as the new independent government of Ireland settled into power—and that was to have a profound effect on the development of Irish dance music on both sides of the Atlantic.

De Valera's Ireland: Public Dance Halls Act of 1935

Éamon de Valera was elected president of the Executive Committee of the Irish Republic in 1932. Under his leadership, through the Fianna Fáil political party, Ireland enacted a host of laws that imposed strict moral codes intended to build a close alliance of government interests with those of the Catholic Church, attempting to enforce a new national identity that was Catholic and also uniquely Irish.

A casualty of de Valera's conservative republic was the dance hall, which both priests and nationalist organizations such as the Gaelic League blamed for the moral decay they perceived within Ireland. The Gaelic League in particular indicated that the growing influence of jazz in the dance halls would seriously undermine authentic Irish forms. According to one statement by the Gaelic League, "Our Minister of Finance [responsible for broadcasting] has a soul buried in jazz and is selling the musical soul of the nation."[5]

In response to sentiments like these, de Valera's government enacted the Public Dance Halls Act of 1935. The act placed ownership of the dance halls in the hands of the clergy and required that all halls be licensed. It also banned country house dances and all-night jazz dancing in unlicensed halls. Crossroad dances—outdoor summertime dances that had gathered musicians and communities since at least the eighteenth century—were also outlawed. Seamus Mulligan remembers this time in Ireland:

> House dances were frowned upon because they were considered
> to be occasions of sin. Well, there'd be a little shenanigans after it.
> What happened was: one of the duties of the junior priest was to
> patrol the towns and watch out. And from time to time they would
> use devious methods, such as going in the back door. When the

lookout had said the priest was coming, all of the women and all of the guys would go for the back door, intending to sneak out, but would knock over the priest, who was attempting to sneak in the same door.

With the formation of the Irish government, Éamon de Valera, in conjunction with McQuaid, who was the archbishop of Dublin, decided that they were going to ban all house dances. That was the end of it. They were going to have dances in a hall in the town that would be chaperoned either by the police or the clergy. Then what happened was they got there and they found out that the fiddler, or the box [accordion] couldn't be heard in these halls. And of course there was no public address system. Consequently, with no public address system to fill the hall, they'd have a little dance here, and a little dance there, everyplace in the hall. From this we see the formation of the larger and louder céilí bands.

The céilí dances satisfied the revivalist cultural mores of the Gaelic League. The Gaelic League in London first used the term céilí in reference to dance in 1897; it felt that the word *céilí*—a term in use primarily in Ireland's northern counties to describe a friendly house visit—would impart a homey feeling and attract a crowd to an upcoming league-sponsored dance. The dance repertoire, consisting of "Sets, Quadrilles, and Waltzes to Irish music," was carefully conceived that evening to create a strong image of Irish identity. The dances had been collected by Gaelic League dance instructors from original sources in West Cork and Kerry. These dances, published in two official texts, were presented as more authentic than the less rigid set dance forms that were in favor at the time. A dance scholar, John Cullinane, indicates that, as a product of revivalism, the céilí dances were new to most audiences. The term céilí dance gained widespread acceptance, and by the 1930s in Ireland, the céilí band had risen as a musical genre.[6]

Céilí bands performed mostly traditional Irish dance tunes. Instrumentation in early céilí bands typically consisted of the fiddle, flute, button accordion, piano, snare drum with woodblock, banjo, and occasionally double bass, Irish bellows-fed pipes known as the uillean pipes, piccolo, or saxophone. All instruments played the melody together, in unison, so that the dance rhythm of the tunes could be heard throughout the large hall.

Despite the best efforts of the government to promote the céilí genre, however, traditional Irish music by the 1940s had begun to play second fiddle to popular ballroom dance music. Since the introduction of radio and gramophone in the 1920s, the Irish in Ireland had become increasingly interested in jazz sounds and the popular music of the United States and England. People were attracted to the glamour of non-Irish dances such as foxtrots and quicksteps. Associated with their American and English origins, these forms seemed big, rich, and urban. Local céilí dance bands adopted them, playing a combination of Irish dance music and popular music.

Irish Music Clubs

While the Irish in Ireland tuned their radio dials to the urban music of America, the Irish in Boston retained their musical traditions in more intimate environments, as they had done in rural Ireland. If they weren't dancing and performing at a dance hall or a kitchen racket, musicians and non-musicians alike found community through the music clubs, which more closely approximated the neighborly, informal gatherings and céilí visits that had characterized traditional village life in Ireland.

One of the earliest of Boston's music clubs was the All-Ireland Music Club, founded by Tom Martin and his brothers Pat and John around 1936. Pat was considered one of the best flute players in Boston at the time, and Tom was a Boston police officer and flute player. As Jack Martin, son of John, recounts, the club

> was started around 1936 or '37. I was just a little kid. My father, my Uncle Pat, my Uncle Tom, and another guy by the name of Steve Carney put this thing together. They got the information out around the network about starting this club up at Emery Hall in Fields Corner, Dorchester. Within a very short time the place was packed every Sunday from two to six. They used to serve Irish bread and tea, and they used to serve beer. It was all free. They paid a little pittance to come in the door, to pay for the hall, the beer, and the Irish bread and all that.
>
> My Uncle Pat was the music director, and he controlled it with an iron hand. He'd call on the different musicians to play. What you'd do is, you'd write your name on a slip to say that you wanted to play. That way, then, you weren't embarrassed or anything. As

little as I was at the time, I used to play, and my father used to play harmonica, and we used to play duets together. I was probably seven or eight years old when that first took place. After about four or five years, they moved across the street to Arcadia Hall. These two halls, every other Sunday, they were packed to the rafters—musicians, and people coming in, people that enjoyed Irish music.

At the music clubs, the music was played in a traditional style: solo, intended for listening or dancing. This is quite different from the modern "session," in which musicians together play tunes drawn from a shared repertoire for their own enjoyment and not necessarily for the entertainment of an audience. In the music club, however, few musicians would share their tunes, because unique tunes helped to define one's musical identity, according to the accordion player Jack Martin:

> Back in the old days, when you had a tune, you kept it to yourself. This generation, yeah, sure they'll share it with you if you read music or do it by ear, but I think a lot of times back in that era, it's, "That's me tune, I'm not givin' it to nobody." I don't think most of the guys read music. Most everybody picked up the tunes by ear.

The music club served as a great training ground for younger musicians, and according to Dick Senier, "nearly every kid born of Irish parents could have a go at a fiddle or accordion, and many had taken step-dancing lessons for years."[7] While it was possible for younger musicians to learn new music at these clubs, Joe Derrane, like Jack Martin, also recalls that some of the older musicians were not generous with their tunes:

> One thing that drove me crazy at the clubs was that some of the old-timers guarded their tunes jealously. It was what they had; they were considered theirs. They didn't share tunes like they do today. When you asked them what tune that was, often they would say they couldn't remember the name of it. Or, if you said, "Play us that tune you played last week," they'd say, "Oh, I played that last week; I'll play it later" or "I forget which one you mean."[8]

Though tunes were not shared as openly in the old days, there was no stopping a young musician from learning by ear, the traditional way. Even at a very young age, it was clear to most who heard Joe Derrane that he was going to become a formidable force on the accordion; he could scoop up

The Dorchester Irish Music Club, c. 1947.

tunes and spit them back out in a form that was far more sophisticated than most had ever heard. Jack Martin remembers how the talented young Derrane was received at the All-Ireland Music Club:

> Joe comes into the hall this particular day with one of the older musicians. At that time, he hadn't made a big debut. He hadn't made records or anything; he was just a fifteen-year-old kid. Of course, back in those days you didn't play music unless one of the older men gave you the nod: "Now it's your turn, boy." The kids that were learning always sat in the background. It wasn't the type of thing that people got up and danced; it was a musicians' club. People played, *all* musicians, there was probably an average of fifteen or twenty guys there playing, on violins, flutes, and accordions.
>
> So my friend is sitting back like a good little guy and behaving himself, and finally my Uncle Pat Martin, who was the music director, called on Joe to play a couple of tunes. And of course, this

kid comes on with the accordion, and nobody ever heard anything like it. I mean, these guys were totally in awe.

Martin and Derrane were to become good friends over the years, seeing each other frequently at the music clubs and finally landing at Dudley Street in the late 1940s.

As World War II was about to erupt, the Irish who had come to America in the 1920s and 1930s were coming of age. They had seen a series of ups and downs in Irish music in the preceding twenty years. The 1920s had been a banner period for Irish music, and both recording and dance hall activity blossomed until the great Depression put a sudden end to any disposable income people had to buy records. Record sales in the United States hit an all-time low of $8 million in 1932, compared to some $32 million in 1927. The end of Prohibition in America in 1934 did provide a temporary boost for the dance hall scene, but this boost was cut short in 1941 by the onset of World War II.[9]

During World War II, transatlantic travel and Irish immigration came to a complete standstill, temporarily ending a long wave of Irish immigration. Many musicians were drafted to serve in Europe, while others concerned themselves with their own families, raising the generation of Irish-Americans who would, together with a wave of postwar immigrants, define the heyday of Irish music in Boston.

4

Strike Up the Band (Again)

Preoccupied with its own domestic affairs, Ireland remained neutral during World War II. As Ireland was establishing its recently won independence, Joe Walsh, secretary of Ireland's Department of External Affairs, articulated the country's position in no uncertain terms, saying, "Small nations like Ireland do not and cannot assume the role of defenders of just causes except their own."[1] The country was not unaffected by the war, however. Wartime shortages and a series of bad harvests in Ireland caused an economic depression that lasted through the 1950s. In *Twentieth Century Ireland*, the Irish historian Dermot Keogh writes: "It was a case of wartime conditions without a war."[2]

These conditions hit rural areas of Ireland particularly hard, starting yet another tide of emigration, mostly from rural areas in the north and west of Ireland, where traditional music still flourished. The U.S. Immigration and Nationality Act of 1952, which allowed unrestricted immigration from the Western Hemisphere, enabled large numbers of Irish people to come to the United States. Between 1951 and 1961, some 57 thousand of them immigrated to the United States.[3] Fiddler Paddy Cronin recalls that those who came brought their music with them:

> The big drive of immigration was always from the west of Ireland. Intercolonial Hall would be full of all those counties—Connemara in Galway, and all the other counties in the west of Ireland. And of

course, all those counties from the west is where the heart of the
music was. Galway and Clare, and Sligo—mighty on the fiddling—
and in my own county, Kerry. So many of the musicians here in
Boston were from those counties, and they all had their own
styles. You'll find that the Irish music that's played mostly around
the states is from the west of Ireland.

The wave of immigration from Ireland that started at the end of World
War II gave a jump start to the dance hall scene on Dudley Street. It
launched a new era that lasted until the mid-1960s and was to become
what people uniformly remember as a distinctive heyday of Irish music in
Boston. Jack Martin traces the start of the new dance hall era to the end
of the war. "The war ended on August 15, 1945, and the immigration
started coming out gradually, a little at a time, from Ireland. Now, these
kids are all into Irish dancing, and the ballroom, the céilí dancing. And of
course they're looking for a place to go, and the dance halls started picking
up again."

Most of the Irish who came to America after World War II were
young and unmarried. Lured by the promises of the American dream,
they were not so much escaping hardship as seeking opportunity and
adventure. With the U.S. economic boom that occurred not long after
World War II, Irish immigrants found it easy to get good jobs and decent
places to live. They also had disposable income to spend on entertainment,
and because they had brought with them from Ireland a predilection for
dance, the dance halls naturally became the social center of their transplanted lives.

In 1946, then, the conditions were in place for a dance hall heyday: a
wave of new immigrants in search of entertainment, musicians to perform
for them, ballrooms to dance in, and, not long after, the economic prosperity to make it all possible. While many of the dance halls had remained
open during the war, postwar plenty signaled a fresh start.

All it took to launch the dance hall scene once again, according to Joe
Derrane, was the leadership of a few enterprising individuals. Musicians
returning from the war revived their old bands to cater to the new influx
of postwar immigrants. Soon Dudley Square's five dance halls—the Intercolonial, the Hibernian, the Rose Croix, the Dudley Street Opera House,
and Winslow Hall—were flourishing again.

Heyday in the Five Halls

Hibernian Hall

The Hibernian Building Association of Boston Highlands built Hibernian Hall in 1913 at 182–186 Dudley Street. It began as a community center, dance hall, and meeting space for fourteen local chapters of the Ancient Order of Hibernians (AOH). The American branch of the AOH was founded in 1836, in reaction to widespread discrimination against Irish immigrants. By the turn of the century, it had shifted its emphasis to charitable activities, community service, and the preservation of Irish culture.

Hibernian Hall, which contained several smaller meeting halls and a large ballroom, as well as commercial space on the ground floor and bowling alleys and billiard tables in the basement, served as the center of Irish cultural life in Roxbury right through World War II, hosting a wide variety of club meetings and events.[4] One of its smaller halls, the John Boyle O'Reilly Hall, hosted performances of Irish traditional music.[5] For example, the fiddler Paddy Cronin played there frequently in the 1950s, though the band at the Hibernian was never as steady as that at the Intercolonial.

Intercolonial Hall

The Intercolonial Hall, situated at 214–218 Dudley Street, in the Intercolonial building, was the largest of Roxbury's five dance halls, hosting a thousand to twelve hundred people every Saturday night, and sometimes even more. When dancers overflowed the main hall, the Crystal Ballroom, the management had to scramble to bring some musicians down off the stage so that they could play downstairs in one of the smaller halls, such as the Longfellow Hall.

The Intercolonial building was designed by the prolific architect Harris M. Stephenson (1845–1909), of Jamaica Plain. The New England Structure Company completed construction in 1906, and the three-story hall opened in April 1907 as a social club for Americans and Canadians of Irish descent. The building included space for two retail shops on the ground floor, as well as several meeting rooms, a library, smoking rooms, a banquet hall, a gymnasium, a bowling alley, billiard rooms, and on the top floor, a ballroom. On the second floor were four banquet halls named the Brunswick,

Hibernian Hall, built in 1915, was the center of Irish cultural activities for more than fifty years. (Courtesy of the Boston Public Library, Print Department.)

the Longfellow, the Evangeline, and the Saint Lawrence, which individuals could rent for business or union meetings.[6]

Dudley Street Opera House

Located at 111 Dudley Street, at the corner of Washington Street, the Dudley Street Opera House opened as a "bright little playhouse" in 1879,

The Dudley Street Opera House, not long after it was built.
(Photo courtesy of the Bostonian Society/Old State House.)

under the proprietorship of N. J. Bradlee. Designed to seat seven hundred, it had a small stage, and its interior was not ornate but functional. After featuring regular performances during its first season, it enjoyed only one more season of opera performance. It was then open only occasionally, to traveling bands, performances by amateur companies, concerts, and public meetings.[7] The Dudley Street Opera House is reportedly where, around the turn of the century, the legendary boxer John L. Sullivan made Boston history by knocking the local fighter Jack Scannell into the orchestra pit and announcing to the crowd, "My name is John L. Sullivan, and I can lick any man in the house."

Over time, the seats were taken out of the auditorium, and a ballroom floor was built. The floor was constructed to have some "give," so that it was more comfortable for dancing. Its wooden surface was kept slippery for dancing by wax granules or cornmeal sprinkled across the floor, particularly in the mucky winter weather or during summer's humidity. Dancers entered the ballroom at the back, facing the stage up front. To the right, there was tiered seating.

The Rose Croix

The Rose Croix Hall was housed in the upper floor of the Knights of Columbus building, located at the corner of 150 Dudley and 60–62 Warren Street. It was designed in 1878–1879 by the prominent Boston architect Nathaniel J. Bradlee, who also designed the Dudley Street Opera House. The building, constructed by T. J. Whidden, housed the Roxbury Council of the Knights of Columbus, businesses on the street level, and lawyers, dentists, insurance firms, and Western Union upstairs.

The Rose Croix was a very popular dance hall among the Downeasters, the Canadian Maritime community of Cape Bretoners and Newfoundlanders who had settled in Boston—"two-boaters," "scadán" (Irish Gaelic for "herring"), or "herring chokers," as they were called—many of whom also had Irish heritage.

The Rose Croix Hall, to the right, was at the corner of Dudley and Warren Streets, in the heart of Dudley Square. O'Byrne DeWitt's shop was on the first floor of the fashionable Hotel Dartmouth, to the left in the photo, taken July 27, 1934.
(Photo courtesy of the Bostonian Society/Old State House.)

Winslow Hall

Winslow Hall was located at 99 Warren Street, on the corner of Dudley and Warren Streets, on the third floor of the building, across from the Rose Croix. Smaller and less ornate than the other halls, it tended to attract smaller crowds. The Waldorf cafeteria and coffee shop was located on the first floor of the building, and many would stop in for a bite on the way home from any of the dance halls.

With its five dance halls, Dudley Street became a mecca for Irish nationals and the Irish-Americans who found community among them. According to Joe Derrane, Irish immigrants created a transplanted subset of Ireland—"the next parish to Galway"—on Dudley Street: "That area was unique to the whole country, maybe the world. The young people were coming out by the thousands. On a Saturday night, except for the architecture and the cars, it could have been Dublin. There were thousands of people out to dance."[8]

After World War II, not only Roxbury but the whole city was bursting with dance music. One typical weekend on the thriving Boston dance scene featured Myles O'Malley, Duke Ellington, Johnny Hodges, Ethel Waters, and Joe Derrane, all playing at different venues.[9] Frank Storer, a pianist who was just a teenager when his father first brought him to perform on Dudley Street, remembers a lively atmosphere, including "full-capacity crowds in all the halls. There were probably twenty-five hundred people on the streets in the Dudley Street area on any Saturday night. In fact, at one time I myself was playing Wednesday, Thursday night, Friday night, Saturday night, and Sunday night in one of those halls."

The war had resulted in a changing of the guard on Dudley Street, however. After the war, several musicians of the older generation who had played there before the war attempted to revive the halls, but these musicians, such as Myles O'Malley, Tom Senier, and Joe O'Leary, quickly discovered that the new young immigrants arriving from Ireland after 1945 had new tastes, as did a whole batch of new musicians. Many of the old-timers had moved on to other venues in the city, such as Wally's Old Timers on Ruggles Street or the Roseland State Ballroom.

O'Leary's band still played on Friday nights on Dudley Street, but the music it played was primarily American swing and big band music, with an occasional Irish waltz. The band also frequently played for events for the Eire Society and Irish Charitable Society, both of which were made up of

*Frank Storer performs to a full house in the Crystal
Ballroom at the Intercolonial dance hall, Dudley Square.*
(From the library of Frank Storer.)

the more established Irish immigrants who had already moved out to sub-urbs such as Milton and Hyde Park.

As for Myles O'Malley, he had been discharged from the navy in 1945 and re-formed a big band that played regularly at venues all over the city, with Johnny Bresnahan on accordion, Joseph Glennon on piano, Vic Alexander on trumpet, and Cookie Pimental at the drums. His band played some Friday nights of modern dancing at Dudley Street but found its crowd in a regular Friday night stint at the Roseland State, as well as legion halls and smaller clubs such as Crescent Gardens in Revere Beach, Brighton Tap and Restaurant, the Irish-American House, and Dick McGinley's Memory Lane in Somerville.

Joe O'Leary's Irish Minstrels also attempted a return to Dudley Street after the war, hosting dances at Hibernian Hall, but the crowds were different, says Joe Derrane:

> The Hibernian was on again/off again. Joe O'Leary tried to make a comeback there, and he only got six or eight weeks out of it. He had been out of the scene for some time, and when he came back, he was still doing the music of the twenties and thirties, and it just didn't work. It was the music of two or three generations ago; he just couldn't get it off the ground.

At Winslow Hall, Tom Senier revived his Emerald Isle Orchestra in the late 1940s—this time with his old friend the accordionist Jack Storer, as well as a new cast of younger members. The personnel in the band changed frequently, and he used the dance halls as a training ground for young musicians. This occurred especially at the céilí dancing nights on Wednesdays at Winslow Hall, when he would be joined by his son Dick, as well as Frank Storer, Jack's son. On weekend nights, Tom's band might also include Walter and Al Deiss, the horn-playing sons of the veteran drummer Dutchie Deiss from the band's Deacon Hall days, and sometimes an Italian saxophone player named Guy Bonanno. Tom Senier's bands, which had played at Winslow Hall from the late 1930s, continued off and on there through the 1940s and early 1950s.

Meanwhile, Matty Toohy of county Kerry, Ireland, who had played in Senier's orchestra, left to form his own band, which performed on Saturday nights in the Dudley Street Opera House. Musicians in his band included Timmy Collins on melodeon, Joe Fahey on banjo, and usually a horn player, such as Al Deiss. The band drew a crowd of Kerry natives and played mostly Irish ballroom selections, including Irish waltzes, polkas, a few jigs, and a few reels. As in the other halls, there were few requests for céilí dances, save for the occasional Siege of Ennis or Walls of Limerick. By day, Toohy worked at Harvard University, but by night, he was playing to growing crowds. Mike Cummings, a dance instructor and Irish football star, recalls:

> When I came out, the place to go was the Dudley Street Opera House. Matty Toohy's band played there, and it was always

crowded. After you danced, you'd be soaking wet with sweat, and the only relief was to go to the fire escape, where you could nearly touch fingers with the people passing by on the elevated. The train took a sharp turn around the opera house into Dudley Station with a grinding and screeching. It was very loud!

Dances in the Rose Croix Hall were run by Bill Lamey of Cape Breton. His band included pianists Mary Jessie MacDonald, Eddie Irwin, and Sally MacEachern Kelly; guitarist Frank Gillan; drummer Jimmy Corrigan; and Jimmy Kelly on the banjo.[10] Many weekends, Bill Lamey invited the great fiddle players from Cape Breton to perform: "Little Jack" MacDonald, Winston ("Scotty") Fitzgerald, the MacMasters, and Angus Chisolm.

The dancing at the Rose Croix was a group style known as contra dancing, which originated in Canada. Herbie MacLeod, one of the founding members of the Canadian American Club in Watertown, recalls a bustling Canadian scene. Interestingly, unlike Irish traditional dancing, Canadian dancing—specifically Cape Breton set dancing—was frequently helped along by the expert dance instruction of a prompter.[11] Malcolm Murray was a well-known prompter.

Attracting a mostly Canadian crowd, the Rose Croix Hall also hosted céilí dance lessons on Monday and Tuesday nights. The hall also later became known for the "Pioneer" dances on Friday nights, for people who had taken the pledge not to drink. The Pioneer Total Abstinence Association movement, which started in Ireland, had a very strong branch in Boston right up through the mid-1960s.

Of the five dance halls on Dudley Street in the late 1940s, people tended to select a favorite hall and frequent it almost exclusively. People often chose according to regional or county association in the home country, and the division of crowds by hall became a microcosm of Ireland within Boston.

As Joe Derrane tells it,

> The Kerry people went to the Dudley Street Opera House. There was Winslow Hall, on the third floor—they all seemed to be on the third floor! You'd get a nosebleed going up there. Most of the people, about three hundred to three-fifty, were from the west of Ireland: Connemara, Mayo, Donegal. Across the street was Rose Croix Hall, mostly Scots and Canadians, and some Irish. There would be about five to six hundred people there. The Opera House fit about six hundred, the Hibernian, a thousand, and the

John Ryan, a Boston legend. In his trademark fur coat, Ryan was a fixture in the Greenville Café. Ryan arrived at the Storer home in the late 1920s. A native of either Saskatchewan or Alberta, Canada, he claimed that he had no family and asked to rent a room for one week, and he stayed there forty years. Mae Storer took him under her wing, as was her style, and immediately got him a job as an orderly at the Little Sisters of the Poor hospital in Somerville. He worked there until he retired. Ryan passed away in the Storer home at eighty years of age.
(From the library of Frank Storer.)

Intercolonial Hall, where Johnny Powell's band played, there were about a thousand to fifteen hundred people there.[12]

According to Derrane, there was very little "ballroom hopping":

Some people did it, but it was a kind of one-time effort to see which they liked the best, and that became their place. Or they'd say, "Well, we like this one" or "We like that one, so we'll go here this week, and next week we'll go there." You didn't get people who would go from ballroom to ballroom to ballroom each night. Not like these days, the pub crawling. There was no ballroom crawling. People pretty much said, "I'll see you at the hall." That's all I used to hear, "See you at the hall. See you at the hall."[13]

While all of the halls were crowded at one time or another, the crowds were fickle. It seemed that every time a new band came on the scene, the dancing crowds would suddenly disappear from one hall without warning and go to another hall. No single event made that more evident than the eve of Labor Day 1948, when Johnny Powell and his brother Mike started running a dance at the Intercolonial. A war veteran and an accordion player, Johnny Powell stepped off the battlefields of the South Pacific and onto the dance hall stage. According to Derrane, "Johnny Powell had been in the service and came back after the war was over. He and his brother decided they'd try to get a dance hall going, and they did, and one hall kind of fed the other. It was just like the whole street took on a life of its own."

Until 1948, the Intercolonial had stood virtually empty, while the Winslow, the Hibernian, and the Dudley Street Opera House blossomed. But almost as quickly as Powell rented three of its ballrooms for dances, the Intercolonial became the most popular of all the halls. Its Crystal Ballroom had massive appeal to young Irish audiences, Joe Derrane recalls. According to Derrane, it

had a huge motorized ball hanging from the ceiling, covered with little one-inch square mirrors, and they had four spotlights with special filters that they would shine on it, so the light was always varying. There would be little sparkles and specks of light all over the place. It was very classy. Physically, the Hibernian was the same size, but it never had the pizzazz of the Intercolonial.

By the time Paddy Cronin arrived in Boston in 1949, Johnny Powell had started his dances at the Intercolonial, and the Opera House crowd had moved over there. Powell's Irish-American mix rapidly eclipsed the strain of more purely Irish music played by Matty Toohy at the Dudley Street Opera House. The same fate befell Tom Senier's Emerald Isle Orchestra at the Winslow. A Galway native who settled in Uphams Corner, Dorchester, Senier favored the traditional Irish music for dances, but the crowds were increasingly drawn to the glamour of Powell's band, with its tuxedos and its modern music. As Paddy Cronin recalls:

> Tom Senier used to run the Winslow. It went good for about three months. 'Twas mobbed. And then something happened, and the crowd started leaving. "The crowd," he says, "it took them three months to close me." The crowds started going and going and going, and in the finish there was nobody. There was nobody left, only himself and the fella on the door.
>
> The other place above [the Intercolonial] had the people. Johnny Powell ran the dances in the Intercolonial in them days, and he was very well known. And he would drag in the crowd, and of course the people followed the people all the time. Senier put over the Winslow for a very short while, but then the crowd started moving, and they never again got them back there.

After Tom Senier's band left, Martin Flaherty, a box player, and his four-piece band took to the Winslow stage. That band included George Derrane on banjo, guitar, and tenor saxophone, as well as Tommy McSharry on piano.

Another musician who performed in Winslow Hall was Jackie (a.k.a. Johnny) Bresnahan, a native of the Mission Hill area of Roxbury. Bresnahan had played in the Emerald Isle Orchestra before the war, and he had kept the music alive in the city after many of Boston's young Irish and Irish-American men were conscripted to fight for the allied forces. Mission Hill locals like Mary Murphy favored Winslow Hall:

> Jackie Bresnahan played there with his band. He was from Mission Hill, and all the people were from Kerry. Such beautiful memories. . . . We did the highland fling, the Varsovienne, the Siege of Ennis, the Irish polkas, the beautiful Irish waltzes—it kept us going all night. We come sweating like maniacs! We just loved it.

Despite the popularity of the Dudley Street Opera House and Winslow Hall among their smaller crowds of devoted fans, the Intercolonial and the Hibernian drew the biggest crowds by far. The Intercolonial got busy so quickly that musicians like accordion player Mickey Connolly got work playing music there as soon as they arrived in America. Recalls Connolly:

> When I came here in '49, Johnny Powell's band was going on Dudley Street, and a friend of mine, Jimmy Costello, had a party for me and another lad that came out at the same time. Jimmy heard me playing the accordion at the party—it was a house party, right up the street here. Jimmy says, "Now, Saturday I'll bring you into Dudley Street. I want you to meet somebody." He brought me into Dudley Street, Saturday night, to Johnny Powell's at the Intercolonial, and I was playing in Johnny Powell's band the next Thursday night. They had to borrow an accordion for me. That's how my thing in Dudley Street started.

It seems that anyone who grew up in Irish Boston during the time remembers even a single visit to the Intercolonial as if it were a pilgrimage. Joanne Keyes, raised in suburban Woburn, went to a dance hall on Dudley Street only once, but she remembers it as if it were yesterday. "My grandmother took my mother and me to the Intercolonial for something when I was only eight years old," she says. "I remember it so well. I still think about it all the time. It was just so fun. They were all there doing the Irish dancing and the music—there were old people and kids, all ages."

The crowds seemed endless. Says Derrane: "If the [halls] were packed, they just kept letting people in."[14] Even though the halls were just steps from the neighborhood fire station, the fire code never seemed to be a concern, and the places were frequently packed well beyond their legal capacities. Frank Devin, who was not a musician but spent many hours serving music-loving crowds as a bartender in Joe McPherson's pub below one of the halls, would watch the crowds go in and out:

> You could hear the dancing from upstairs, the feet. It was wild. You couldn't move in the place. I don't know how they ever danced up there, it was so crowded. The streets would be packed before the dance, and suddenly would be deserted. You would wonder where everyone went and how they all fit in there. But when the place emptied out at midnight, the streets would be filled with people again. Nobody sat; they all danced.

All together at the dance hall but far from home, people from all of Ireland's thirty-two counties would recognize their similarities and ignite a sense of pride in being Irish, something they may have taken for granted back home. And they were proud of being from not just Ireland but from a particular region of Ireland. The real and imagined traits—accents, senses of humor, names, and idiosyncrasies—that distinguished the Kerry "culchie" from the Dublin "jackeen," the Galway fella from the Corkman, didn't melt away in America. Not just in the dance halls but also in numerous social clubs, the Irish would organize their transplanted communities in America by county of origin.

Irish Social Clubs

In addition to hosting the dances, the Intercolonial and Hibernian Halls served as home bases for Boston's numerous Irish county clubs. At one time, the city had a social club for each county in Ireland, and a Central Council of Irish County Clubs unified the counties by gathering seven delegates from each county club at Hibernian Hall on the fourth Friday of each month. In addition, each club had regular meetings at the Hibernian, the Intercolonial, or the Rose Croix, followed by a social, which usually included music and dance. If the club didn't have musicians as members, it would frequently hire musicians to play for céilí and set dancing, which might go on for several hours after the business meeting.

Kinship networks had always been particularly strong among Irish immigrants to America, and county clubs helped to ease the transition into American life. At the county clubs, greenhorn arrivals could find work by hobnobbing with fellows from their own area at home. They found other important things there, too. As Michael Quinlin of the Boston Irish Tourism Association puts it, "Immigrants to America quickly learn that loyalty to one's own is a valued trait, not just for jobs and housing, but for upholding the cultural and social values that seem more important than ever once you leave home."[15]

Most clubs met once a month, as a social event and often to raise money to support charitable causes. The highlight of a club's year was, without question, the annual ball. The occasion often included installation of officers, club announcements, dinner, and dancing. Larry Reynolds, a fiddler and a perennial figure in Boston's traditional Irish music scene, recalls that "most every club had a ball every year. Everybody got dressed up—tux, the hall, big gowns. That was the highlight of the year for that county. Each county would try and have a bigger ball than the next one. They'd have them in a hotel, like the Commander in Cambridge."

In addition to the county-based clubs, the Irish Social Club brought people from all counties together. Founded by Mary Concannon in 1945, it raised funds to send busloads of young Irish step dancers and musicians to New York to compete in the annual Irish dance competition and festival known as the *feis* (pronounced "fesh"), because Boston didn't have its own feis until 1950. Every Sunday, Mary Concannon would host Irish Social Club meetings in a back room on the first floor of Hibernian Hall. In the early years, the meetings were family events, intended mostly for mothers whose children were learning step dancing. Patsy (Flavin) Hurley, born in Dorchester, whose parents were from Ireland, grew up listening to Irish music. She recalls going to the Irish Social Club every week after her step dancing lessons. At the club she learned popular ballroom dances like the highland fling and Shoe the Donkey.

Mary Concannon would invite musicians such as the fiddlers Johnny Fitzgerald and Pat Connolly, as well as the accordionists Johnny Bresnahan and Connie Hanafin, to play for the children. Of course, the gatherings were as much for the adults as for the children, but because of Boston blue laws, adults were not allowed to dance on Sundays. But so often, to the Irish, law serves as a creative challenge rather than a deterrent. Within just a few years, the Sunday meetings became so crowded they were held in the upper halls, until finally they were moved all the way up to the large Hibernian Hall itself, on the top floor.

A young accordion player named Joe Joyce attended regularly in the late 1940s. He says:

> People would sit around in those folding chairs like you have in the choir—gum on the bottom of the seats and all. They were low-slung, fold-up seats, four of them bracketed together. The cops did show up from time to time. You had to pay the cop five bucks or something to get them off your back. Mary's husband, Jimmy Concannon, was looking out the peephole: "Jeez, it's a cop."
>
> This was 1947. The blue laws were in effect in those days. It was like a secret society on the top floor. The music could be

heard out on the street, so they shut the windows. Now it's ninety-two degrees heat in the place, and they're fanning themselves with the napkins. "It's a bit schtuffy in here." "Shhh . . . the cops'll be around agin, and they'll git ye." After cops left, they all started singing again, with Tommy Shields directing them in some song.

Mike Cummings, who emigrated from Ballygar in 1947, also recounts colorful stories of the Sunday dances:

> The Hibernian Hall was three floors, and the lights on all three floors could be turned on and off by a chain that came down to the first floor. Down at the door was stationed old Mr. Concannon, and the cops would come down to the hall and ring the bell. This one cop named Burke was a heavyset man, and when he rang, Concannon would pull the chain and the lights would go off and on, on all three floors.

Upstairs in the upper hall, continues Cummings, the emcee would see the light and rush all the dancers off the floor. By the time Burke had lumbered his way up the stairs past the Céad Míle Fáilte mosaic on the second-floor landing and then climbed the final creaky stairs to the big hall, Mary Concannon would have the kids out on the floor step dancing, and the club members would sip their tea, shout encouragement to the young dancers, nod to the cop, and wink to each other. Says Cummings, "It was all right to watch the children dance, but you couldn't dance yourself."

By and by, Burke would catch his breath and make his way back down the stairway. Old Concannon would bid him good night, and no sooner would the door latch click shut than Concannon hit the chain again. As the lights flickered on and off to give the all clear, the emcee would take to the floor and announce, "Everyone up for an auld Irish waltz!"

5

If We Only Had Old Ireland Over Here

Dance, Music, and Irish Identity
in the Postwar Dance Halls

The Ireland that so many left behind in the 1940s and 1950s was in transition. With only a few decades as an independent nation, Ireland at that time was self-consciously modernizing. Some there regarded the old rural ways with shame, as symbols of the impoverished past. Increasingly influenced by American music and the cultural values associated with it, many Irish began equating traditional music with rural Ireland, and by association, with all that was backward and poor. Fiddles, flutes, and accordions were guilty by association. Larry Reynolds recalls having to carry his fiddle under his coat so he wouldn't be branded a "bog man," a "mucker"—a country bumpkin.[1] "The influence of pop music," he recalls, "had put Irish traditional music behind the door, so to speak. It had overwhelmed the Irish music. If people'd hear you playing traditional music, a jig or a reel, they'd sometimes be laughing at you."

Reynolds and traditional musicians like him were pleasantly surprised to find that Irish music was thriving in America in the dance hall bands, alongside "Irish-ized" renditions of the modern pop music of the time. Indeed, there was more Irish music in American dance halls than in the ones at home, and some said that coming to Dudley Street for the first time was like taking a step back in time. In Boston, Irish music was popular and attracted large crowds, and yet it was slightly different from the Irish music played in Ireland. The music that sent people sailing across the American dance floor was a mixture of Irish and American sounds—a jig, a reel, a fling interspersed with more modern popular waltzes, tangos, and fox-trots.

It was not uncommon for a Siege of Ennis Irish céilí dance to follow a medley of waltzes. On the dance floor, Irish met American in a way that reflected the increasingly cosmopolitan Emerald Isle, but in a balance that displayed the immigrants' longing for what they had left behind.

The dance bands that gathered crowds five nights a week followed the precedent set by the swing bands of a generation earlier. Like the swing bands, the fifteen-piece Irish bands squeezed onto a small stage, the band name emblazoned on a low stand set before each musician. But something was different: accordions and fiddles often led the bands, banjos picked the

Irish and American flags surround the Tara Céilídte Band as they perform for a New Hampshire television program to celebrate St. Patrick's Day, 1959. Front row, left to right: Paddy Cronin, Mickey Connolly, Des Regan. Middle row, left to right: Larry Reynolds, Johnny Murphy, and an unidentified piano player. Back row, on drums, George Shanley.
(From the library of Mickey Connolly.)

melodies alongside them, and saxophones followed along, reading the tunes from *O'Neill's Music of Ireland* as best they could. And instead of the lush, meticulously arranged harmonies of the swing era, the musicians played traditional jigs, reels, hornpipes, and other Irish dance tunes in unison, the way an Irish céilí band would.

The mix of music spoke to the mixed crowds of new Irish immigrants and to first- and second-generation Irish-Americans. Irish-Americans in this era were most often born to Irish parents who had come to America during the early decades of the twentieth century. Though this generation of Irish-Americans may have gone to American schools, they lived in Irish neighborhoods, and their parents socialized almost exclusively with Irish people. Living among them, new immigrants from Ireland were torn by dual desires: an eagerness for a new, modern life and a longing for the old, familiar one. Together, Irish-Americans and Irish made up the market that promoters had to cater to if they were to build a successful dance hall.

"Dancing Our Shoes to Pieces"

In America as in Ireland in the 1940s and 1950s, Irish dance and music brought people together. Larry Reynolds, one of Boston's most active and longstanding supporters of Irish music, remembers his youth in county Galway, Ireland, where young people met for a few jigs and reels at Sunday evening crossroads dances. It was a tradition with roots dating back at least to the seventeenth century. In the Ireland of his youth, he says,

> there was always dances on Sunday night. In summertime there were Maypoles. There was a little stage set up outside, and dancers would go up and down, like in somebody's field. There'd be a band playing, and everybody came. It wasn't very expensive to get in, but you had a great dance on the long summer nights. You'd dance all night long. Then, of course, if there was the dance hall on, you'd go to the dance hall after, but the Maypoles were great; you were dancing outside, and it didn't seem to rain as much then as it does now in Ireland. It would start about six or seven o'clock, and you'd dance until eleven or twelve o'clock at night.

Modern music had risen in popularity in the cities, but most Irish immigrants to Boston came from small towns in the west of Ireland, where work was scarce and traditional music was ever-present at local dances—though modern music was making its way to rural areas, as well. Dance was a big part of Nora McGillicuddy's rural upbringing:

> There was a lot of dancing in Ireland where I lived. Céilí and modern. There were two halls in a place called Salt Hill in Galway. There was a big modern hall called Sea Point. That was where the modern dancing was. That was more expensive. And then we went to the other hall; it was all céilí. We also had a dance hall right in the village, about two or three miles from where I was brought up, in Moycullen village, a lovely dance hall. And we used to go to another one six miles away. There was a lot of dancing. We used to go two nights, at least.

Dance continued to be important for immigrants in America. The dance halls provided an Americanized substitute for the céilí sounds they were familiar with from the small towns and villages of Ireland. While early dance hall bands in America were not called céilí bands, the term eventually came into use in the United States. It made an appearance in the 1950s, for example, in the Copley recordings of Joe Derrane and his All-Star Céilí Band, though American céilí bands like Derrane's included far more American material in their repertoire than did their Irish counterparts.

It was clear to successful dance hall promoters, whose task it was to rent the halls, hire the bands, and attract the dancers, that the most celebrated dance hall bands were the ones that specialized in both American and Irish music and performed on both traditional and modern instruments. The Intercolonial and the Hibernian halls both had two floors: upstairs for the more modern music and the smaller halls below for the Irish music. The bands that played in the large upstairs ballrooms were adept at playing both styles, though.

Upstairs at the Intercolonial, in the Crystal Ballroom, bands tended to play primarily waltzes and instrumental versions of popular American tunes, though with several Irish traditional instruments, such as accordion, fiddle, and occasionally, flute. Downstairs in the Longfellow Hall (at the Intercolonial) and the John Boyle O'Reilly and O'Connell halls (at the Hibernian), the music was primarily traditional Irish jigs, reels, and hornpipes. Here's how Storer describes the division of music by floor:

You had a band on the top floor playing big time, playing charts, playing nice American ballads, and playing a good bit of Irish stuff, too. They had the two accordions, Billy Caples and Johnny Powell. Johnny would also provide music for several weddings each weekend, and by some miracle he would show up at all of them.

The top-floor bands like Joe Derrane's identified themselves as Irish, but in reality, they played very few of the most traditional Irish dance tunes. Derrane recalls:

We were doing a large, large percentage of waltzes. We did a fair number of highland flings, hornpipes, an odd barn dance thrown in. We also did a good number of polkas, and . . . that'd be the meat and potatoes of it. You'd even do a couple of sets of fox-trots, you might even throw a rumba in there. Once during the night, you'd play reels to a "Siege of Ennis" dance.

American-born musicians like Storer and Derrane recognized that Irish and Irish-Americans did not necessarily share dance tastes, so when playing with Johnny Powell's band, they catered to both groups. Says Derrane:

The Powell band was versatile. His band was the most flexible. . . . Instead of the traditional ad lib way of playing the air, they put it to a dance tempo—waltzes like "The Snowy Breasted Pearl," "Skibereen," "Connemara Shore," and "She Lived Beside the Anner." And Johnny's band would play Irish-American tunes— "Danny Boy," "When Irish Eyes Are Smiling," and "My Wild Irish Rose."

If you were going to dance, you'd need the music, but as it turned out, the music needed the dancers just as much. If they wanted a crowd at the next dance, bands had to play music that kept the dancers on the floor. It was more important for the music to be danceable than identifiably Irish. Derrane recalls:

We'd play medleys of three waltzes, so those who might want to dance with a few people would get ample time to spend with each. Also, we'd play a medley of polkas, or highland flings, which no one really plays anymore, but they were very popular to dance to in those days. People liked the heel-toe steps. We'd often play the

Siege of Ennis, which was like one part of a full set. We didn't play Clare or Galway sets; Irish-Americans couldn't learn the [more complex] dances well. We tried to keep everyone happy.[2]

Musicians recognized that more important than playing specific styles or genres of dance was simply *playing*, so they kept up the pace of their sets. Storer says:

With the Irish it was always sets of three—three highland flings, three waltzes, three polkas. When you did the American music, you did two short fox-trots, then you'd do a short jitterbug, jives, but American style, then you'd do a tango or a rumba, then you'd take a break. That was ten-thirty. You took a break till quarter of eleven, then at quarter of eleven, you went back to the waltzes, flings, and polkas routine.

Some of the American music would have a mixed American/Irish feel. Joe Derrane explains that the bands frequently played "six-eights," a type of dance tune in which familiar American tunes or marches originally in 6/8 time were played almost like jigs. He says:

They would be tunes like "The Hundred Pipers." We used to make that distinction between the jigs and the so-called six-eight. That tune was originally a Scottish tune, but it would have been done pretty much like a waltz time. We did it for years also in jig time. Once in a while, we'd do it as a waltz. Sometimes at the end, you might do two of those six-eights, then throw a jig right on the end of it.

The Dances

The dances of the day were primarily couple dances. However, Irish group dances—such as the oft-mentioned Siege of Ennis—were a small but indispensable part of the evening. The Siege of Ennis was a popular céilí dance that was interactive. Couples started the dance across long lines, and as the music played, progressed together down the lines, alternating with other couples, so that by the end of the dance, they had danced with nearly everyone on the floor.

Mike Cummings of county Galway, who came to America at the age of twenty-two in 1947, brought with him a collection of Irish dances that he had learned back home. Recalls Cummings:

> In my town of Ballygar, there was a group of people that wanted to learn the Gaelic dances, so we petitioned to the Irish Folklore Commission to send a teacher to teach us to dance. Every Monday night, the teacher came to us, and we had just enough people to pay the teacher and an accordion player. We learned all the steps for the most popular group dances at the time. The teacher taught us the Siege of Ennis, the Walls of Limerick, the Four-Hand Reel, and the High-Cauled Cap.

While some smaller circles of avid dancers were familiar with the relatively new Siege of Ennis dance, Cummings brought the dances to a much larger audience in Boston. Once he got to Boston, he immediately went looking for places to do the Irish dances he had enjoyed so much in Ballygar. He says:

> After I came over, a group of us started to inquire about Irish Gaelic dancing here in Boston. I was already captain of the GAA [Gaelic Athletic Association] football team by this time. We found that the Eire Society, the most prestigious of the Irish cultural organizations, sponsored a group of girls who were teaching folk dancing. The society was formed to spread the culture of the Irish and was made up mainly of Irish-Americans who had achieved some status in the community—lawyers, doctors, teachers, businessmen.
>
> Looking to dance, I went out there and joined the club. An Irish-American girl, Mary O'Keefe, was the teacher. She would teach the dances by reading them from a book that she got from the Irish Dancing Commission. She had never learned them herself. They were delighted to find that I arrived with these dances already in my head. That was very successful, and our club also went on to join the Harvard [University] Folk Dance Club, as well.

Mary O'Keefe was teaching from a book published by the Coimisiún an Rinnce (Irish Dancing Commission) in 1939. The book featured written descriptions of many of the approved céilí choreographies—including the Waves of Tory, Walls of Limerick, and High-Cauled Cap, dances that were widely disseminated throughout Ireland, and eventually made their way to

America. Before this, the set dances performed in Ireland consisted of a mixture of Irish steps, Irish music, and French figures that had been brought to Ireland in the eighteenth century via England and Scotland, by travelers, dance masters, and soldiers.[3]

Prior to Mike Cummings's arrival on the scene, dancers in Boston would dance sets—which would include a polka, a jig, and a reel—that could last an hour. Everyone joined the dance, even the musicians occasionally. Tom Senier's son Dick recalls playing with Joe Derrane, reportedly a fine step dancer at the time. According to Dick, Derrane would hand over his accordion to another musician and jump down off the stage for a dance. By the 1940s, however, set dancing gave way to céilí dancing, a more strictly choreographed form of group figure dancing.[4]

Mike Cummings, who had learned the newer dances firsthand in Ireland, soon made his name as a teacher of the Siege of Ennis, without question the most popular group dance at the time. He taught with the Gaelic League president and staunch IRA man Walter O'Regan, to the music of accordion player Tom Senier. The dance classes were so successful that Senier, veteran of the Emerald Isle Orchestra from before the war, suggested that they take their show on the road to Dudley Street, and he'd revive his Winslow Hall band. Cummings tells the story this way:

> We started up in Dudley Street about 1948. After about five
> nights, we weren't making enough to pay for the hall, to pay for
> Tom and his band, so we gave it up. Johnny Powell was just start-
> ing up his band at the Intercolonial at the time—and Johnny, by
> the way, was a very good step dancer in his own right. For a heavy
> guy, he was exceptionally light on his feet. Well, he came down to
> us one night, and he was watching us. He asked me if I would come
> up to the Intercolonial on Saturday and start the Siege of Ennis.
> The dancers had tried to get it going week after week, but it
> would get all fouled up.
>
> So I started going to the Intercolonial, and I would line up the
> dancers, four facing four, and not long after Johnny started, we'd
> go through one set. The Siege of Ennis became the mainstay of
> the dances. It stayed that way for years—even today. The Irish
> love it. It gave them an opportunity to meet. You met everyone in
> the hall, and you danced with everyone. We also tried the Walls of
> Limerick, but it was too involved, so it dropped out of favor.

The Siege of Ennis's popularity was no surprise, given the environment: a large group of young, single people away from home. The dance allowed each dancer to enjoy the company of several dancing partners. For Nora McGillicuddy, it was the best part of the evening. She says: "The funniest part of the dancing was the Siege of Ennis. Swinging with all different ones. We'd laugh through the whole thing. They all swing a little different. They weren't the best swingers, some of them, and sometimes you'd almost fall. It was so fast, you'd really almost fall."

While Cummings was always very much aware of his Irish and Gaelic cultural roots, the accordion player and singer Joe Joyce felt that people enjoyed the dances not because of their Irish authenticity but rather because they were well-known dances that a large number of people could participate in. Overall, he indicates, most dancers at the halls preferred non-Irish forms, such as waltzes. He says: "The Gaelic societies did keep up the céilí dances and the set dances: the Walls of Limerick, The Waves of Tory, the Siege of Ennis, those kinds of dances. But people weren't into a rejuvenation of the traditional culture. They were just happy to go down and have a few old waltzes; then they'd go home."

In addition to the group dances, solo dancing was also popular in some circles, though that was done more frequently at weddings or kitchen rackets. Referred to in Connemara as *an bhatráil* (the battering) and in Boston as a "breakdown," today it is more formally called *sean-nós*, or "old style," dancing. A freer form of step dancing, it was originally performed mostly in the Irish-speaking area of Connemara (the Gaeltacht).

All would stop at an Intercolonial wedding when Johnny Powell's band struck up "Miss McLeod's Reel" or "The Stack of Barley," and the best breakdown dancers from Connemara would take to the floor for a solo dance, while crowds gathered around them. South Boston native Éamon Connolly's mother brought her dance steps with her from the stony hills of Rosmuc, Connemara, to the hard streets of South Boston, and on to Roxbury weddings at the Intercolonial, where she was known as one of the best breakdown dancers around. Says Éamon of the dance style, "This wasn't like the Riverdance style—it was the old style of dancing, where they'd give a good goddamn kick at the floor."

Still, the old-time waltz was probably the dance most commonly performed at the dance halls, though according to Connie McEleney, waltz style in America was different from what he had been accustomed to back home. In Ireland, old-time waltzing had emerged during the 1920s as a medium-tempo derivative of céilí and ballroom dance styles, done to songs like "The Wild Colonial Boy," "Maybe Some Day I'll Go Back Again to Ireland," and "A Mother's Love's a Blessing."[5] Though old-time waltzing had roots on the European continent, Mike Cummings recalls that the Irish had completely absorbed and transformed it, and it had become an inextricable part of any evening of dancing in Ireland.

> In Ireland, you had plenty of ballroom dances, but in the 1940s, it was only on the Gaelic dancing nights that you had strictly Irish dances. The only concession to ballroom dancing on the Irish nights was the old-time waltz. At that time, the old-time waltz was a big deal in Ireland. Every dance would include an old-time waltzing contest. It was a great honor to win. But the old-time waltzing was very different than here. Here, they danced any old way, but in Ireland it was very formal. It had more structure. You move counterclockwise for five counts of one, two, three, then you turn and dance five counts of one, two, three clockwise.

The waltzes were, in fact, the mainstay of an evening of dance on Dudley Street. Dancers would rush up the stairs to catch the first waltz, "The Snowy Breasted Pearl," which was always followed by the highland fling, a dance done in couples or threesomes. Arm in arm, the dancers would toestep their way across the hall to a highland fling tune, one of the more popular of which was "Johnny, Will You Marry Me." Unself-conscious fun was the order of the day, and no one thought anything of the silly antics associated with dances to songs like "Shoe the Donkey," a comical, almost childish song written to the tune of the classic mazurka "The Varsovienne."

Musical Styles

On any given night upstairs in the Intercolonial, people could expect to hear familiar American waltzes and Irish-American songs such as "When Irish Eyes Are Smiling" and "Star Spangled Molly," as well as chart hits like "Mona Lisa." The music was neither exclusively Irish nor exclusively American. It was *Irish-American* music.

At the Intercolonial and the Hibernian, the larger bands played Irish-American music and songs in the upstairs ballrooms, while the downstairs bands remained the haven for Irish traditional music. Brendan Tonra, a fiddle player and composer, arrived in America in 1959 already an accomplished musician in the traditional genre. Born in Gowlane, near Doocastle, county Mayo—the same region that gave rise to the fiddling legend Michael Coleman—Tonra excelled in music from a very young age. He played at parties called "porter sprees" and house dances from the age of sixteen, and in the autumn of 1954, at age nineteen, he had already written his first tune, "The Gowlane Reel," while digging potatoes on the family farm.

Nurtured in a modest but vibrant, music-rich community, "a warm society where money was scarce and land was poor, but music was highly respected, for many even more than work,"[6] Tonra describes the patrons of Boston dance halls matter-of-factly. "The real Irish stayed with the céilí band," he says. "The big shots were upstairs with the fox-trots."

The pianist and flute player Gene Frain describes the halls as buildings full of music, with very different music in each hall: "There was the first hall, downstairs, the big hall upstairs, but before you get all the way up top, there was one hall in between, and the Irish used to go in, Paddy Cronin, Johnny Cronin, myself. We did the traditional stuff, the jigs. Real traditional. And they didn't do that much upstairs."

Paddy Cronin performed frequently in the downstairs halls. A skilled fiddler with a distinctive traditional style, he was a big sensation in the music circles when he first arrived. Though he played in Johnny Powell's band, he seemed to prefer the loose camaraderie and the authentic traditional music of the downstairs halls. He says:

> From time to time I played a bit for Powell. Then they started getting an Irish group to play downstairs in one of the three smaller halls while the modern band played upstairs, which was a better idea. Powell used to send us downstairs to play. Various Irish fellas that were around that time played with us; there was nothing steady about it. There were different personnel all the time.

Having several halls within one complex gave the dancers a choice of music, allowing for bigger crowds and more profits for the dance hall. Having the choice appealed to dancers such as Mary McEleney, who immigrated to America from Ireland in 1955. Mary danced in halls on both levels. "If there was a dance on upstairs that you didn't like," she says, "you went downstairs for the Siege of Ennis or something like that. And when that was over, you went back up."

It was hard to deny the overwhelming popularity of the American-style musical arrangements on the top floor, and it was no accident that Irish traditional music, which drew smaller crowds, was placed in the smaller halls. Gene Frain, a pianist and flute player, believes that Irish traditional music alone would not have had the draw. "Either they liked it [downstairs], or it was too crowded [upstairs]. We wouldn't be there if they didn't have a gang upstairs, you can be sure of that," he says.

Dudley Street bands had to select music that would appeal to people from a mix of backgrounds. Though Canadians and Scots came to the dance halls, Joe Derrane reports that the crowds were predominantly a mix of Irish and Irish-American:

> The number of Irish versus Irish-Americans could vary on any
> given night, but it was predominantly Irish. I would say, like sixty-
> five or seventy percent the Irish and thirty to thirty-five percent
> might be Irish-American. Enough so that they had to play some
> commercial or American tunes during the night. We'd do one or
> two sets of them—by a set I mean at least three medleys.

Within the Irish and Irish-American communities, musical preferences varied, but American, or popular, music was clearly the majority's preference. Promoters were careful to put musicians like Joe Derrane, who had mastered both traditional and popular styles, in the largest halls. Frank Storer's recollection of his first night performing upstairs in the large hall shows how promoters organized musicians according to ability and musical background. "One night, Joe Leavey, a very fine pianist, had a heart attack," says Storer. "Johnny Powell came down to the second floor and ordered me to the top floor. I was totally unprepared for it, because I was unfamiliar with their musical scores, but we got by."

As both Storer and Derrane attest, the upstairs bands would always select a significant number of American medleys, for popularity was key to a ballroom's success. "The ballrooms were geared to giving them what they wanted, sell what they were buying," says Joe Derrane.

> Especially at the Intercolonial, because they had a sax section
> there, and a trumpet player, which in itself was very, very unusual.
> A piano player, Carlton Bates, used to do most of the arrange-
> ments for Powell's band. We'd play "I'm in the Mood for Love,"

maybe some contemporary waltz at the time or something, maybe a little swing beat. Maybe even a Dixie tune now and then.

Popular music appealed to the Americans and the Irish. The appeal was so great that most of the larger bands played only a couple of sets of traditional Irish tunes a night. In fact, Paddy Cronin suspects that too much Irish music could lead to a hall's demise—so much so that it nearly seemed as if people avoided a hall specifically *because* it was very Irish, and the less genuinely Irish a hall was, the more successful it would be:

> The two big halls, the Intercolonial and the Hibernian, did all right. The others were a failure. A couple of Irish fellas would start running a dance hall, and there'd be nobody there. A fella said to me, "Ah, Christ, Paddy, they're doing the wrong thing." I said, "How are they?" He said, "If they could get some Englishman that had crucified some Irishman, and let him run it," says he, "it'd be mobbed! There wouldn't be standing room!"

Mickey Connolly, who played in Ireland with the well-known ensembles Ganley and Rush and the Brose Welsh Band, says the Irish in the 1940s wanted to hear only the most modern music:

> Oh, God, there were fussy dancers that time. You should have seen the lads coming over from England to Ireland. If you didn't play the quick steps and cha-chas and sambas, the modern dances, they didn't want to hear you. . . . These were lads just coming home from work in England, for vacation. God almighty, when I got here to America, I played tunes here that none of them knew. Listening to Radio Luxembourg, I learned the fox-trot "The Gypsy," and I'd play it here, and they used to just look at me. They didn't play that here. But Billy Caples and I used to play them, the two accordions.

The author and musician Gearóid Ó hAllmhuráin describes an environment in Ireland in which traditional music was considered backward:

> In the socially polarized Ireland of the 1940s, the status afforded to the traditional musician was well beneath that accorded to his "high art" counterpart. Shunned by the educational establishment, ignored by the popular press, and derided by urban music

societies, many traditional performers had a low self-image of
their role in Irish music and of its place in contemporary Ireland.[7]

American Armed Forces radio, established in Germany during the war,
had brought the sound of swing music to Ireland, and it had quickly taken
over. Swing bands popped up all over Ireland.[8] By the late 1940s in America, however, the swing era had swung. Big band ensembles led by Duke Ellington and Tommy Dorsey were replaced by solo crooners such as Frank
Sinatra, Nat King Cole, and Ella Fitzgerald. But while the larger jazz ballrooms were giving way to cabaret-style entertainment, the Dudley Street
dance halls were just opening their doors. Throngs of Irish people rushed
in, looking for a touch of home, though under an American veneer.

Larry Reynolds, who later went on to cofound the Boston chapter of the
Irish traditional musicians' association, Comhaltas Ceoltóirí Éireann, in
1975, had been more accustomed to modern music in Ireland. He describes
his first impression of the music he heard when he arrived at Boston's Irish
dance halls: "The great Joe Derrane was all the rage. The music at first I
didn't care for, but there were great musicians. . . . It was different than
what we were used to [in Ireland]. It was actually even more Irish than what
we had left, in a way. . . . They had their own touch to it."[9]

Reynolds's own céilí band in Ireland included a saxophone, to cater to the
audience's growing taste for popular music, but the modern music was only
a very small part of the repertoire. "We played mostly céilí music," Reynolds
says. "The modern was kind of a fill-in, you know. Or at least it got the
people that didn't care for céilí. You got them to come if you played the
modern music."

The Songs

The dance hall bands, whether they had a vocalist or not, would frequently play instrumental versions of popular Irish-American songs. The
Irish-Americans have always had their own repertoire of songs, which
they feel are just as Irish as the songs any Irishman knows; many, indeed,
are not even aware that there is a difference between Irish songs and Irish-
American songs.

For Irish-Americans, singing songs is simply part of being Irish. According to the radio host Seamus Mulligan, there were practically two parallel universes in America's Irish music world: operatic parlor-type songs written by Irish-Americans for Irish-Americans, and ballads that emigrated with the Irish. Over time, he came to know the Irish-American repertoire well, though many of his countrymen didn't particularly care for the songs. He says:

> Songs like "I'll Take You Home Again, Kathleen," "When Irish Eyes Are Smiling," "It's a Great Day for the Irish," and "My Wild Irish Rose"—stuff that the Irish wouldn't tolerate at all—I know a lot of them, and I learned a lot of them in Ireland, but they were manufactured in America. They were going to the Irish-Americans, and of course they were the ones that had the money. And at that time, a lot of that stuff was all sheet music.

Popular recorded Irish singers like the McNulty family, Connie Foley, Ma Burke, Mary Carton, Mickey Carton, and others covered a wide range of material from both the Irish and the Irish-American repertoires, singing Irish-American songs made popular on the vaudeville stage, as well as saccharine songs of longing for home, sentimental ballads of emigration, and rousing anthems of rebellion brewed in Ireland. The New York–based McNulty family band, consisting of Ma McNulty on the accordion and her children Peter and Eileen, began the first of many recordings on the Decca label in 1936. Their *Irish Show Boat* theatrical revue had raised national attention with a radio premiere in 1932 and a stage performance at the famed Radio City Music Hall of Rockefeller Center in 1933.

In America, the traditional Irish ballad form had been combined with popular American music into a new form designed specifically for mass musical culture. These new song forms had been introduced in the theater, on the comic stage as "stage Irish" repertoire, and in sheet music since the beginning of the nineteenth century. Many of the songs popularized as Irish were actually artifacts of the Tin Pan Alley era, a period that lasted from the turn of the twentieth century through World War II, in which songwriters worked for hire, pumping out sheet music destined for the piano of every middle-class family in America.

Joanne McDermott still knows all the songs from the annual Irish show at St. Patrick's parish in Roxbury, and her family sang the songs at home:

Frank Storer, left, plays the piano while Connie Foley sings. Foley came to America from Tralee, county Kerry, and served in the Korean conflict with the U.S. Army. A prolific recording artist, he was best known for his rendition of "Wild Colonial Boy," and he was adored by audiences on both sides of the Atlantic. In both his singing style and his choice of material, Connie Foley was a musical link between the tenor John McCormack, of the early twentieth century, and great ballad singers such as the Clancy Brothers, who were to emerge in the 1960s. Tommy Shields, rear, speaks to sax player Clary Walsh.
(From the library of Frank Storer.)

We would have tons of house parties, and we had a piano. Almost everyone had a piano, and everybody sang, because that was the Irish tradition. Irish-American songs, we knew them all. At the St. Patrick's show, we did all the Irish, well, the Irish-American songs. "It must have been the Irish who built the pyramids 'cause no one else would carry up the bricks"—that was one of them that we sang. And the other one was "Who Threw the Overalls in Mrs. Murphy's Chowder":

Who Threw the Overalls in Mrs. Murphy's Chowder,
Nobody spoke, so they shouted all the louder,
It's an Irish trick, it's true,
I can beat the Mick that threw [She interjects:] *("the Mick," that's a*
  derogatory term)
The overalls in Mrs. Murphy's chowder.

In Ireland, they would say, "What is that? That's not an Irish song." But ours were Irish-American songs. Things like "I'll Take You Home Again, Kathleen," "Danny Boy," and "Did Your Mother Come from Ireland?" Those were written on Tin Pan Alley in New York by American songwriters. Most of the songs we knew were Irish-American. They weren't truly Irish songs. But we didn't know any better.

Did Your Mother Come from Ireland?

Among the Irish-Americans in Boston, there were two camps: those who became even more Irish in America and those who just wanted to blend in, and often the difference was in whether your parents had arrived before or after the Irish had come into their own in America. The young people of the 1940s and 1950s were children and grandchildren of those who emigrated shortly after the bitter struggle for Irish autonomy that finally ended in the early 1920s. Memories of the blood and gun smoke of the War for Independence, and the Civil War that followed it, were still fresh in many minds. Many of the Irish who emigrated in the 1930s were old Irish Republican Army (IRA) men. One Roxbury native said that family legend had it that his father made $22 a week, on which he raised nine children, and until the day he died, he sent $2 a week home to Ireland to support the IRA.

Young Irish-American children grew up singing thinly veiled songs of Irish rebellion, such as "The West's Awake," "The Snowy Breasted Pearl," and "Come Back to Erin, Ma Vourneen." One such family, the Hansens, grew up in Jamaica Plain and were taught all the Irish songs by their mother, Mary Ann, who had immigrated from county Mayo. Even when rock and roll came on the scene in the late 1950s, the family's love for Irish music remained. Her daughter Janice Hansen Kleinbauer, who was to take the stage at the Intercolonial Hall in the late 1950s, said, "It just came natural, this love of Irish music. We knew every Irish song since we were so little. We knew every one."

Perhaps more Irish than the Irish themselves, it was often felt that first-generation Irish-Americans in the 1940s hung on to the Old Country more tightly than the immigrants themselves. Says one Irish immigrant, Mame O'Shaughnessy, of her Irish-American relatives: "Irish-Americans, such as my cousin Patsy [Flavin] Hurley, they seem to have a stronger sense of Irishness than we do. We just came and lived; you could say we took our Irishness for granted."

The Irish-Americans whose parents had been of the generation that immigrated while Ireland was still recovering from the famine, however, had witnessed the days when the Irish were at the bottom of the ladder in Boston. Their experience had shown them that to get ahead, you had to get along—even musically. As Joanne McDermott says:

> We learned the ballroom dances. We didn't really do Irish step dancing. . . . In fact, when I was a kid, and my mother was first-generation American, there was a little bit of shame attached to being Irish. You didn't want to be *too* Irish, outside of your own group. My mother never let me take step dancing. Instead she . . . brought me to a friend of hers from Roxbury who had a little studio in Roslindale Square, and I took tap dancing. And I was very young, and I often thought later, why didn't she let me take step dancing? That would have made sense, but there was a little shame. . . . You wanted to blend in. So she wouldn't let me take step dancing.

Frank Devin, raised in St. Patrick's parish in Roxbury and second-generation American, has similar recollections:

The Three Colleens practice for "A Night in Ireland," a concert of music and dance at John Hancock Hall, 1957. Many such events were hosted by the radio personality Tommy Shields to showcase the talents of Boston Irish musicians, dancers, storytellers, and comedians. Left to right: Maureen Murphy, Maureen Cloherty, Dorothy "Dolly" Cussen. (Courtesy of the Boston Public Library, Print Department.)

Not a lot of people took step dancing. It was looked as another culture's dancing. Step dancers appeared in St. Patrick's Day parades, and they performed on St. Patrick's Day at school. But it was a *performance*, as opposed to part of our culture. It wasn't looked down on, but it was just looked at as different. People wanted to be Americanized in those days. It was something you went and saw or heard. It wasn't something you *did*.

But many *first*-generation Irish-American children in the 1940s did learn step dancing. Maureen Hansen Keohane opened her first step dancing school at the age of sixteen, and it was an immediate success, she says:

My sister Chris and I had been taking lessons since we were very
young in Somerville from two teachers, Joe Mulcahy and Theresa
Dempsey. Joe played the accordion. My mother used to take us to
his house on Friday nights, Chris and I and my cousin Peg, and
we'd go on the elevated trains, like around six-thirty or seven, and
we'd get the last train home at around twelve-thirty A.M., then
walk up from Green Street Station. It took us the good part of an
hour to get home.

At this point, Chris and I were dancing here and there for the
Columban Fathers, and my cousin and Chris used to sing songs
together, like "Back to Donegal"—all those old songs. . . .
People in the neighborhood asked me about dancing lessons,
and I started teaching in the dining room, and it just kept growing and growing. . . .

My father would take all the dining room furniture down every
Friday night and move it and roll up the parlor rug. We'd have
our recital rehearsals in the two front rooms every Friday night.
All the mothers would come, and the babies, and our mother
would be out making them all tea.

By the time of Hansen Keohane's first recital, which she held in 1950,
during her senior year of high school, her dancing school had expanded to
thirty-one students after just two years. For the performance processional,
she needed thirty-two dancers to represent the thirty-two counties of
Ireland. The children were choreographed to walk down the center aisle,
each bearing a banner across her chest representing a different county in
Ireland. Though that year she had to recruit a young neighbor to step in to
carry the thirty-second banner, it was only a few years until her recitals
were showcasing nearly four hundred student step dancers at Boston's John
Hancock Hall.

Still, some first-generation Irish-Americans concerned with getting ahead
avoided Irish music and dance altogether. Gene Frain's sisters wouldn't dare
go to Dudley Street, opting instead for the city's "classier" nightclubs. As
Frain put it, "They were 'upper-crust Irish.' Dudley Street wasn't high class
at that point."

The musician Mickey Connolly, who came to Boston right after World
War II, came from a traditional music background but had been influenced
by the modern music on American Armed Forces radio. He says he brought

the modern music with him from Ireland to the Boston dance halls. "Powell and them weren't playing any modern music," he says. "It was mostly Irish here. But in Galway I used to stay up till two o'clock in the morning to hear a station from Belgium that used to play modern music. That's where I got 'Buttons and Bows,' at two o'clock in the morning. The next night at the dance over there, I was the king of the dance." But though his modern tunes made him popular in Ireland, he, like many other new immigrant musicians, found that Irish music was much more popular in Irish-American dance halls.

However, living in a transplanted Irish environment, according to Larry Reynolds, reinforced many musicians' desires to maintain their Irish identities. While the push for assimilation was strong, it only encouraged Reynolds, Connolly, and many others to preserve their Irishness. "I believe that I became more of an Irishman than I was, because you never thought of it when you were home," he explains. "But if you thought there was any threat to your Irishness, I was always very quick since I came here to let someone know, if I met them, that I was Irish. And proud of it. A lot of people felt that way."

While Reynolds certainly wasn't the only one to feel this way, other musicians indicate that they did not consciously make a decision to assume an "Irish" musical identity. Irish traditional music clearly was appreciated in some parts of Ireland, but overall it had declined in popularity and in Ireland, it wasn't really part of what it meant to be "Irish."

Until they got to America, that is. Despite traditional music's dormancy in Ireland, many people's interest was rekindled once they reached America because Irish music represented a taste of home. Asked if the "Irishness" of the music was what drew them to the dance halls, many would reply, "No. It was just what I was used to." Rather than being drawn by the Irishness of the music, they were drawn to the social community that formed around the halls, says Joe Derrane. "The music was familiar, maybe not their favorite, but it was familiar at least," he says. "You had this common bond, and the meeting place. It was just the right place at the right time."

The combination of the music and the social community that formed around it created the dance halls' magnetic atmosphere. Not too Irish, and yet just Irish enough—not the same as at home, but similar; foreign and yet familiar.

Curiously, the years in which traditional music lay dormant in Ireland were the very years during which the dance halls thrived in Boston. In ef-

fect, the lively dance halls in America played a critical role in preserving traditional music while it suffered a temporary decline in popularity in Ireland.

Maybe Some Day I'll Go Back Again to Ireland

Thanks to increased affluence and the flexibility of immigration laws, Irish
in America in the 1940s and 1950s were free and able to travel back and forth
to Ireland as they pleased. But even though going to Ireland the legal way
was entirely possible, some still found mischievous ways to travel.

Joe Joyce traveled to Ireland for the first time in 1953. Joyce and two
friends accidentally (or maybe not so accidentally) stowed away on a pas-
senger liner bound for Ireland. Joyce's band, which included Joyce, Frank
Keough, Johnny Sullivan, Jack Doherty, and Jimmy Kelly, had been per-
forming the night before. After the Wednesday night novena at Mission
Church, they were playing for a dance just down Tremont Street at the
Knights of Columbus Hall. Keough and Doherty had spent the night at
Joyce's house on 79 Wyman Street, and then the three went to Boston's
Commonwealth Pier the next morning to bid farewell to a few girls who
were traveling to Ireland.

Joyce and his mates parked his car on the wharf, left the keys in it, and
bought fifty-cent tickets to board the ship before it left port, which was allowed in those days. When the signal sounded, however, they did not disembark; they planned instead to get off at the next port, Halifax, a name they
recognized as that of a small town south of Boston, where they would disembark and hitchhike back. Of the three, only Keough knew that Halifax,
Massachusetts, was landlocked and the ship was bound for Halifax, Nova
Scotia, but he kept it to himself while the other young men, in crumpled
suits, curled up to sleep in the ship's lounge.

The next morning, a deep voice came over the loudspeaker. "Mr. Joseph
Joyce, please report to the purser's office." Joyce reported, sure that he had
been discovered. He reached the office to find his friend Eva Connors
there,[10] with a young boy named Joey Joyce whom she was accompanying to
Ireland. Without a passport and caught red-handed, Joyce spent the re-
mainder of the journey in the galley, "cleaning lipstick off six hundred cups
six times a day," as he puts it. It was only a matter of days before the others
were discovered as well.

The young musicians arrived in Ireland with no passports, and no more than a hundred dollars between them, along with their instruments and the blue suits they had been wearing since the dance the week before. They were turned over to local authorities immediately.

Meanwhile, back in Boston, the police had become suspicious of the car left on the pier, and contacted Joyce's mother. Not long after, the shipping authorities contacted her as well, and she made hasty travel plans. Much to Joyce's surprise, upon his arrival in Ireland his mother ambushed him in Cobh with fire in her eyes. She ushered him into a big green taxi, and they drove straight to the passport office in Cork city. They stayed with Joe's cousins in Connemara until the passports were processed, and then they spent ten weeks traveling in Ireland. Joe came home on a Pan American flight and was drafted to serve in the Korean conflict within a week. The story made front-page news in papers on both sides of the Atlantic.

6

There's a Sweetheart Waiting for You

Women and Romance

Romance, Irish Style

A woman brought her husband in to the doctor. He was very sick, and the doctor asked the wife to step outside the waiting room so he could talk to her. "Your husband is very ill. In fact, he may die. The only way he has a fighting chance to recover is if you reduce his stress in all ways. Wake him gently in the morning with a nudge; then make his favorite breakfast. Then, when he comes home from work, give his feet a rub, and make him a nice hot supper, his favorite meal. If he says something and you don't agree with him, just smile and go along with it. And when he's sitting on his chair, don't nag him or bother him; just let things be. Then at night before bed, give him a nice back rub to help him sleep, tuck him in, and give him a nice good-night kiss." She listened and nodded. On the way home from the doctor, her husband asked her what the doctor had said when he had pulled her aside. The wife replied, "He told me you're going to die."

—*Joke, as told by Anne Powell O'Connell, age seventy-nine*

Promoters of Irish dance events typically leased a dance hall from a building owner who lived outside the Irish community. The promoter also hired the musicians and organized refreshments. Admittance to a dance hall cost about fifty cents in 1948. Except for limited income from the sale of coffee, Irish soda bread, and other desserts, dance promoters like Johnny and Mike Powell of the Intercolonial relied on admittance fees. That money paid the musicians and the lease on the hall, and left them a sum of money for themselves. Because they made so little on each admittance, promoters had to fill the halls in order to make money. Their most important task, then, was to attract an audience. Those who were most successful catered to a number of desires among the young, mixed crowds: the desire to see familiar faces, a longstanding cultural love for dancing, and the ageless yearning for romance, with music as the backdrop.

Familiar Faces

For the thousands who came to the Dudley Street halls, the chance to see familiar people was perhaps the most important draw, even more important than the music. Many of the young women from Ireland were working in homes in wealthy parts of the Boston area, the young men were working at whatever they could get, and many were living with distant relatives, with friends from their hometowns in Ireland, or in rooming houses. They were lonely and homesick, and like anyone in such a situation, they longed to be with their own. Joe Derrane, who was born in Roxbury to Irish parents, sees the desire for community as one of the most important reasons Irish people frequented the halls:

> They're here, they're homesick, they're lonely. These places were jammed. Jammed. And all of them going at the same time; it was really something. They wanted to be with their own, you know. It became known, look, if you went to Dudley Street for two or three Saturday nights, you're bound, you're *bound* to see somebody from home. That was the kind of reputation it had. This place became the mecca. It actually got to the point that you could put four chimpanzees up there with washboards and tin cans, and I think they still would have come.

For many immigrants, America was a land of economic opportunity and also a land of romantic possibility. There was money to be made and money to be spent. As in earlier waves of immigration, most of the Irish emigrating to the United States in the postwar era were under thirty-five years old, and most were unmarried.[1] These facts worked to dance hall promoters' advantage. Musicians say that the postwar decades were times of plenty for them. They were hired to play gigs four and five nights a week at the dance halls, and before long, several weddings a week—the fruit of romances that had first blossomed on the dance hall floor.

Larry Reynolds, who emigrated from Ireland in 1953, agrees with Derrane that Irish people came to Dudley Street to be among the Irish community. "They came to meet the Irish, being lonesome for one thing. Longing for home would bring them together," Reynolds says. The dances were successful in that regard, as Reynolds's bandmate, the fiddle player and composer Brendan Tonra, attests. When asked if he found the American experience lonely, he replied, "Lonely? No, I wasn't lonely. It was easy to meet people. You'd meet everyone at Dudley Street."

The Pull: Romance

Promoters such as the Powell brothers at the Intercolonial Hall recognized early on that the presence of women was an important way to attract men to their venues. The Powells, according to Joe Derrane, devised the idea of holding dances on Thursdays, when most Irish women working in domestic service ("kitchen mechanics," as they were called) had the afternoon off. Thus began the institution of maid's night out. Many people, Derrane adds, left Ireland because the prospects for romance were so slim there. Derrane, whose parents and wife were born in Ireland, describes the system as he understands it:

> It was the custom then historically in Ireland: you take a man that owns some land, and he dies; he might have two sons, two or three daughters. Historically, the holdings went to the eldest son. The youngest son, he just worked the place, depending on his relation to his brother. The girls, they got nothing.
>
> In terms of marriage prospects . . . I mean there were some great guys there, but God, you know, the women had to wait for an older brother to die to inherit any of the land. . . . They didn't have a hell of a lot to look forward to. Here they are, working in their families, taking care of the man of the house, the father and the mother, so what were their prospects? To marry a guy and just

A group gathers in 1957 in the Intercolonial's Crystal Ballroom for a senatorial fund-raiser for John F. Kennedy. The Four Provinces Orchestra is onstage. This photo was taken at 8 P.M., and as the story goes, by 10 P.M., the crowd had multiplied fivefold. (From the library of Frank Storer/Joe and Karin Joyce.)

trade one household for another. That's what brought most of them out, the opportunity for employment.

According to Connie McEleney, men would go to the halls without a date, but they were likely to meet someone there. He says, "You'd end up talking to someone. They could end up a date before you went home, if you were lucky." The same was true for women: "My cousin had a bunch of girl-friends that used to meet and they would get together and go over there, and look for their prospective husbands," says Jack Martin.

Mary Murphy, a first-generation Irish-American from Mission Hill in Roxbury, recalls the excitement of going to the dance halls when she was seventeen years old. "I was a teenager when I went to the dance halls," she says. "I went from about 1947 to 1951. That was a wonderful era to grow up in. There was so much to do, and we always went to the dances. Even if you went by yourself, we got there and knew everybody!"

Mary's Irish-American contemporary Maureen Hansen Keohane of Jamaica Plain, who had just started up her own step dancing school, started going to the dance halls while she was still in high school to meet friends and Irish relatives who worked in domestic service in Boston. Says Keohane, "I started going down when I was about eighteen. A lot of girls, juniors or seniors in high school, would meet and go down to the Irish dances. Some had Irish cousins who we'd meet on Thursdays and Saturdays, when they were off work [in the houses around the city]."

One such young Irish woman, Nora McGillicuddy, was working for a family in Newton. All week, she looked forward to the fun of dancing on Thursdays, when she would travel alone on the bus and trolley to get to the dances:

> I was working for a family in Newton Centre by the name of Gross. They treated me very well. I had my own room and my own bathroom. But you worked a long day. You worked through suppertime, and then you'd have to do dishes. In those days, you also did a lot of ironing. Tablecloths, napkins. We ironed everything.
>
> But I was so lonely out there. So I used to go in on the Thursday nights by the train and see everyone at Dudley Street. You'd just go upstairs and have a Coke and a few dances. We used to wear those taffeta dresses, and the stiff petticoats. The red lipstick. I used to buy a new dress like every other week! And new shoes, because you'd wear out the shoes dancing. Those taffeta dresses would cost maybe twelve dollars, and I only made forty a week my first job, living in.
>
> The Intercolonial had a nice, high stage. Lovely velvet curtains. The floors would be so slippery, shiny. When the music started, you'd be looking to see who'd ask you to dance. You'd be standing on each side, watching all the nice guys coming in. And if your friend got a dance, you'd be jealous. You'd always get a dance, but the women seemed to outnumber the men then. There was hardly anyone that didn't dance.
>
> After the dances, we used to go to a place called the Waldorf for tea and pie and cake. It was just down the street from the Hibernian. Most of them would go; you'd have to wait in line, because you'd be starving, after the dancing.

Then you'd go home. We all had different directions to go to. We'd have to get the last train; then you'd have to wait for the streetcar. I had to walk a good bit, too, when I got off the streetcar, and I'd be by myself. It would take me three hours sometimes. And we'd get up to go to work in the morning after all night dancing. Oh, they were great times. Dancing all night long.

I really didn't know anyone when I came out. Some I met down at the dance. We were always so friendly. You just talk to people: "What part of Ireland are you from?" Everyone was so sociable.

Promoters went to great lengths to ensure the presence of women at the dances, and savvy doormen admitted women free into the hall. Women had great independence, and would visit several halls in an evening. While the pianist Frank Storer performed onstage in the dance hall, his wife visited several other halls:

The point was there that she'd say, "Okay, see you later." "Where're you going?" She'd say, as the saying went, "I'm going up the street," meaning up to the Hibernian. She'd leave, and she wouldn't tell me, but she'd also go over to the Opera House, Rose Croix, and the Winslow Hall. They'd make the whole circuit around the halls. It was a dollar to get in, or fifty cents. Plus, lots of them, they see a bunch of girls, they're not going to keep them out. They needed to get girls in to dance with the guys, so a bunch of girls come to the door and say, "What's it going to cost to get in?" "Oh, give us fifty cents each," or "Just go 'head in," you know. And they'd always do this after ten o'clock, so there weren't many hands out looking for another admission; they were just trying to get a mix of a crowd in.

Dance promoters also used raffles to attract women to the clubs. For example, nylons became a popular raffle item for the dances. Joe Joyce recalls that nylons were used at the House of Eire Club to attract a crowd on off-nights:

They used to give away nylons on Tuesday nights, at eleven o'clock, Charlie Porter would. Someone would take back the tinfoil that the nylons were wrapped [in], and use the tinfoil again the next week. I used to have to run to the kitchen to give the winner a brown bag to take them home in.

Some of the raffle items were more significant, intended to attract larger crowds of both men and women. Connie McEleney remembers rather sizable prizes: "A brand-new car would get raffled off. There used to be a prize every weekend."

Joe Derrane describes the raffle draw as a memorable part of the evening, and also as a way to hold the crowds from leaving for another hall during the band's break. He says:

> We'd play from eight to twelve. You'd get a ten-minute break. They'd bring the coffee and a slice of Irish bread, and serve it right backstage, that's it. And that fifteen minutes, that's when they were announcing the winners. They had a lot of drawings, you know, save your stub when you come in the door, because the winner might get a hundred-dollar prize or some real special thing. They may have a free trip to Ireland.

Dishes, Diapers, and Dictation

Most Irish women in the late 1940s worked in domestic service. Many found it hard when they first came to America. Though most women were sponsored, if they didn't have relations or close friends already living here, they were sponsored by a family who would employ them. These families would pay their passage to America, and the young women repaid them by working. In these conditions, they were expected to stay with the families for better or worse. Says Mame O'Shaughnessy:

> I had a friend who came out here probably in the late 1950s. She had never left Ireland, and she was very quiet. She was met in Boston, and was brought all the way to Portland [Maine]. She said that she looked out and she never saw a building. She didn't see roads, tunnels, nothing. All she saw was so-and-so's house at home, the mountains, the fields. That's where her mind went. She

was miserable. It was hard working, and a lot of people did a lot of crying when they came here.

Nora McGillicuddy, who came to America in 1956, started out in domestic service but eventually ended up working in a Boston-area hospital, the Shattuck Memorial Hospital. But it was not to escape hardship that she came:

> I came over in 1956. September 9, 1956. I always wanted to travel since I was about sixteen, and my aunts from here wrote to me and asked if I'd like to come here. They owned their own houses, in West Roxbury. To make a living, one of my aunts used to take in laundry, because she had six children. Then she'd be home and do the laundry, all that ironing, washing, and everything, every week to make a few dollars.
>
> I said I'd try it. I just wanted to come to America. It wasn't to get away from anything. I was very happy at home. Well, we hadn't a lot of money, you know, but we survived. I could have eventually got a good job at home. When I got here, though, I didn't like it at first. But then I started going to the dances on Dudley Street and that was it. . . . From then on, I was there every Sunday night. I missed home always, but I'd never go back to live.

As hard as the young women worked, dancing on Dudley Street was the highlight of their weeks. According to all accounts, it was a happy time in which women felt free and safe. Enthusiastic dancers such as Mary McEleney, Nora McGillicuddy, Evelyn Storer, Ann Derrane, and Patsy Hurley all report having had simple fun. Mary McEleney says, "We'd go and have a great time. We used to wait for the train on Dudley Street, and we'd be lilting away, and swingin' and dancin'. You were always on the last train."

Evelyn Storer, who was born in Ireland and emigrated to America in 1955, has similar memories:

> I'd get out of work, get dressed, meet my girlfriend, take the train to Dudley Street. We used to go to the five-and-ten, and I'd put my hair back—you know how you put a bun at the back of the hair—and we'd dance all night. We had a ball. Then, we'd go to the Waldorf. That's where you met everybody. The girls were all

having apple pie and ice cream. You'd swear we never saw an apple pie, but it was just so good. We had a ball. We didn't drink; we'd just dance.

Joan Gannon, was just seventeen years old when she came from Killarney, county Kerry, in 1961, and the dance hall was her first stop. She says:

There really wasn't very much employment in Ireland then. My sister Noreen was here on her own, and she really wanted me to come. The first place that I went to was the Intercolonial. The first Sunday night. Then, on Thursday nights, another girl, Maureen Spain from Galway, the two of us went to school Thursday nights to learn shorthand and typing. But instead of the shorthand and typing, we ended up at the dances at the Intercolonial. We loved it.

Gannon even enjoyed the trip from Allston, a Boston neighborhood that was over an hour to Dudley Street on public transportation:

Actually, a lot of the fun was taking the bus there, rather than taking a cab. I would take a bus from Allston to the Intercolonial, and we walked from Dudley Street Station to the hall. You were never alone. You were always with a group, and there might be other girlfriends coming off the bus from Jamaica Plain, and you always met someone on the bus. I would go with my sister, and we'd pick someone up on the way, some Irish girl. There was a lot on the bus from different parts of Ireland coming. We all went because there was nothing else around, really.

We had the dresses—the dresses that started then to come out; they had the petticoats under them. You never really wanted to get on the bus with the dresses, but you had to. They were a pain to wear in the bus—you took up half the bus in them! But when you got off the bus, you could hear that Irish music all the way up the street, and when the dance was over, you went up to the Waldorf for breakfast.

And then, you took the trolley home to wherever it was you were living or working. For many of the young Irish women who were working for families, the journey was long, but they were sure to get home early enough to catch a bit of sleep before rising early for morning Mass. According to Dick Senier, dance hall people looked after each other, and no one was left behind:

> Those who came in from [towns north of the city] such as Lynn or Peabody had to contend with a couple of buses or a combination of bus and el, so that they would have to leave the dances early to get the last bus out of Haymarket Square on the Eastern Mass. system. Either that, or they would get a ride from someone. We rarely left anyone stranded.[2]

Crinoline and Pearls: Dressing for Dudley

Getting dressed for the dances was a task not taken lightly. If the dance started at eight o'clock, then at five o'clock the curling iron would be heating on the stove in the corner, while starched crinoline petticoats stood at attention in every conceivable corner of the house—hung on the backs of doors, draped over chairs, or stuffed into nylon stockings in the closet, deliberately crushed and wrinkled so as to maximize their puff power under the dress on Saturday night.

Sisters Maureen and Chris Hansen had seven petticoats between them. Starched rigid in sugar and water, the petticoats seemed to act on their own volition. "There were petticoats everywhere!" said their youngest sister, Janice. Like most of their friends, the Hansen girls would regularly go to the popular Filene's bargain basement in downtown Boston to buy dresses for ten or twelve dollars—in a day when cigarettes were seventeen cents a pack, movies were ten cents plus two cents tax, dance lessons were fifty cents, and the trolley trip to Dudley Street was fifty cents.

Looking good mattered in a city where competition was so tight; in Boston Irish women far outnumbered Irish men. Larry Reynolds recalls: "There were many, many more women than men at that time. [At] home, there were three or four men to every woman. But here, it was like ten [women] to one [man]. And the finest-looking women you ever saw would be waiting all night for a dance. They couldn't get a dance!"

Early in the night, it was women at one side of the hall and men at the other, but when the music started, men moved en masse across the ball-room floor to find a dance partner. "The poor guys," recalls Chris Hansen Knopp, "they'd have to walk across the hall to ask you to dance. And if you ever said no . . . I mean, you wouldn't say no unless the guy was so drunk or something, but that was very rare."

If you were a woman and you wanted to dance with a male partner, you had to stand right out front on the women's side, or you'd be left standing. But most women didn't seem to notice the shortage of men; if they needed a partner they would simply dance with each other. It was very common for women to dance together, according to Janice Hansen Kleinbauer, who says, "The women would arrive before the men, so the girls danced with the girls. That was the funny part of it; it didn't matter. Girls could dance with girls all night."

Mame O'Shaughnessy, who had come to America from Ireland via London, was shocked at how acutely the women outnumbered the men. Throughout the 1950s, the Irish emigration patterns reflected where the demand for workers was: men went to England to help rebuild after the war, and women went to the United States. Shaughnessy recalls:

> There was no work in Ireland in the 1950s, really, and London was full of Irish. They were actually needed. Work was plentiful there—there was plenty of road work, and many buildings were still being rebuilt after the war.
>
> The thing that surprised us in Boston, coming from Ireland, was the women dancing together, waltzing and doing the high-land fling. That was a surprise when you saw it for the first time, because in Ireland the women did not dance together. . . .
>
> In London, there was no need for girls to dance together. There were so many men that if you wanted to dance, you just stood there and you danced. It was quite different. It had to be three to one, four to one. I liked America, but the first time I went to an Irish dance hall in Boston, I was disappointed. . . . In Lon-don, there were so many men. Then later in the evening, after you've already been dancing for two hours, you practically had to hide in the ladies' room if you didn't want to dance. By this time, some of the men have had a few drinks and all of a sudden they're ready to dance.

Long Harvest Tables, Button Box Players, and Women Dancing with Women

But the men weren't complaining. Connie McEleney tells it like it is: "You went looking for your wife, and that was it. If you weren't going to look for an American, that was the place to go to look for an Irish one." In fact, he met his wife, now Mary McEleney, at the Intercolonial Hall in 1959. They married in 1960. For them, the dance halls were an integral part of the courtship process. They spent their early years together dancing every week on Dudley Street, three nights a week. McEleney remembers:

> In them days, if you were going with someone, you'd just say
> you'd meet them at the hall. There was no such thing as going to
> the house and picking them up. What they used to do, if you were
> going to the dance on a Sunday, you went down to Carson Beach
> in [South Boston], say at eleven o'clock, and you went to the
> dance from there. You stopped in a diner, got something to eat,
> then went to the dance. That's where the Irish used to all go.

When it came to marriage, the Irish tended to choose Irish or Irish-American mates. Though the likelihood of mixed marriage had increased significantly by the 1950s and 1960s, there was still very little intermarriage at that time. Frank Devin says:

> My family was outspoken about it. "Stay with your own," and all
> that kind of stuff. "Don't marry an Italian." My brother married an
> Italian, and my father wanted to throw him out of the house. An
> Italian! And now, the ways that people marry, nobody cares about
> that kind of stuff. It wasn't mean-spirited; I think it was just a
> comfort level. They wanted to be with their own.

Dudley Street was indeed a good place to go to meet one of your own. Musicians could chart the dance halls' successes by the increasing number of weddings they were asked to perform at. By the 1950s, musicians played weddings as often as they did dance halls. Joe Derrane explains, "You have single girls, single guys; romance blossoms. Then you have weddings, christenings, private parties, bowling banquets, anniversaries. . . . It was an unbelievable time." He describes the many wedding engagements he played during those years:

> Friday night weddings were very, very popular back then in the
> fifties. Almost every Friday night, we'd have a wedding, and, of
> course, on Saturday, you were good for two. Sometimes, there
> were three weddings in a single day. It was not unusual for me to
> leave the house at nine o'clock on a Saturday morning and not get
> home till, oh, one-thirty Sunday morning, playing all the time,
> and running from one job to another. There was no downtime in
> between. Then you'd do another wedding on a Sunday.
>
> At a wedding, I'd do three, four hours. . . . The Irish would go
> to Putnam Hall in Dorchester, Metropolitan Hall out in Brighton,
> Codman Hall—Red Gallagher, Metropolitan Caterers, he had
> that place. . . . An awful lot of the Irish tended to go to these halls
> for their weddings, so often enough, you . . . were there for this
> wedding from say, eleven to three o'clock, then you just stayed
> there for the four to eight, then you ran like hell into the ballroom.[3]

Weddings became defined by the music as much as the music was defined by the wedding. Next to the cake and the tables, the band and its omnipresent accordion were part and parcel of the typical Dudley Street wedding. Says Peg Reidy, a Roxbury native:

> I went to weddings with my mother at the Hibernian Hall. I re-
> member the long harvest tables, I remember the button box play-
> ers, and the women dancing with women. And I remember the
> cakes. Back then you always took a piece home, wrapped it up,
> and put it under your pillow as good luck when you get married.

According to Derrane, most of the weddings were for people who had met on Dudley Street. "If you didn't get their actual weddings," he says "you'd get their cousin's or friends of their relatives." It seems that any Irish musicians you talk to today who married in the 1950s in Boston met their spouses in Irish dance halls in America. Mickey Connolly met his wife in the dance halls the week he came back from the service in Germany during the Korean War:

> I came back, and I met Cathy the week I came back, actually. In
> Dudley Street, in the Winslow Hall. I went in, and I stopped at

the Intercolonial to see Billy Caples. . . . Billy says, "Come on, let's go down to the Winslow. I'm playing with Martin Flaherty down there." So the two of us walked down. He borrowed Flaherty's accordion, and we went up on the stage, and we raised hell. And Cathy, on the way out the door, she says, "Where do you live?" I said, "Norwood." "I live in Dedham," she said. I said, "I work in Dedham." So, right off, I asked her for a date for the next night. But she didn't show up. I almost got away [Laughs].

While women were seen as an important part of the dance audience in the late 1940s and early 1950s, very few made regular appearances as performers on the dance hall stage. One exception was pianist Sally (MacEachern) Kelly, and the other was Mary Irwin, a piano and accordion player. Both women played primarily in the Canadian scene in Boston, but they were known to play in some of the Irish halls, as well.

By day, Mary Irwin worked as a switchboard operator at Boston City Hall during Mayor John B. Hynes's tenure, and in the evening, she was a fixture on the dance hall scene and a welcome guest at any musical party. A great organizer, she had the telephone number for just about every musician in Boston. "She practically ran an agency," says Joe Joyce. Paddy Cronin was also a good friend and musical companion of Irwin's. Cronin says, "Every party we ever had, Mary was there. She sat at the piano some nights and never left it till morning. She was a very, very nice woman. Every time I'd call her to play, oh, she'd be right over! Oh, she was good."

Later in the 1950s, as singers became more common in the dance halls, Boston vocalists such as Anne Marie McNally, Barbara Doherty (Walsh), and, after them, in 1959, Jana Louise (Janice Hansen), increased the prominence of women on the dance hall stage. Overall, however, women in the dance halls played traditional roles: wait for an invitation to dance but never invite someone to dance except during the occasional ladies' choice dance. Otherwise, said Derrane, "it wouldn't be 'proper.'" It was thanks to ladies' choice that he met his wife, Ann. For two years, he says,

> I moved to New York and played at the Tuxedo Ballroom with the singer Mary Carton. That's where I met my wife. One night, I had hurt my shoulder so I wasn't able to play. The doctor said I'd need a week to rest, so the hall owner gave me a night's pay working in the checkroom—he was great that way, because he knew I depended on music for income. I was working there in the coatroom

this night, and they had this thing back then, the ladies' choice dance. Well, this lovely little thing kept walking around in circles around me, and finally she tapped me on the shoulder, informed me it was ladies' choice, would I like to dance, and I said yes, and that was it. I was gone.

I remember it was cold, the latter part of October, maybe first of November, and she was living in a room on the West Side, and I was living in an apartment on the East Side. I brought her home to meet my folks at Christmas, and I proposed to her. Just like that. It's been great. And we've been married ever since.

Tea and Buns or "A Beer and a Beatin'"?

On and off the dance floor, men at the dance halls were expected to treat women with respect. Frank Storer explains that disrespect of women was one of the major grounds for removal from the dance halls. Though alcohol was not served in the halls, occasionally a few men might arrive late on the scene after having a few drinks in the local pubs. Such men were quickly removed, says Storer:

> These guys were going down to the bar and coming back up with a strange package on them. Then you'd notice the cops—you didn't see them all night long, and all of sudden you'd see them in a certain area, where these guys were, and they'd be watching them, and all of a sudden, bing! They'd be right out the door. A lot of times, they'd let them back in. They'd take them down to the second floor, have a talk with them, say, "Now, you want to go back upstairs and be a gentleman?" And they would, they'd go back up, and they would behave. Sometimes, they wouldn't behave and they'd take them right out, take them down to the station if they really got out of line, or being obnoxious to the girls, insulting, things like that.

Overall the dance halls were a wholesome scene. Derrane recalls:

> In both the Hibernian and the Intercolonial, there was a balcony. You had to go up another flight of stairs, and they had a little cof-

fee shop where you could get a cup of coffee, a cup of tea, a slice of Irish bread, or a cold drink. No alcohol, just a soft drink, coffee, or tea, and maybe some fresh Irish bread and butter, or a piece of cake, or a turnover or something. You'd take that and go up and sit on the balcony and enjoy your tea and your company, and watch the dance for a while.

In the hot summer months, dancers could cool down from the stuffy air of the dance floor with ice cream provided by Deering Ice Cream of Maine.[4] However, Winslow Hall in particular become known for a bit more than tea and buns, according to Derrane, who says:

The Winslow became known as "the bucket of blood." There were an awful lot of fights downstairs outside the hall. Well, they probably started upstairs until the guys got thrown out. Most of the people were new from Ireland, and they brought their customs with them. They're fresh off the boat. And you got some of them at this time trying all the different halls, and you get someone who doesn't know when to shut their mouth. . . . These new immigrants from Ireland . . . had their customs and ways of doing things, and then the Irish-Americans would come in, and they weren't aware of these customs, and they were stepping on toes and not even knowing it. That all tapered off as they got used to each other, but it was tough for a while. There was a learning curve on both sides. Once they realized when to keep their mouths shut, there were no problems. You didn't get that so much at the other halls.

The problem was that there were barrooms all over that place—there were four or five bars within just a few blocks. The Irish guys were slow to start the dancing, and they'd go in and drink until ten, ten-thirty, and now the fun starts.

Though it was common for men to step out for a pint or two at the barrooms located just outside the halls, that was not the main draw of the evening. Those who wanted to drink found their ways, but the overall purpose of the evening was to dance. Frank Storer recalls that "if you wanted a legitimate drink, if you didn't have it on your hip, you went down to the first floor, out of the building, and into the bars that were located on street level. But as far as a cash bar in the dance hall, no. You came there to dance."

But for those who were not avid dancers, that half-pint of liquor in the pocket could be more important than the dance itself. Joe Derrane observed from the stage that alcohol served as a catalyst to loosen up the crowd:

> You'd come in earlier in the night, all the women would sit on one side, and all the men on the other side, and you didn't get too much going until maybe ten, quarter of ten. Then about eleven, a little after eleven, you'd notice a marked increase in the dancing, because all the guys had gone down the stairs a couple of times to check out the bar and have a few pints. *Now*, they're ready to come dance.

And just as well, according to the girls. "They always danced better when they came back," says one dance hall veteran who asked to remain anonymous.

As for the musicians, some abstained altogether, while others partook freely. Johnny Powell kept his musicians from straying to the bars by sending in trays of Irish bread or cake from the concession stand to be served to musicians in the cloakroom behind the stage during their breaks.

Keeping up with the busy pace of performing at three and four weddings a weekend, then evenings at the halls, was demanding, and some forsook drink altogether, according to Mickey Connolly. He says:

> I was a Pioneer, and took the pledge and wore the pin. I brought my Pioneer pledge to Germany with me during the Korean War. But after that Thursday night that I met my future wife, Cathy, she drove me to drink, I guess [Laughs]. We were in Joe McPherson's place, myself and Bill Caples, and Joe says, "Ginger ale, Mickey?" That's all he ever saw me drink. Billy says, "Give him a shot of VO and a beer and be a man, he's out of the army now!" So Joe reached down, and he took my pin, and he says, "I'll save this for you." I never went back for it.

Occasionally, a musician would drink too much, but it was taken with humor. Joe Joyce describes one such occasion: "Johnny Connors, a.k.a. Peter Feeney, he liked his tea. He would stop playing if he hit a flat note. We were playing at a bowling banquet, and midway through the waltz, he slipped off his piano stool. Red Maloney says, 'Johnny fell!' I said, 'Keep playing! He'll get up!' He was half in the bag!"

Though alcohol consumption was generally accepted, drunkenness appeared to remain minimal, controlled by the vigilance of police as well as dance hall staff. Fortunately, most of the police in the area were either Irish or Irish-American, and most would make sure that the perpetrator was covertly seen out safely, without incident, as Frank Storer relates:

> It was quite wholesome in those days, I thought. You had an occasional person that had too much to drink, but they were pretty well escorted out by the police; they'd be right on top of them. Officer Frank McEiver always had the hall detail. He was very patient and most of the time persuaded the person to behave and have a good time.

Even by the late 1950s, when Larry Reynolds arrived, it was still wholesome: "Everybody waited for Saturday night again. People would go to the Waldorf and have coffee afterwards, then spend half the night walking home, because they'd miss the transportation. But you could walk anywhere then; whether a man or woman, you had no fear of walking."

Whether this picture was accurate depends partially on whom you speak with, however. The guys on the corner in South Boston looked upon the Irish weddings as a chance for free booze—when you could drink all afternoon for "the donut": zero. Éamon Connolly recalls:

> Sunday afternoons for entertainment, if there wasn't a wedding up at the Pierre Marquette in Southie, we'd go up to Dudley Street for what we called a beer and a beatin'. I could wangle an invite with the older guys because I could play the guitar and sing a few songs. They'd say, "We're going to the Intercolonial. Get a sports jacket, get a tie, we're meeting on the corner, down at the car barn at one o'clock. And don't bring anybody with ya."
>
> We'd all throw on the one-button-roll zoot suits of the times, with the stovepipes—the pegged pants—and the *Blackboard Jungle* look. We'd comb the hair back like Tony Curtis, and we'd go drinking, just looking for trouble. That was the name of the game. There'd be ten to twelve people going—the Kineavys, the Roques, the Wards—getting on the streetcar at P and Second, right down at the station, one block down from where we hung around.

Mikey Ward would hold inspection, make sure we got the knots in the ties. The only ones that could go were the ones that could dance. You'd want to start ducking the ones who couldn't bullshit and would get you into trouble or fuck up the wedding names after the free drinks. Mikey used to crash the weddings so regularly that he only wanted guys that could enjoy the day and not have to fight our way out of there. The worst thing in the world you want to do is get caught, 'cause you got a hundred guys in the dance hall saying, "They're crashing!" You're outnumbered big time, so you didn't want to screw up.

The deal was, Terrence O'Malley and Mikey Ward were the operators of the group. Nineteen-year-old war heroes. Mikey Ward would be the grand master. He wasn't the toughest in the crowd, but the real toughs didn't have the savoir faire. Mikey Ward would send Terrence O'Malley up to bullshit his way through. He looked like an altar boy, so he could go in through the wedding tribe, while we'd drink down in the joint next door. He'd use a bit of a brogue, depending on how much brogue was needed, and find out the maiden name, the groom.

After a while, Terrence O'Malley would report down, "They're doing the first waltz." Johnny Powell was almost a resident player at the Intercolonial. That's all the Galway people wanted. He had it tied up to a fare-thee-well for the Galway weddings where the Irish was being spoken.

So down at the bar Mikey Ward says, "Okay, we'll make this the last round, because Johnny Powell will be starting up with the two-step." He had it down to the time. They wouldn't buy a full round down there for money if they knew, once Johnny Powell went to "Miss McLeod's Reel," it was full bent for the afternoon. They were a Connemara tribe up there and everybody's on the floor, dancing, and they'd be three deep at the bar. Nobody knew anybody, and that's how you played it.

Then Mikey Ward would go through the joint, check the thing, get the names. He'd say, "The maiden name of the bride is Callahan, the groom's name is Grealish." He'd say, "Now think of it three times fast. We don't want a fucking horror show. Come on up one at a time, every fifteen minutes."

Once you got up there, the question you'd ask is, "Whose side are you on?" And then whatever name they had, you went automatically the other way: "Oh I'm the second cousin to the Grealishes." You had to get the right side so you could bullshit your way through the afternoon. We swallowed like Apaches, getting whiskey for nothing, until somebody'd come over and say with a big brogue on him, "Who are you related to? No one seems to know ye." You'd be dancing around with a girl, maybe taking up too much of the young girl's time, and all of a sudden . . . well, eight out of ten times you could get away with it, but when you tried to do it with ten or twelve guys—and then all of a sudden, oh shit, there's another six. . . . So you'd either get caught out or make an afternoon out of it. If you got thrown out of the Intercolonial, you'd scurry over to the Hibernian. There was a little Irish café in between the two that was a watering hole when you were thrown out of both, that at least you could meet there.

The worst-case scenario was that you get caught, and sometimes you did. Terrence O'Malley was recognized once from a wedding he'd been at four weeks before, and the men in the wedding party took him out and stuffed him in a barrel. Mikey Ward's response to the rest of the guys: "We'll have to change the strategy. Terrence can go home now." No one wanted to get found out, and they weren't going to be exposed by one person's mistake. As Éamon Connolly says:

> If the people found out that you're interlopers, well, that's when the gloves are off. And you had to fight; it was all honor. It was usually when somebody was flirting with someone else's girl who was a regular.
>
> At the Intercolonial, the worst place was the stairs. If there was only a donnybrook or a fucking scat [skirmish], you'd be okay. Hopefully it'd be only two on two. If it was more than two on two, which it often was, the guys that went to the ambulance were the ones who fought on the stairs. If you're in over your head and somebody's kicking your ass, you're going down. But not only he might hit you with a shot that sends you down; you gotta worry about everybody else when you're rolling, holding your head, because they're falling, and they're fighting on the stairs, too.

Even if you were just trying to get away from a fracas—maybe you thought you were in love and running for a drink for your prospective fiancée—you could get caught on the stairs. And there were some big-ass Connemara guys. I don't even care if the guy's the father of the bride. Some of them, for chrissake, they could be like 260. These big goddamn guys, old-timers, half in the wrapper. I mean, that's like getting hit with two guys anyway if he falls on you. Once somebody hits, you had to get out of the way. There'd be some awful pileups. You'd be sure there were a couple dead underneath—and these fights were a common occurrence.

The Greenville Café

While the dances went on upstairs, a popular spot for a drink was downstairs in Joe McPherson's bar, the Greenville Café. Opened in 1934 at 233 Dudley Street, it moved in 1937 to 208 Dudley, directly under the Intercolonial Hall, where it stayed until McPherson sold the pub to Pete Lee and Timmy Walsh in 1961. Though Canadian himself, McPherson was a great supporter of Irish music. According to Joanne McDermott:

> Joe wasn't a musician but he loved music, he loved the people, and they did spend a lot of time [in the café]. The reason that McPherson's Greenville Café was so popular with the Irishmen was because it was right next door to the Irish dance hall . . . and they didn't have a bar in the dance hall. It was mostly men; there were a few women in there. In those days, there was a double standard. If you were a *nice* woman, you wouldn't be sitting up at the bar at that time. You know, the fifties were very proper. It doesn't mean that [women] weren't drinking. It just means that they didn't want to do it in public. Especially sitting up at a bar stool in that period of time, it wasn't considered exactly proper. But we really didn't drink much in those days, in the fifties, in Roxbury; it was okay for the guys to drink, and they did.

Frank Devin worked nights as a bartender in the Greenville Café during the dance halls' height. While he attended Boston College, from 1948 to 1952, he recalls that the café had a long, long bar, probably about forty feet long. During the week, I could sit at the bar at night and do my homework. Every once in a while I would get a beer for somebody, then sit back down again. But Thursday they were ten deep at the whole bar, all the way back to the booths. That's because of the music that was upstairs. The owner, Joe McPherson, was from Big Pond, Cape Breton; his wife Annie was from Prince Edward Island. My brothers used to give me the business for working for the "herring chokers"—that's what we called people from Canada. Even in those days there was a little bit of a division between the two groups.

Thursday and Saturday were wild nights, and I mean wild. Joe McPherson made his fortune, if he had a fortune, on those two nights. Sometimes there were two or three bartenders on duty. Joe and the Powells had an agreement of sorts. He would congregate all sorts of people in the bar and cater to them with their kind of music. The dancers all went to Joe's; they didn't go to the other bars around. Obviously it was in the same building as the dances, but even when the dances were at Hibernian they would come over to Joe's.

A few drinks would always help loosen up the men's feet in the dance halls, so the arrangement worked to their mutual benefit. Generally, the environment was orderly, though Devin recalls one exception, when a fight broke out:

> There was a policeman on duty there, as there was on all of those nights—Thursday, Friday, Saturday, and Sunday. Every one of those nights, there was a cop, and he sat at the end of the bar. He was so ossified he couldn't get up to help out. The next day, when I met him coming in, I said, "Thanks a lot; you were a great help yesterday." He was in uniform, too, by the way. He was an Irishman, born and brought up in Ireland.

It was for reasons like the atmosphere described by Devin that few women would patronize the bars. That didn't change until the late 1960s, when women's employment options expanded, and many worked as nurses, clerical workers, and waitresses. Frank Storer recalls trying to convince his wife to join him at a tavern: "I'd say to Evelyn after the dance, 'Come on, we'll get an after-hours drink.' 'Well, I'm not going up there!' I could get in, but the old-timers would say to her, 'What are you doing in here?' The old standbys [didn't] want them drinking in there."

That would change as time wore on. In the 1940s and 1950s, women would remain on the ballroom floor with their high heels and highland flings, their puffs of crinoline, and their Stacks of Barley. There was still another ten years until they would join the barroom crowd. For now, it was time to find a husband and raise a family.

7

The Kings of Dudley Street

Johnny Powell and His Band

If the Rest of the World Were Like Ireland

Do your thoughts ever roam to the land you call home,
To the place where you're longing to be?
Were there tears in your eye when you waved her goodbye,
As you sailed across the sea?

Chorus:
If the rest of the world were like Ireland,
What a wonderful world it would be.
For a friend is a friend in my Ireland,
Surely that's how God meant it to be.
You've a song in your heart if you're Irish,
And a smile ev'ry one likes to see.
If the rest of the world were like Ireland,
What a wonderful world 'twould be.

I remember and sigh as the years pass me by,
That I've been like a bird on the wing.
Sure, it's Erin's green shore that is heaven's front door,
For it's there that the angels sing.

—Lyric by Johnny Powell, music by Carlton Bates.
Copyright 1951 by William Carlton Bates for O'Byrne DeWitt's Sons,
Boston, Mass. #3308-3, Copley Recording No. 9-175

There were five halls on Dudley Street, but the one that drew the biggest crowds was the Intercolonial, run by Johnny Powell and his brother Mike. Johnny Powell had served in World War II. When he came out of the service in 1945, there were already a few active dance halls on Dudley Street, but the bands seemed to cater to the older prewar generation. Powell saw what was happening in Boston and made a move: there was a large Irish-American population there looking for a place to go, and there was a huge influx of new, young immigrants from Ireland, and there was a desire for both Irish and popular music. So they started organizing their own dance band to play at Intercolonial Hall, debuting Johnny Powell and His Irish Band on the eve of Labor Day, September 1948.[1]

Though the Intercolonial was run by both Johnny and Mike, Johnny was the personality and the musician, and Mike was the businessman, according to Joe Derrane:

> The brains behind the whole thing was Mike. Mike controlled the purse strings, while Johnny just wanted to play. Mike was trying to operate from the point of view of making the hall ever more successful, and at one point was trying to cater to a more Irish-American crowd. But Johnny was more interested in the people and having a good time, and he was reluctant to draw more Irish-Americans in. He wanted to keep it as Irish as he could. They were two different guys altogether—totally different.
>
> Mike was all business. He was very good, and very fair, very honorable. He'd sit you down if he wanted something, and say, "Here it is: A, B, C. I pay the money. This is the way it's going to be," and you didn't mind because you knew it up front.
>
> Both of them were very honorable. They never cheated anyone. Mike took a little bit of knowing, but Johnny, you'd meet him the first time and after talking to him for five minutes, you'd feel like you'd known him your whole life. You'd be saying, "Come on up to the house, stop in for a visit anytime!"

While the brothers had their differences behind the scenes, the compromises they made were ideal for the demand that was there. One thing the two agreed on was the importance of musicians. They always selected the best and brightest. According to Mickey Connolly, "Powell had the number-one band in Boston for Irish bands. There were others, but they weren't qualified like Powell's was. See, Powell picked his men."

When Joe Derrane attempted to start a dance at a competing hall with a new band, Johnny and Mike Powell actively recruited him to the Intercolonial. Derrane had already proved himself a prodigy on the accordion, and the Powells knew he'd draw a crowd away from their new dance at the Intercolonial. Recalls Derrane:

> I was starting my own dance on Thursday nights at the Dudley Street Opera House, which was not running on Thursday nights at the time. I had a five-piece band playing there. The Powells were trying to get the maid's night out thing off the ground, and word got around that we had started getting a crowd in there in the Opera House. I was making money, not big money, but I was paying my bills and making a night's pay.
>
> Mike Powell finally approached me, and he wanted me to come work for him. . . . Mike was the treasurer and comptroller for the MTA, the transit system, so he had a lot of business sense. He laid it right onto the table; there was nothing sneaky about it. Mike said, "Look, how many people can you draw over there? A couple hundred, something like that?" I said, "Yeah, about that." He said, "Well, that's $250 that I'm not getting. Why don't you come work for us? No expenses, no hassles, you just play, then go home. And we'll get the people. You do the math. You get paid, and you're helping the hall." I figured out that I'd end up with the same amount of income, and no headache. So, I went with him.

Powell's appeal was partly rooted in his family's contributions to the Irish community in Boston. Johnny's parents had come from Connemara, county Galway, in the 1920s, his mother, Nora Theresa McDonough Powell, from Cararoe, and his father, Jacob, from Rossaveel. Frank Storer says their home in America quickly became a kind of "underground railroad," and it was well known that the Powell family had sponsored "half of Galway" to Boston.[2]

Because the Powell family looked after their own, they earned the deep respect and admiration of the Irish community in Boston. According to Mickey Connolly, "Johnny Powell's mother and father were Irish and lived in Quincy. His mother and Peggy Rutledge—Harp Caterers—used to run the cafeteria up in the Intercolonial. Oh, she was great for the Irish lads. 'Come up here, you'll be starving.'"

Even after losing her young husband in 1931, Nora Powell continued to take in boarders—five of her brothers' and sisters' boys from Ireland—partly because she had to, to support her own nine children. She looked after her children during the day and then worked evenings, frequently waking at 3:00 A.M. to bake bread to feed the boys and send them off to work at 5:00 A.M.

The respect the Powell family earned in the Irish community contributed to the success and longevity of both the bands and the dance hall that Johnny Powell ran. Frank Storer refers to Powell as "the King," saying that he essentially controlled the Irish music business in Boston. Indeed, Powell was widely recognized as the main man on Dudley Street, and his band was booked sometimes two years in advance for weddings. Frank Devin calls him "the impresario of the day. He was behind everything. If you wanted a band for your wedding, you went to Johnny Powell. He ran the dances [at the Intercolonial] and at the Hibernian."

Johnny Powell maintained rigid control over what was played by his band and how they played it. "He set the tempos, the sequences, the whole thing," says Derrane. "There was a very cohesive kind of a unified approach to everything." Powell also maintained tight control over who was playing what and where in the hall, according to Mickey Connolly, who played with him before joining the service, during the Korean War. Says Connolly:

> We had three bands. Well, there was twelve of us normally in Johnny Powell's band, up in the Crystal Ballroom. Johnny would send four down to the Longfellow, and he always hired extra musicians on the weekends. He'd send another two or three down to a third hall. They had to close the doors one night, the fireman came in to close the doors. There was twenty-two hundred people in the hall! At fifty cents apiece, he was charging.

While a few musicians came and went from the band, Powell's band had a core of steady musicians. Johnny Powell played the lead on accordion, with Billy Caples, Joe Derrane, and Mickey Connolly also on accordion. Other musicians included Harry Hanbury or Pat Connolly on fiddle, Joe Leavey on piano in the early years, later followed by Carlton Bates and Mike Fahey on banjo. Drummers changed often, but the one there most frequently was Johnny's brother-in-law, the chiropodist Dr. John "Tut" Connolly, who Joe Derrane describes as the "best Irish drummer I've ever heard." Al Deiss played alto saxophone, and Clarence "Clary" Walsh was on alto and soprano sax. Frank Murphy also played alto and soprano. Though most of the musicians in the band were Irish-American, born in America of Irish-born parents, Duke Jyllka, who was of Lithuanian or Polish descent, played tenor sax, alongside the Italian musician Mike Portenova on clarinet. Walter Deiss would sometimes join the band on trumpet and later on C-melody saxophone, and occasionally Sonny Coakley, a young Irish-American accordionist, would be called in. Johnny Powell's band did sometimes have vocalists, but only on rare occasions. The band sometimes accompanied such singers as Connie Foley from Tralee, county Kerry, or Dorothy McManus, who was from Ireland but living about a half hour north of Boston in Winthrop, Massachusetts.

The Powell band's musicians dressed in tuxes, adding to the Intercolonial's reputation as the classiest of the dance halls. Says Derrane:

> I had three tuxes—you had to. We were playing Thursday, Friday, then a couple of weddings on Saturday, then the ballroom, then weddings on Sunday. You couldn't get a weekend out of a tux. There was no air-conditioning, and there might be two or three big fans. It was ninety-five degrees in the hall. And you get twelve hundred people in there, and they're all dancing and jumping around like crazy—you'd be wringing your clothes out. The sweat was lashing off them, and they'd be red and flustered, and we'd be red and flustered with the heat. It was just nonstop. Unbelievable.
>
> This is where Mike Powell's thinking came in. Give them something nice to look at. The bands in the other halls were dressed neatly, but you'd have one guy with blue pants and the other guy with brown pants, but not in tuxes.

A dynamic character, Johnny Powell was an enthusiastic bandleader who, when wedding bookings started pouring in, rose to the occasion. Enlisting the assistance of musicians in his own band, as well as those who played in other Dudley Street halls, he would arrange the musicians into small combos and send them to any one of the five weddings he might book each weekend. Joe Derrane describes the typical wedding band as a blend of Irish and American, appropriate for the time:

> For weddings, he'd take a piano, a drummer, with himself and a sax player. A large portion of the people at the ballrooms were Irish-Americans, hence the sax player, the piano, the drummer—the typical trio—plus an accordion. They would play Irish music, then a fifteen-minute set of American tunes: "Dancing in the Dark," "I'm in the Mood for Love"—the popular songs of the day.

Powell was welcome at every wedding in Boston, and his arrival would inevitably cause a flutter. "When he'd get there," recalls Frank Storer, "all the old biddies would crowd around him—they loved him. People would say, 'Now, the music's really going to get good!'" It was not necessarily Powell's musicianship that improved the music, however, Storer notes. It was his mere presence. According to Storer:

> Johnny would have five weddings going on a Saturday, and he may call me and book me for a job. I may get to the job and Billy Caples would be playing accordion, and Johnny would be on the other job. He would bounce around. He was like a diplomat type of guy; he would show up at all the weddings. They loved him, and he had a lot of charisma.[3]

Powell's diplomacy extended beyond weddings. Jack Martin calls him

> the father of wakes. This guy, that's all he ever did was go to wakes, because he knew so many people! Everybody knew John. He was a big, big man. He was about six foot three, and he had a big brogue on him, even though he was *born* in America. But you would swear he came from the Old Country. I worked with John at Boston Edison before I went in the police force. On a few occasions, we used to have Christmas parties in the company, and I'd bring my accordion in, and John'd bring his in, and we'd razzle-dazzle them until everybody got drunk; then we'd have to put 'em away! He was all personality! Just a big happy-go-lucky guy. He liked everybody, and everybody liked John.

Behind Powell's gregarious exterior, his sister Anne recalls, was a man who was kind and soft of heart. But he was not without his own struggles, though few would recognize this from his public persona. Says Anne:

> Many times he was in a crowded room, he was lonely. A wake was his only way of getting out. He was taking care of his mother, who had a massive stroke. Johnny was tired, but he liked to get out and talk to people. He never married, though. My brother Mike came out in the hall . . . and he started running the show. They had little conflicts, and Johnny started drinking heavy. He was never a fighter; he was like a goodwill ambassador. See, there's a thin line between saints and sinners: he stayed on the drink, but he never played anyone dirty.
> Instead of dealing with my brother, he took to drink. Mike was

the oldest boy in the family. My father had gotten killed in 1931, working on the old Boston el down by High Street. A wall collapsed on him and killed him. Mike was the oldest, so he had to quit school. He got a job in the MTA, and went from messenger boy to clerk all the way up to comptroller. Without my father, Mike used to rule the roost. He was tough. A lot of us feared him.

But Johnny got lost in the shuffle. Johnny and I were right in the middle of nine kids. The oldest ones are the king and queens, the youngest ones are the princes and princesses, and the middle ones get lost.

That was the private Johnny Powell. The public Johnny Powell was magnetic, which helped him maintain a loyal cadre of musicians. According to Joe Derrane:

When you saw Johnny, when you talked to Johnny, and when you listened to his music, what you saw was what you got. There was nothing false about him. His folks were from Connemara. He spoke and read Irish fluently, and when he'd get in with the Connemara people he'd talk Irish like the best of them. Johnny was Irish to the core. He was very down-to-earth and very lovable.

Johnny was very nice to work with. He was straight as a die. If Johnny called you up and said he needed you on Saturday, you didn't have to ask anything, how much the pay was or anything. He was straight, he was fair, and you always got paid. Sometimes things would happen and Johnny wound up working for nothing—but the guys always got paid.

Musicians who worked for Powell were sure to perform frequently and be compensated fairly, but this meant that they had to be at his beck and call. Powell would frequently call a musician at the last minute, often flirtatiously charming the musician's mother or wife, and, according to Frank Storer, "He'd use some old Gaelic phrase that had a double entendre and get her laughing. Then he'd say, 'All right, tell Frank I need him tonight, and to be at the dance hall at eight.' Then, he'd just hang up."

While this often meant a suddenly canceled date with a wife or girlfriend, the women in the musicians' lives tolerated Powell's last-minute bookings, for employment with him held a certain status in Boston. There was a widespread opinion in Boston: "You can't let Johnny down."

Johnny Powell understood his dance hall crowd, a mix of Irish nationals and Irish-Americans. He carefully catered to both, but he knew that his bread and butter was with the Irish-Americans. Powell had an almost intuitive sense of who his crowd was, and Joe Derrane counts that as one of his biggest strengths:

> Johnny was not a trained musician in the traditional sense. He was a self-taught musician. He wasn't a reader. What he did, like a lot of us did, was listen to a lot of records. He was always steeped in music. We wasn't so much interested in céilí music, but he had a feel for the ballroom music, for the dance tempos—for what people *liked*, which is critical.

Powell was a kind man, but also, with help from his business-headed brother, he watched the money carefully, and patrons paid to enter the hall whether they came in at the beginning of the evening or near the end. Says one musician, "There was no one going in free with Powell. Other than that, he was all right. I played for him, and he treated me all right."

In later years at the Intercolonial, Mike suggested to Johnny that they put a kitchen in, to serve sandwiches in addition to the usual Irish bread and tea. Johnny said no, it wouldn't go over. He maintained that the Irish in Boston were watching their money to pay for bringing the next ones from home over to America. But Mike felt strongly about it. He proceeded to build a stainless steel–clad kitchen in the Intercolonial, and over time, it turned out that Johnny had been right. All the Irish really wanted was their tea and Irish bread. According to his sister, Anne, "He knew the Irish like the palm of his hand."

Johnny Powell's mother died on February 13, 1973. He had been very loyal in taking care of her, and was shaken by her death. A month later, Powell had a heart attack himself. He had been experiencing some heart troubles, and his doctor had warned him that his music days were over, but that didn't fit Powell's plans. Joe Derrane recalls Powell's reaction: "What does he want me to do, spend the rest of my days in a rocking chair? If I'm going to go, I'm going to go doing what I enjoy." And so he did. Johnny Powell passed away on March 16, 1973, while playing onstage. Mickey Connolly remembers the night Johnny died:

> We were playing in the 1200 Beacon, in town there on Beacon Street, and we were playing for an Irish club. And ten o'clock at

night, we took a break. I said, "Let's take a break and go have a beer." The next thing, I see a big crowd of people coming in the door. I said, "Jeez, I know them all. . . . What the hell are they doing here?" They were up at St. Mary's Church hall in Brookline at a St. Patrick's dance. Johnny Powell was playing, and Johnny dropped dead on the stage. They closed the place, and they all came down to us. It was the right way to go.

All-Star Band Members

Without question, the star of the Johnny Powell band was Joe Derrane. According to Frank Storer, Derrane was well known as Powell's "number-one man. The two were practically synonymous at Dudley Street's height."[4] Many even describe Joe Derrane and Johnny Powell as "one and the same." Even at the age of fifteen, Derrane was a well-respected musician, says one observer of the dance hall scene.

> "Little Joe," they used to call him. Before he was ever doing those albums at twenty, he would direct the bands. You'd see him up there with a bunch of older guys, calling the tunes, meanwhile playing a tune and responding to dancers on the floor at the same time. What focus, what amazing focus he had! He played as ornamented then as he does now.

Joe Derrane was born in 1930. The oldest of three brothers, Joe started playing the accordion at age ten under the tutelage first of Johnny ("Jackie") Bresnahan, then of Jerry O'Brien, an accomplished melodeon player and radio personality featured with O'Leary's Irish Minstrels. Derrane was a mainstay on the dance hall stage and on the original "Irish Hour" radio program, hosted by Tommy Shields and broadcast every Sunday night for many years. Derrane was just eighteen years old when he recorded his first album, which was the beginning of a busy recording career. His recorded repertoire reflects the favorites in Boston: "The Salamanca," "The Union Reel," "The Mason's Apron," "The Boys of the Lough," "Harvest Home," "The Jackson Polka." He also recorded a selection of jigs, reels, hornpipes, and waltzes with his teacher Jerry O'Brien and with the Joe Derrane Irish All-Stars.[5]

Everyone wanted to play as well as Joe Derrane, but no one succeeded, save Billy Caples, the other all-star button box player in Powell's band. Billy Caples (1928–1986) had been with Johnny Powell's band right from its inception. Caples was born in St. Joseph's parish in Somerville, to Helena (Noonan) Caples and William Caples, both of the Fermoy region, county Cork. He began playing the single-row accordion in his early teens, inspired by his mother, who played the concertina. Later, he also picked up a piano accordion, a "flashy gold accordion that he went down to New York to buy."[6] Caples served in Guam with the U.S. Army during World War II and then worked for thirty-two years at the Steel Canvas Basket Company, in Cambridge, Massachusetts, while maintaining his own active musical career.

Caples was inspired both by the musical agility of Derrane and by early 78 rpm recordings of the fiddler Michael Coleman, whose renditions of popular tunes Caples learned note for note. Caples's style was different from Derrane's. He didn't sprinkle his tunes as generously with triplet ornamentation the way Derrane and many other Boston players did, but his playing was solid, consistent, and sure.

After playing with the Powell band for many years, Caples eventually formed his own band, the Billy Caples Orchestra, which played frequently at the Hibernian. Recognized as a musical genius by many who knew him, he was legendary for stomping his foot while he played, which lent rhythmic support to his steady, hard-hitting style. Billy also attracted strong players to his band: Frank Storer on piano; Clary Walsh, Finbar Storer, George Derrane, and Vic Kirby on sax; Frankie Wilson or Bob Martus on bass; and Frank Meyers on drums. Joe Derrane and Billy Caples, both Boston-born, were old friends. Derrane says:

> I met him when we were both fifteen. He was with Johnny Powell since the very beginning. Billy did writing for the band—the lead sheets. He had a ton of old tunes—"The Old Rustic Bridge" and other pop songs of Ireland. "Inisfree." Some that were on the commercial edge and some that were deeply rooted in the tradition. Those were the songs heard in the dance halls in Ireland.
>
> Billy was Irish-American. He loved waltzes and could play them all—Viennese waltzes, all types of music. Billy and I were exposed to a much wider variety of music year after year than they would have been in Ireland. Our tastes and appreciation were different—but not better—than theirs.
>
> Billy had brought in a lot of music to the Johnny Powell band.

He would work with Carlton Bates. He would write what he
thought were acceptable chords, and Carlton would make sugges-
tions, and they got more and more complex as time went on.
They made a couple of 78s together on Copley Records.

Billy became well known among musicians for having a brilliant musical
ear. Mickey Connolly, who had a nice collection of waltzes he had learned
in Ireland, recalls Billy transcribing the tunes Mickey played onstage, nearly
as fast as Mickey could play them. One of Caples's students, Skip Toomey,
recalls that he did something similar during lessons:

> He'd always write out a tune while he was talking to you, and he'd
> put in the fingerings and everything. One time, he was writing out
> a piece of music for me, and in the meantime, I had given him a
> tape of something I wanted to learn, and he was playing that on
> the tape recorder and listening to the tape. At the same time, I was
> playing a different tune, and we were talking all at the same time,
> and he would do it all with absolute facility. His head could work
> at that level. He was an absolutely amazing guy. And they weren't
> Mother Henry tunes. They were fast tunes!

If You Have an Accordion, You Have a Party

Accordions, which were by far the most commonly played instrument of
the day, were at the lead of Powell's and most other bands. The most popular accordion at the time was the D/C# Irish button box, though some
musicians also had piano accordions. Loud and clear, the accordion was
well able to project over the shuffling feet of eight hundred dancers. Flutes
and whistles, by contrast, were fairly uncommon in the larger dance hall
bands, for they could not project adequately—especially over the accordions. Gene Frain, who started as a flute player, ended up playing saxophone instead. "I got the sax," he says, "because no one's going to hear a
goddamned flute. You get one accordion, and forget it. You can't hear nothing. I decided I was sick of playing second fiddle to the goddamned accordions. With the sax, I could drown out two or three with no trouble."

If you had an accordion, you had music, and if you had music, you had
a life of dance, music, friends, and good times. Mickey Connolly's wife,

Cathy, fully supported his music, buying him an accordion from the most famous maker of the time, Frank Walters. Mickey Connolly says:

> Cathy and I got engaged on her birthday. I took her down to New York to meet my family. We went to my aunt and uncle's place in the Bronx, and I had no accordion, but there was a Sligo man lived upstairs. "Mickey," he says, "I'll get you an accordion." He went up and he borrowed an accordion. "Now," he said, "you're here now in New York. Go downtown and order an accordion for yourself. Go down to Walters, Frank Walters, he's a German, and he makes them. Order one."
>
> Well, I got to the shop, and Frank says, "It's a shame with your talent not to have a box. It's normally five hundred dollars. But for you, I'll give it to you for four hundred. I'll have it made for you." He custom-made them, so he says, "Call me within a couple weeks." And Cathy said, "I'm going to buy that for you," and she gave him the deposit. Most women want to keep their husbands out of the music racket. But she paid for that for me, for her engagement. She got a diamond and heartaches to go with it! [Laughs]

The Walters accordions were made for the dance halls: square, solid, and powerful. And the accordion was *the* instrument. Says Jack Martin:

> The people that enjoyed the Irish music, and I'd say most of them probably were from the Old Country, loved the accordion. Irish-Americans did, too. I mean, you get a certain group of American kids like myself, I always loved the Irish music. I still do. I will till the day I die.
>
> It was easier to learn because there was a special accordion notation system that didn't require that you know how to read music. The system that they used to use those days was what they call the press-and-draw system, which indicates which button to press and when to draw or compress the bellows. After a while you got so you [could] do it like you would read music.
>
> Back years ago, it was just the straight accordion; it didn't have the sharps and flats on it like you have today. They were in the key of D, and they were very limited on production. Most of the accordions that were built were Italian accordions—Paolo Sopranis and the Baldoni company in New York. There was also Frank

Walters in New York, who built a great accordion. He was German. He had hands on him like baseball gloves, and he'd run over those keys like greased lightning.

I always say, God forbid, if there's a fire in the house, two things go: the accordion and my wife! Everything else stays there. I go for that first, then grab Annie. . . . Of course, the question is, which one first? [Laughs]

A Piano in Every Parlor

The piano, usually a grand piano in the large ballrooms, provided simple textural accompaniment. Since Irish music is melody-based, the piano's role was to support the melody and help to drive the dance rhythm in the dance halls—thus the rhythmic style of Dudley Street pianists. Common piano accompaniment style in the Boston dance halls was to place a single bass note, the root of the chord, with the left hand on the strong beats of the measure, beats 1 and 3. Then, on the upbeats, piano players would typically strike the triad of the chord. This emphasized the offbeats of the music, creating a percussive, swinging feel that would help to project the rhythm across a large hall.[7]

According to Gene Frain and Frank Storer, pianists were expected on no uncertain terms to play the correct chords, so they needed to be familiar with the tunes. The prevalent feeling was that the best piano accompaniment supports a tune but does not overwhelm it. As Storer puts it:

> The accordion player and fiddle player are playing their style. They're doing a little improvisation with what they're doing. You'll hear Joe [Derrane] play a lot of triplets and riffs, but if I'm there trying to do the same thing in the back, what you get is a clash. If you're accompanying anything, you *accompany* it. The piano is a supporting instrument. It sits back there, and the lead instruments will play. And you will hear the bass player, the piano, the percussion, the drum—they're all providing the beat.

Accompaniment also helped to set the tempo. The music in Boston was played at an upbeat dance tempo. To judge from the Copley recordings of Joe Derrane and his All-Star Céilí Band, reels and jigs were played at about

126 beats per minute (bpm). (For reference, that tempo is just a little faster than "The Stars and Stripes Forever" is usually played.) Hornpipes and barn dances were played at about 96 bpm, and highland flings at about 104 bpm.[8] Musicians were not encouraged to think of beats on a metronome, however. Instead, they were instructed to keep an eye on the dance floor. Pianist Frank Storer remembers the words of bandleader Johnny Powell, who repeatedly advised, "Watch the dancers. If they don't look comfortable, you're going too fast." Irish music was composed to be danced to, and Powell's halls were such a success because he knew that and enforced it with his musicians.

Not all of the musicians were well-versed in Irish traditional music. This depended in part on what instrument they played and in part on where they had grown up. Saxophonists, trumpeters, and the occasional trombone players were in most cases trained jazz musicians who had made their way to the Irish dance halls after the swing era had effectively swung for the steadier work on the Irish circuit during that period. Joe Derrane, who performed with some of these displaced jazz musicians, reports that, while they were not from a traditional Irish background, they were able to read the tunes from sheet music. Derrane says: "These guys had played in some of the local big bands and the radio shows and stuff like that. They just read everything."

These musicians were such good readers, in fact, that Derrane says they could read Irish tunes from O'Neill's *Music of Ireland*, transposing them at tempo from either B-flat or E-flat to concert key, though many tenor and alto sax players eventually went to soprano, because it was easier to play the fast Irish jigs and reels on that instrument.

The musical emphasis in the dance halls was on melody, rhythm, and tempo. Using multiple instruments did lend texture to the sound, but in a day of less sophisticated amplification systems, the primary contribution made by multiple instruments was an increase in volume. Some bands would have one microphone that they'd set up in front of the band in the middle of the stage. They put the boxes and the fiddle, and maybe the banjo, in the front row. Then there was a short tier, maybe six or seven inches high, behind them for the horns, and behind that again, another, third, level was for the drummer to drive the whole band. The setup was organized so that the lead instruments were up front. A minimal system of two speakers hung from the walls of the hall permanently, since bands tended to have a residency at a hall. Fiddles sometimes would be amplified, and by the late 1950s, fiddlers such as Larry Reynolds and Brendan Tonra carried small amplification systems.

The person who orchestrated and arranged the music for a band was typically also a band member, and many of the special treatments of the tunes were improvised on the spot. Dance hall music arrangers sometimes composed multipart harmonies for American selections, though these arrangements did not utilize the rich, sophisticated jazz harmonies associated with Count Basie– or Duke Ellington–style swing bands. Derrane recalls that trumpeters and saxophone players, who were more likely to be familiar with jazz, would sometimes improvise harmonies or other complementary lines of music. Frain says he attributed it to boredom, rather than to a conscious effort to create texture in the overall sound of the band:

> The sax players got sick of playing the melody. If you knew anything about jazz, you could put in the bass lines. It's easy, if you know the tunes, to figure out something to do. There's only two or three chords going. I know I would get awful sick of playing the same thing over and over and over. Irish music can be very repetitious.

The traditional style of ensemble playing in Irish music accords with the precedent set by the céilí bands: to duplicate the melodic line. As a result, some Irish musicians on Dudley Street were not accustomed to hearing harmony. Thus, the jazz players' attempts to improvise complementary musical lines were met with a mixed response at first. Derrane recalls that

> Frank Murphy, the tenor and alto saxophone player, told me that the first night they played with Powell, everyone was just flying by the seat of their pants. This ballroom was just getting off the ground, and one of the first things they did was to import a saxophone player. So Johnny Powell and they were playing "When Irish Eyes Are Smiling" or "My Wild Irish Rose," or something like that, and Frank—that being more of an American tune than an Irish tune—Frank was comfortable in the tune, but the key was strange. He was playing little harmony lines, and nothing was said. As soon as there was a break, Johnny Powell leaned over and said to Frank Murphy, "If you don't know the damn tune, don't play it." Powell didn't recognize harmony for what it was! So there were twenty instruments, all playing lead, but Frank adjusted to that. This is how foreign this whole thing was at the beginning. But it caught on, very much caught on.

Carlton Bates was the piano player and arranger in the Powell band. Disabled as a result of a motorcycle accident, he would take his place onstage with the aid of two canes. Because most of the musicians in the band could read music, Bates arranged a few American or popular tunes into two- and three-part harmonies. Joe Derrane recounts that Bates's breadth of musical knowledge was an inspiration to him:

> The Powell band started out with Joe Leavey on piano, but he had to leave the band. His wife was very sick, and he needed to be home to take care of her. So Carlton Bates came along to play piano and eventually became the arranger. He was a very nice guy and a top-flight musician. He would arrange the waltzes. The accordion and fiddle would play leads, and the two saxes and the trumpet would play harmonies. We did these American arrangements, but we still kept the Irish music out there. Carlton Bates got me interested in learning chords and harmonies. I would listen to what he was doing and ask him about it. He would try to explain it to me—which created an interest in me to learn harmony, which eventually led me to the piano accordion.

Bates would provide separate written parts for each musician. Adds Derrane, "The guys used to fool around a little bit with harmonies themselves. There were a few tunes that he had arranged, but not a whole lot, because I don't know that he was getting paid for them as such. It was more for everybody's enjoyment."

Having Carlton Bates arrange a few tunes in a more contemporary style was evidence of Powell's ability to move with the times. While Powell was attracted to Irish céilí music, he knew his crowds: the Irish, who were interested in modern music and just a little bit of home on the side, and the Irish-Americans, with an entire repertoire of Irish-American tunes and of course an interest in the popular music that surrounded them everywhere but at the dance halls. Powell's flexibility when it came to repertoire secured the band's long-term success.

The Johnny Powell Band enjoyed a long residency at the Intercolonial, playing there until well in the 1950s. The Intercolonial was the finest of the halls, and the band, in tuxes, had a professionalism that brought the Irish halls right up with the times: the finest musicians playing exactly the music that the Boston Irish and Irish-American crowd wanted to hear. Johnny Powell and his band were the characters behind the single dance hall that became synonymous with its era.

8

The Musician Crowd

A Community of Differences

Whether Irish born or American born, musicians on Dudley Street formed a tight community, playing together and seeing each other frequently at performances in the hall, at music and social club events, in the bars after hours, and at wedding gigs. The makeup of the various ensembles that were pulled together for any given event was constantly changing, so musicians had frequent opportunities to meet and play with any number of others. Within the musical community there were certainly cliques, but these subgroups were based on interpersonal affinities, not a provincial sense of territoriality. Still, new musicians weren't always welcomed with open arms. The musicians ran in "crowds," according to Paddy Cronin, who says: "If you came from the outside, they had to look you over. It wasn't just sit down and just be lovey-dovey with it. They're the same way in New York, and they're that way in Ireland right now. Oh, Ireland could be the worst of all."

And working conditions weren't always luxurious. The halls were heated with steam systems that used coal-fired basement furnaces, and you couldn't always be sure whether the building superintendent would be shoveling coal or bending his elbow in McPherson's pub. Musicians wanting to escape from the cold hall would go in to the barroom for a few pops themselves to warm up during breaks.

The Intercolonial could be the coldest of all. Its stage, thirty feet across and twelve feet deep, had two small doors that led to a backstage coatroom where musicians could store their coats and instrument cases. Opposite the doors, inside the coatroom, there were two windows in the back of the hall. Several public housing projects had been built behind the hall, and the hall owners never seemed to be able to keep the windows from being broken by thrown stones. In the summer, musicians kept the windows and doors open to keep a flow of air onstage. But in the winter, it was an altogether different matter. Joe Derrane recalls very cold nights:

> One particularly cold night—and I mean, it was bitter—and we're all in there, and I remember Cookie Pimental was playing drums that night. We couldn't close the doors, because the windows were broken, and the wind would just come howling through there and slam the doors open. It became very distracting, so we finally put something in front of them to leave them open. Now you're out onstage, and there's no heat in these bloody halls. You'd have a little heater in the corner, and another one in that corner, but it was a huge ballroom! One by one, the guys were going out and getting their sweaters; the next thing you know, we all wound up with our overcoats on.
>
> In those days we had music desks on stage—the collapsible stands, and they're shaped like a V in the front, with a little platform on top. And there's a little light there for the guys that had to read music. But what the guys were doing was taking the forty-watt bulbs off the top of the stands, and they were putting the bulbs down on the floor, and they were taking their shoes off, and they had their feet wrapped around the bulbs! I looked around at one point, and Cookie Pimental was sitting there with the drums, and he had his overcoat on, his gloves, his hat, and earmuffs. And he played the whole night like that!

Good humor tempered tough times like that, recalls Mickey Connolly:

> We were playing Dudley Street one night and there was six, seven of us, I guess. Walter Deiss was on the sax, and Larry Reynolds on the fiddle, Paddy Cavanaugh on the drums, me on the accordion, Tommy Garvey on the piano, and Joe Joyce on the other accordion. It was so cold that Walter Deiss went out and put his gloves on; he was playing the sax with the gloves on. In the Intercolonial, they had to shut the heat off. . . . I don't know why; maybe they didn't pay the guys that were running the place to heat it. Joe said

to me, "Mickey, you're running the band. If you don't go down and tell these guys to turn the heat on," he says, "I'm going to put my gloves on!" And Larry looks at [Joyce's] accordion and says, "Jeez, Joe, it sounds like you've had them on all night."

This camaraderie helped musicians balance full-time jobs, personal lives, and frequent gigs, for it was a long night for musicians performing on Dudley Street. Derrane explains: "There was one ten-minute, fifteen-minute break; that was it. They used to bring the coffee to us. They didn't want the guys going off for break, because some of the guys might go downstairs and decide they'd have a beer, and one can lead to another." Though the playing schedule was fairly rigid, things loosened up after hours. According to Mickey Connolly:

> The dance would start at eight o'clock. One break. Maybe ten, ten-thirty, fifteen minutes. Then back onstage again. You couldn't buy a drink or anything in the hall. We used to go up to the coffee shop. I wasn't drinking at that time, most of us weren't. Even when Larry and I got together, we weren't drinking. Twenty-minute break, you went then until quarter of twelve. The cops were pretty strict about the hours.
>
> Most times, we would go out afterwards. We'd go to a party—there was always parties: "Come on to my house, bring the accordion, we'll have some music." A cousin of Bill Caples, Matt Caples, lived down near the O'Byrne DeWitts', and he was music mad. He'd never let you go home from Bill Lamey's house until you played a few tunes.

Joe McPherson's bar was also a popular after-hours spot for musicians, recalls Frank Storer:

> I remember going from the dance hall down to the bar below and set up playing down there again until three o'clock in the morning. We'd finish the dance in the ballroom, come all the way down to the first floor, into the gin mill, as we called it in those days, the bar. Someone would say, "Hey, Joe, go out and get your accordion, bring it into the bar." I'd sit down at the piano, and the banjo would start. The place would close at twelve o'clock, but it wasn't really closed. It would go all night long. The police would sit there at the bar. And we had a wedding to play the next day.

*Johnny Caples (left), with button accordion, and Billy
Caples, with piano accordion, stand outside their home.*
(From the library of Frank Storer.)

Humor and mischief were Irish coping mechanisms that musicians brought with them in their fiddle cases, and these personality traits extended into the second generation. American-born Billy and Johnny Caples helped Paddy Cronin through a tough morning in the most Irish of ways. As Cronin tells it,

> I used to love to hear Michael Coleman records. Billy and Johnny Caples knew that. I went out one Saturday night, and I was very sick. I drank too much. They called me out of the bed early the next morning, and they were after being in town, the two of them. "Paddy," Johnny said. "You have to come over right away! We got a new record of Michael Coleman"! I said, "I can meet you . . . ," and he said, "Oh, no, you have to hear this. You'd better come now." When I came in the door, they had the phonograph in the middle of the house, and they had a big bottle of beer, you know, unopened.
>
> Here they are, the two of them, working on the machine, and they opened the bottle and gave me the bottle. They were walking around the phonograph, you know, looking and turning the record upside down and everything. In the finish, I took a look out the window or something like that. The next thing I heard is singing: "Chck, chck, chck, chck, chck, chck!"
>
> They had bought a Greek record! When I looked around, they had the machine going, and there was no one in the room, only myself! And I was sick as a dog. . . . Johnny said to me, "He's not Michael Coleman, you know. He's his cousin Johnny Coleman!" Oh jeez, I'll never forget that! [Laughs] They were only winding me up, calling me up out of the bed to hear it!

Humor was generally the accepted way to deal with band politics. One band had had ongoing problems with a particularly arrogant band member. When it came time to register the band with the city, they neglected to write the name of the self-proclaimed "most important member" on the application. The jilted musician issued a lawyer's letter to the band, notifying its two leaders of his intent to sue. Not to be shaken, one of the band members swiftly made several hundred copies of the letter and then posted them on every pillar and post in the Intercolonial Hall. Embarrassed, the musician rescinded his lawsuit and spent the next several months repairing his reputation.

Another bit of mischief ensued one night when Frank Storer and a well-known banjo player were playing at one of the Dudley Street bars. Storer says:

> The owner, who knew us well, was away on vacation and left an idiot in charge who didn't know the Irish crowd. He was interfering all night with our presentation, so when we were finished, the banjo player says, "We'll fix him!" He "borrowed" the amplifier and microphone and removed them to our car.
>
> The next night, we had to play there again, and we told the individual that the amplifier and microphone were missing, and that we couldn't play without them. He was worried that he would catch hell from the boss when he returned and asked us what to do. Of course we had the amp and the mic all the time in the banjo player's car.
>
> We said to him, "We know where you can get one just like the missing one for about fifty bucks." He said, "Go get it." We went to the car, came back a little while later, and sold his own equipment back to him. Served him right. He paid out of his own money and said to say nothing to the boss. Ha! He never bothered us the rest of the night.

A Few Extra Bob

Playing music provided a necessary supplemental income for most musicians. By the late 1940s, Boston had become a worn-out city where one in five housing units was considered dilapidated, manufacturing jobs were leaving, and only one new private office building had been built since 1929. More than four decades of ward politics under James Michael Curley had been good for the immediate recipients of his political favors but bad for the city. No major city had as many municipal jobs per capita, and the city's universities were gobbling up real estate, leaving only crumbs for a tax base. That all began to change in 1949, with the mayoral election of the reformist John B. Hynes, a middle-class Irish Catholic. Once in office, Hynes focused on weeding out "Curleyism" and rebuilding the city. Slowly things began to improve for city residents.[1]

Among the first Irish immigrants to come to Boston after World War II, fiddler Paddy Cronin witnessed the economic revival that led to the happy days of the 1950s. Steady work was scarce in Boston when he first came in 1949 from Gneevguilla in the Sliabh Luachra, a mountainous region on the border of counties Cork and Kerry, but it wasn't long before he was work-ing and performing regularly. He says:

> I came to America with my cousin looking for work. We had lots of it in Ireland, but no money from it. I came in July of 1949 on the *Marine Flasher*. It was a troop trip during the war and we had a damn good old time on it. We had a step dancer from Galway; her name was Bridget Barrett. I had the fiddle, and I was playing away for her, and we had a dance every day on the boat. We enjoyed it, and if we stayed on for another five days, we wouldn't mind it! We were having a good time.
>
> When we got to Boston, we went out every day filling applica-tions to see could we get a job, and we couldn't get one. If you got a job, it was only temporary, and it paid nothing. I mean, you were putting in your time and getting nothing for it, and that's the rea-son you left Ireland. The Irish would ask you, "Are you working? Are you working? Are you working?" It was very bad.
>
> Jobs I had for quite a while after coming out were dreary. Bits of construction here, and bits of this and bits of that. My cousin said to me, "We were able to make enough money in Ireland to get here, but by Jesus," he said, "if we want to go back, we have no money!" 'Twas after the war, but then things started to open up, and they started building the cities, and things got good then. That's when it opened up, and it really put things going like mad.

Most musicians had full-time day jobs, but even when gigs were most plentiful, they still had families to support. To make ends meet, Mickey Connolly and his band traveled to play in Irish halls throughout New En-gland. He remembers:

> 'Twas a good income. Music helped me pay for this house, I'll tell you. Playing music, we were making ten, fifteen bucks that time. When I worked with construction here when I came to this coun-

The Joe Joyce Band at the Intercolonial Hall, c. 1956. Left to right:
Eddie Irwin, piano; Joe Joyce, accordion; Dick McNaught, drums;
Joe Elwood, sax; Chris Murphy, guitar; Jimmy Kelly, banjo.
(From the library of Joe and Karin Joyce.)

try, I was getting a dollar an hour. When the war was going in Korea, they paid us whatever they wanted. I'd go up and ask for a job, they tell me what the pay is, I couldn't walk away. I had nowhere else to go.

Despite a hard week's work at their day jobs, the musicians hit the bandstand and worked just as hard there. The few attempts at creating a union were short-lived, because musicians felt fairly compensated for their time. Derrane says:

We were getting thirty-five [dollars]. All the guys were getting at least twenty-five, and a lot of them were getting thirty, thirty-five. The union scale was running about the same thing, maybe five dollars more. The union, we felt, was too restrictive. I said, "We're here, we don't have any hassles, we don't pay any dues, we don't do anything else." I'm not going to join the union to pay dues and go through all the restrictions. For what? Five bucks per gig?

According to Storer, however, some musicians were paid less. Their pay rate depended on seniority:

When I was first started playing with Tom Senier's group—and this is no reflection on Tom because it was the going rate—for me, being a brand-new player, not being a solid contributor, latecomer, I was getting like three dollars a night. Three dollars for the whole night. I was glad to get it because I was new, and I met a lot of musicians who took care of me in years to come. Later, when I worked with Johnny Powell, I was getting like eight dollars. Then the rates went up to fifteen dollars, maybe twenty, then twenty-two, then twenty-five, thirty. When I retired from active music in 1992, I was making one hundred fifty per night. My, how times changed!

The musicians playing traditional music downstairs in the Intercolonial were paid somewhat less than the upstairs musicians—around ten dollars—and the halls weren't paying any more than they had to. No one appeared to expect to make a living solely from music, though some musicians were making more than others. Derrane worked a regular job during the day, but he still made ample money playing music. "Bands made great money on Dudley Street," he says. "I made about eighty dollars a week for my job, but playing on Thursday, I'd make twenty dollars, then maybe twenty-five to thirty for each wedding."[2]

Dick Senier relates a story of the challenges his father faced in getting paid at weddings, challenges that were unique to the Irish because there was no union among Irish musicians:

> My father, Tom Senier, played countless weddings and other gigs. He would supply as many musicians as were needed, usually accordion, drums, and piano. If a fourth was needed, it would usually be a sax. It never occurred to him to bring a bass. That kind of sophistication came later.
>
> Sometimes he would have a "divvil of a time" finding the bride's father at the end of a wedding celebration so that he could get paid. Occasionally, he would get burned. When I came back to Boston after grad school at Georgetown, my father asked me to play solo accordion at a post-wedding house party in Dorchester. I really didn't look forward to it because the Irish accordion has always been of very little use in such gatherings, where people want to sing and dance. But I went along.
>
> At the end of the night I couldn't find the bride's father because

he had passed out from drink. I was told that the family would contact my father. A few days later, my father got hold of the man. My father was told that I took too many breaks and that I wasn't as good a player as *himself*, and he refused to pay. From that day I insisted that my father let *me* book the jobs. When a call came in for the next wedding I took the phone. I said that for five men the price would be $25.00 each, plus an extra $25.00 for my father, who was the bandleader. That was a common union custom but unknown among the Irish. I said further that a fifty percent deposit would be required at the outset. My father was agape through this little scene, but once the deal was finished and he had the deposit in hand, he was a willing convert! Up until that time he had never taken anything extra for himself, though he had to do all the work and take all the risks.[3]

A Dudley Street Style

Although musicians in Boston formed a tight community, musicians from Ireland had come from many parts of the Emerald Isle and represented a great diversity of localized playing styles and musical "accents," so to speak. Most counties of Ireland have a distinctive regional style, and musicians from different regions may play the same tune markedly differently. Some may play it more slowly and with flowing lines, while others may play it more rhythmically or choppily. Likewise, the same or a similar melody may be known by different names, and tunes with the same name may have slightly different melodies.

In the early part of the twentieth century, radio and recordings did a great service to Irish music by bringing the music of isolated regions to a wide audience. Yet they also dimmed the intensity of colorful regional style differences. Similarly, the immigrant experience in Boston, New York, Chicago, Philadelphia, and other Irish strongholds, in which people from many regions of Ireland were suddenly living and performing together, contributed to a confluence of styles.

Musicians from all over Ireland found themselves in close quarters in Boston. On Dudley Street, musicians from Sligo, Mayo, and Donegal would be likely to find themselves sharing a stage. According to the regional styles learned in Ireland, one musician might "swing" the music more than another, or have a different setting, or version, of a tune. When played together, differing versions and performance styles might create a new texture or a new whole—a pan-Irish sound. Or they might clash.

Irish-Americans who learned to play Irish traditional music in Boston had a regional "accent" of their own, and some Irish nationals had the sentiment that one must be Irish to play Irish music—a sentiment that contributed to occasional friction between the two groups. Gene Frain describes a well-known Irish fiddler, saying: "He doesn't like Americans. If you were American, forget it. A lot of them think if you're American, you shouldn't be going near Irish [music]." Joe Joyce, born in Allston to Irish parents, also attests to this attitude, quoting the father of the bride at a wedding that he played: "What the hell do you know about Irish music? You're not even Irish."

The tensions between Irish and Irish-American musicians during the Dudley Street era were most often the result of specific personalities involved, not an overall trend, according to Larry Reynolds, who says:

> There was a little bit of a conflict there at times. And it was on both sides. But you could chalk that up to individuals, too. Some of the Irish guys would think that the Americans shouldn't be playing, that they couldn't play as good as the Irish could. On the other side of the coin, some of the Americans would more or less have *learned* music [formally], whereas the Irish hadn't, for the most part. Americans would have learned to read the music. And of course, that could be a sore point. It could be a point for contention [for some people].

The American style and approach were different, no doubt. Some Irish people felt it was lacking that distinguishable but undefinable element that makes music authentically Irish. A great fan of Joe Derrane, Paddy Cronin recalls a conversation about this with Joe's parents, who had grown up in Ireland: "The father and I were talking about Americans playing Irish music, and he says, 'The Americans are good you know, but they don't have that "yock!"' They didn't have the 'yock.' Whatever he meant by 'the yock,' I don't know. But Joe is plenty good. I like Joe's music. He handled that accordion like a machine."

Strong, rhythmic, light, supple, and steady—machinelike, if you wish: Derrane's energetic, driving, and precise, consistent style was exactly what was needed to sustain the dance beat. Like Derrane, every musician had a personal, unique style. The styles of accordion players such as Joe Derrane, Joe Joyce, Billy Caples, Johnny Powell, and Mickey Connolly—and before them, Jack Storer, Tom Senier, Johnny Bresnahan, and Jerry O'Brien—were distinct and recognizable. But musicians had to meet on common ground in America if they were to play together in a way that would be pleasing to play and pleasing to hear. On the American dance hall stage, musicians from different regions of Ireland exchanged tunes and were influenced by regional styles they may never have encountered had they stayed in Ireland.

Opinions within the Irish community differ as to whether such stylistic confluence is a good thing or bad thing. One thing is certain, however: the varied musical backgrounds of these musicians allowed the bands to cater to the broad range of tastes in the audience. It also made the bands more musically diverse, and allowed them to feature the strengths of individual musicians, as appropriate. As Derrane points out:

> When the American music was played, we were smart enough to know that three Irish button accordions just weren't going to fit that, so we laid off for those sets. So we'd let the saxophones, trumpet, piano, drums, whatever, let them go and do their thing. We carried pretty much the Irish stuff, if you will, and they carried the American stuff. And we were able to get that medium ground because of the level of musicianship. Everybody worked hard.

Although it was acceptable to bring an Irish feel to an American popular tune, it was altogether intolerable to infuse Irish traditional tunes with a jazz or swing feel. But you couldn't always help it. When playing Irish music, dance hall musicians played in a style that they considered appropriate and traditional. Though they recognized that their music was not pure Irish, they were mindful of their place within a musical continuum. Frank Storer, for instance, was careful to play only what was appropriate to the music, even if he did occasionally introduce more complicated harmonic accompaniment to the tunes. When asked about how popular music influenced his style of accompaniment, Storer says, "Oh, you would play some progressions, but you can't get too cute with traditional music. I think that once you start to jazz it up or improvise, it ceases to become what you're trying to present."

Storer understands the variations he introduced were quite conservative, for he views his own innovations in comparison to the music of his father's generation—a musical inheritance that was already one generation removed from the homeland. Over time, however, these variations had a cumulative effect on musical style that, while imperceptible to musicians like Storer and Frain, appeared more radical to new arrivals from Ireland.

Joe Derrane's playing was certainly influential on Dudley Street, for he was one of the most sought-after and admired musicians of the day. It is likely that musicians like Derrane unknowingly helped to create a Dudley Street style. People frequently refer to Joe as "ahead of his time." They likely are referring to his highly ornamented style, an approach that distinguished him—and still does—from many other traditional players.

Derrane is well aware that his style is partly the result of musical influences from outside the Irish tradition. His playing today reflects subtle hints of influences from forty years of commercial music work that included Top 40, Jewish music, Italian music, show tunes, and jazz. Still, then as now, he is careful about what he includes in his music. Derrane says of his playing style:

> Years of playing so many things that have more complex chord progressions, resolutions, or passages—they stick to me. . . .
>
> We're all products of our environment. My environment compared to most people in the traditional Irish music is very, very broad. Of course, I'm Irish-American, and I've been exposed to so many different kinds of music. I mean, my God, just the elevator music from years ago. . . . You turn on the radio, in your car, any of these things over an accumulation of years, some of this stuff starts to set in.
>
> The challenge is to make sure that you use that hopefully not too often, because then the music loses its appeal, and it invades the traditional senses too much. Some people would not agree. They say I've overdone it; other people think not. My own sense is, I play it the way I feel it, and gee, I hope and pray that they like it. But that's it.

Derrane has indeed been lauded and criticized, then and now, for his highly ornamented approach to Irish music. While playing the familiar melodies, he decorates the music with passing triplets and chord inversions, and he may use musical effects that are more often heard in American-style music than in Irish traditional music. Sometimes, for instance, he changes the melody subtly, suggesting a slight change in the underlying harmonic structure. While this may be a departure from what some would feel is pure Irish traditional music, Derrane recognizes and incorporates outside influences in a way that is meaningful to him but fits within the confines of the musical tradition.

The Irish musician and scholar Fintan Vallely takes a positive view of multicultural influence, and hails the creativity of contemporary Irish-American musicians:

> The variety of cultures in the United States has left musicians there more open to other music influences, so producing a versatility which gives us truly adventurous interpreters of tunes. [Many contemporary players] combine intelligent and skilful adventure with a solid understanding of traditional music gleaned from being immersed in it since childhood. The performances and recordings of these players [are] experienced sometimes as threatening to older, native musicians back in Ireland, but often [they are] inspiring to the younger. But such players will say they are not reflecting their experiences in the world in which they live any more than the previous generation reflected theirs.[4]

In reflecting their musical environment, it can be said that musicians are indeed learning in a traditional manner. Irish music has traditionally been learned by osmosis—and many say that the "yock" can't be taught. But within the tradition, there are a variety of teaching and learning methods and no guaranteed results. Much depends on environment, and far away from Ireland, the very close musical community that formed around the Boston dance halls served as a surrogate Irish environment that nurtured a generation of young musicians.

9

At My Father's Knee

Learning Irish Music

Irish music is traditionally taught and learned not from written notation but orally. Traditional Irish fiddlers, accordionists, and flute players historically learned their jigs and reels from friends or relatives, or from a musician in the neighborhood in informal or formal lessons. Players absorb a traditional style and repertoire by being completely immersed in the culture.

The Irish-Americans: Learning the Irish Way

Most Irish-Americans in Boston in the 1940s and 1950s learned Irish music the traditional way: from their parents, a relative, or a friend. In Boston, Gene Frain's parents hosted musicians on a weekly basis. "They used to wind up at my house every other Sunday, a bunch of musicians," Frain recalls. His father, Owen Frain, had been a flute player in Dan Sullivan's band. Born in Roosky, county Mayo, around 1898, he was surrounded by music as a child, and took up the flute at an early age. According to Gene:

> My father told me when he was young, every house in his neighborhood had a flute and violin hanging on the wall. He said everyone could play the violin. I said, "What the hell did you bother with the flute in the first place for?" As far as I'm concerned, the

violin is miles ahead of the flute. He said, "I played the flute because everyone could play the violin, and I got sick of listening to violins."

Another musician reports that his father, a pub owner, used to invite itinerant musicians into the house for Sunday dinners. "We had a big roast every Sunday, and these guys would come in. An old guy would pull a packet of newspaper from his jacket and he'd unroll it and pull out three black sticks, or a fiddle in a plastic bag," this musician says.

Dick Senier, son of the legendary Tom Senier, came from a family of eleven, of whom all were taught music from the age or four or five, first by their father and only later by a music teacher. Tom's philosophy was, "You aren't ready for lessons until you can play your instrument." Tom encouraged his sons to learn by doing. While he might rail at his sons for playing ball too noisily outside his bedroom window, he would never complain when they sat down to play the accordion or piano. When his son Dick was a teen, Tom often invited his son's band, the Stars of Erin, to join him at playing engagements at the dance halls—sometimes for pay, sometimes not. Dick suspects that sometimes his father may have even paid others to *allow* the young band to perform. The Stars of Erin was made up of Joe Derrane on accordion, Alan ("Red") Maloney on drums, Dick Senier on piano, George Derrane on banjo, and Finbar Storer on sax.

Frank Storer, whose father, Jack, was a close friend of Tom Senier's, also grew up in a musical family. Like Tom, Jack urged Frank and his brother Finbar to play. Recalls Frank:

> My father played with Tom Senier in the Emerald Isle Orchestra—he had done this before me, back in the thirties and the forties. His children were *required* to take music lessons. I studied piano, and my brother John, better known as Finbar, took lessons on the saxophone. My brother was the first to actually enter the playing scene, outside of the house, with my dad.

Frank Storer studied piano first with the Irish pianist Johnny Connors, then later with an Italian classical instructor, Giulio Gianotti. However, when Gianotti encouraged him to attend conservatory, he declined, reasoning that there were more performance opportunities with the Irish music genre. "I loved classical music," Frank said. "I played it for lessons, but in the nighttime, I'd be banging out jigs and reels. It was a big difference."

Jack Storer (right) encouraged his children to learn music.
Here he performs with his son Finbar in the Hibernian Hall.
(From the library of Frank Storer.)

In the late 1940s, Frank's father encouraged him to perform on Dudley Street with Tom Senier, Jack's old friend from the Emerald Isle Orchestra. Johnny Powell had just started with his band at the Intercolonial, and Frank was just a junior in high school at the time. Frank says:

> I was coming along well on piano at the time, with the Tom Senier/ Winslow Hall setup. Richie [Dick] Senier, who was the piano player, was the son of Tom. Joe Derrane and his brother George Derrane on the banjo were also in that band. Richie played the piano and the flute, but was going to the seminary at the time. Since my father and Tom were very good friends, and with my father out of the business due to paralysis, Tom called my father and said, "Do you think Frank could handle it, with the band?" So, I said I'd try to do it.

I was just a chubby, red-headed kid at the time, a junior in high school. After the dances were over, I used to have to take the trains back to Somerville from Dudley Square. I'd get off in Central Square, and then take a bus home from there. There was a curfew in Cambridge at the time: kids under sixteen had to be off the street by ten o'clock. Well, I would come up from the underground in Central Square, and there was a cop standing there, and next thing, there's a hand on my neck, and I hear, "Where are you coming from, son?"

I tell him I'm coming home from playing in the dance halls over in Dudley Square. He said, "Sure you are, kid. And I'm going to buy the Brooklyn Bridge." He's an Irish cop, so of course he knows my father, and I tell him my father was Jack Storer from the Emerald Isle Orchestra. So he walks me over to the phone booth and makes me call my father to check. My father answers, "Yes, that's my son. Make sure he gets on the bus home." Where I really wanted to go was to Wimpy's across the street for a burger and a frappe, but as soon as he sees me, it was "Hey. On the bus!" He was on the beat every Saturday night, and it got to be that as soon as I came up from the train, I'd get a stern look and an "On the bus, now, son."

The nuns at St. John's parochial school in Cambridge, where Storer was a student, were none too impressed, but Storer continued to perform with that group in Winslow Hall until the hall closed down in 1951. He then began to play in Billy Caples's band, until he was drafted by the Boston Braves baseball team and sent to Myrtle Beach, South Carolina, for training. From there, he was drafted again, this time for the Korean War. When he finally came home from the service, his baseball opportunity had passed, so he returned to the Dudley Street music circuit.

Joe Derrane's parents, unlike Storer's, were not performing musicians, but they encouraged his interest at an early age. His parents told stories of him standing in front of the radio at home as a very young child, listening to Sunday night radio broadcasts featuring the singer Terry O'Toole, "The Boy from Ireland." Jerry O'Brien, an accordionist, also performed live each week on the program, and Joe would come running from wherever he was in the house to listen with rapt attention as the sounds of Irish accordion filled the room.

> My mother said even from the time I was three or four years old,
> when the accordion would come on, I'd be standing in front of the
> radio and bouncing and dancing. Once the accordion stopped, I
> was gone, back to whatever devilment I was up to. I just had a fas-
> cination with it right from then. When I got old enough, I still had
> that fascination, and I pestered them until they contacted Jerry
> O'Brien through the radio station, and they arranged for lessons.[1]

Joe's father, Patrick Derrane of Inis Mor, the largest of the Aran Islands,
played a single-row, ten-key accordion known as a melodeon. His mother,
Helen (Galvin) of county Roscommon, played fiddle, though Joe has no
recollection of having heard her play it in the house until he got his own accordion at the age of ten. Joe's first accordion was a Globe Gold Medal Professional single-row melodeon. A few years later, Tom Senier, a great friend
of O'Brien, spent a day in New York and spotted a nineteen-key, two-row
D/C# Baldoni-Bartoli accordion that he thought would be perfect for
young Joe. O'Brien and Joe spoke with Joe's parents about it, and they
agreed that it was a good investment. His parents came up with around
$400—no small sum in the 1940s—and soon Joe and his teacher, Jerry
O'Brien, were on the train to New York to have a look. As he tried out the
instrument, Joe loved the accordion immediately. He played this accordion
for years, using it in the dance halls and for the sixteen record sides he was
to record on the Copley label.

Joe Derrane studied intensely with Jerry O'Brien, even spending a
couple of summers with O'Brien and his family. The two shared a close relationship, and O'Brien took Derrane along to performances, introduced
him to Dudley Street, and even made several 78 rpm recordings for Copley Records with him.

According to Derrane, O'Brien taught accordion in a style that emphasized learning by physical repetition, rather than by following written notation. But this isn't to say he dispensed with notation altogether. O'Brien
used a "press-and-draw" tablature style that indicated which fingers to
press according to numbered buttons, with symbols over each number to
indicate when to draw or press the bellows. He focused on accuracy and
crispness, traits that still come through on Derrane's recordings today.
Derrane describes a typical lesson:

> Lessons would be an hour, sometimes two hours. It was not un-
> common for Jerry to come into my house for two hours. He

would listen to me play, then he'd play, and say, "No, not that way. That's too short. Do this. You're dragging. No, it's not clean enough. It's muddy. Lift this finger. Then, play the next one. Lift that. Then play the next one. Clean, clean, clean, clean. Steady, steady, steady." Very demanding that way. Very fair. But he kind of didn't teach reading—you know, it's a tough way to learn, but it does work. Jerry wasn't a strong reader.

O'Brien taught with an oral method that focused on demonstration, imitation, and repetition. He also emphasized memorizing and acquisition of repertoire. Derrane recalls intensive summer studies with O'Brien:

I spent most of my summers at his house, growing up with his own kids while he went to work. Then in the evening he'd give me a tune. Then he'd say to me, "Have that learned." He'd go off to work the next day, and I spent all day—*all* day—practicing that tune. When he came home after dinner . . . actually I'd wait for him to come in, and play for him. I was there from Monday through Saturday, and I'd go home Sunday to check in. I would get a tune every day, sometimes two. This is when I was thirteen or fourteen. I practiced two or three hours every day—eeeevery day.

Derrane and O'Brien became a familiar duo. O'Brien frequently took "little Joey" along with him to gigs, and they recorded together in 1948 and 1950. After Derrane had studied two years with O'Brien on the Irish button accordion, O'Brien's accordion was stolen, after which Derrane taught himself to read music and then took up the piano accordion at age fifteen. Downstairs in the basement at O'Byrne DeWitt's, Jerry O'Brien served as *the* teacher for a whole generation of young people who wanted to learn to play the box.

For Joe, music was a family affair. His brother George also was a talented musician who played banjo, clarinet, and saxophone. Jack Martin calls George "a very talented guy. He played banjo, one of the best banjo players in Boston. And then things changed, and he went into clarinet and saxophone. Great player. But George was a reader. Joe has often said, 'As well as I read, I could never read as fast as my brother,' as far as just looking at stuff and boom, boom, boom, boom, boom. . . ."

Joe and George Derrane and their first-generation Irish-American contemporaries, such as Dick Senier, Frank Storer, and Gene Frain, were completely engaged in the dance hall scene as soon as the halls opened after World War II. As Dick Senier says, "Our whole life in our last years of high school was in the Irish scene."

Jack Martin, whose father and uncles founded the Irish music club in the 1930s, learned in a variety of ways. He says he was surrounded by music from the start:

> My father was from Galway, and both my uncles played flutes. Pat was considered one of the best, maybe the best, flute player in Boston at the time. Pat Martin. . . . And my Uncle Tom, he's deceased also, he was a Boston police officer, and he was an excellent flute player, too. The music was in the family. It was always around.

Other Irish-American musicians also had an uncle or parent who played. As children, these musicians sneaked opportunities to play the instruments when their elders were not home. "My father never encouraged me, but it was around," one musician recounts. "I remember at the age of five, putting two chairs together to climb up into the closet and pull the accordion off the shelf. I don't know why I picked it up. Some people have an openness to music. I think it's an ancestral memory—that we inherit it."

Joe Joyce must have inherited it from his uncle Pat Mellett, who lived in his house. Mellett told young Joe not to touch Mellett's accordion, which only made him more determined. The instrument, Joyce recalls, was

> a melodeon . . . a Globe, with a picture of a Globe on it. It had the fingers on the keys, painted red and gold, and you'd hear them: clickety, click, click. When he used to wrap it up in a shopping bag with string, jeez, the string must have been five feet long. "I'm going to put this away, Joey." And he'd tie it in a knot and put it in the bottom drawer of the bureau. "Get out, now. I gotta go to work." So he was gone to work, and Joey went back into the bottom drawer and untied the cute little bow he had on it. He'd come in, up the stairs, and I'm squawking away on the accordion. "Joe, is that you?" My mother said, "Ah, that's okay, put it away now." From that day on, he'd have to tie it up, put it away in the top shelf of the closet, so Joey couldn't get at it, chair or no chair.

Later, Joyce's neighbor Tom Faherty, who was an Irish immigrant, gave him an accordion. Joyce recalls:

He handed it to me. I was sitting in a chair, and I almost fell down. My own accordion, you know! They were worth about thirty bucks. That's three hundred now. So I started doing what the musicians around me were doing. I learned how to play "There's No Place Like Home . . . be it ever so humble," you know. I learned that; then I used to play "Bold Jack Donoghue" and "Maggie in the Woods."

Boston-born Gene Frain learned from his father first, but then took lessons in school. However, his flute teacher was unfamiliar with and derisive

Owen and Gene Frain play together on Irish wooden and Boehm system silver flutes. Owen played in the Dan Sullivan band in the 1920s, replacing Thomas Ryan and Danny Murphy on flute. Owen also played the pipes, though Gene says he remembers having seen his father play only the flute and the chanter, a removable section of a set of bagpipes that has finger holes on which the melody is played.
(From the library of Frank Storer.)

of the Irish musical style. Frain showed up for lessons at school with his father's black six-hole wooden flute. "I probably did know better," says Frain, "but that's what I had. I thought he was going to laugh in my face, but I had a technique that he didn't." The teacher had him change to a silver flute, which has a more complex system of keys, springs, and pads.

Only a few musicians studied music formally at a conservatory. Billy Caples studied at Berklee School of Music, in the college's fledging years as a small school on Newbury Street in Boston. Despite his formal training, when Caples himself began to teach, his approach to teaching remained Irish. As a young boy in the 1950s, Skip Toomey studied with Caples. Toomey says:

> I took lessons on Thursday nights . . . in a room that was beneath the Intercolonial Hall. There would be music blaring everywhere, in the two halls, and you could hear the stomping through the ceiling. In his breaks, Billy would come down and teach me a lesson—now, this is a guy who was working all week, playing at night, and would have to go to work the next day, and he'd come down on his break and teach a ten-year-old kid to play for three bucks.

The Irish: Learning at Home

Musicians who came from Ireland were less likely than Irish-Americans to have had a formal teacher, according to Brendan Tonra. In Ireland, he says, musicians learned to play by imitating the techniques of musicians who were close to them, such as parents, friends, and relations—and from recordings:

> My father played the fiddle, and my mother knew all the tunes, but I didn't learn the fiddle from my father. I just picked it up when I was seven or eight years old, and my mother showed me how to get the notes. Then my grandfather John Henry left me his fiddle, and my father and I would sit in front of the fire and play tunes. After that I learned to play, listening to recordings at my Aunt Peg Regan's house. She had a phonograph, and there I heard recordings of Michael Coleman and Paddy Killoran.[2]

Mickey Connolly, of Williamstown, Galway, says he had a similar experience:

> My mother played the accordion, and I had two, three uncles that
> played. My mother taught me to play the accordion. I was six
> years old when my aunt came home from New York, and she
> brought an accordion. It was a year after my father died. My
> mother put me sitting on the floor with the accordion in my lap,
> and from there—my mother was a nice player. My uncle lived
> here with us in later years, and he was a great player, too.
>
> Later, my aunt brought a gramophone to my mother. Big deal, I
> tell you. It was one of these "His Master's Voice" machines, and
> she brought records as well. I picked up a lot from listening to
> those records: the McNulty family, Michael Coleman, Ma Burke,
> Seamus O'Brien. All Irish stuff.

Connolly took lessons from his mother, and then he learned from older musicians by playing with a local band, Ganley and Rush. He'd cycle ten miles with his accordion to get to the céilí hall that they played in.

Larry Reynolds started playing fiddle in Ireland at ten years old. Like many Irish musicians of his day, he picked up much by ear because he had been surrounded by music since he was very young, but he also says he studied with a teacher in his hometown:

> My father used to sing, and my sister used to sing. There was always music in the house. My brother bought me a fiddle. My sister, Betty or Elizabeth, paid for my lessons. My cousins were taking them at the time, and so I took lessons for a while. Most of the time, you see, you'd be playing at home anyway, or you'd be going to someone's house. Most of them you were picking up by ear anyway. But lessons were a good start for me.

Paddy Cronin studied in Ireland with Patrick O'Keefe, who was known as a great fiddler and a great character in their area, the Sliabh Luachra region that runs along the Blackwater River between Kerry and Cork. Says Cronin:

> My aunt was out in America, and she took a fiddle back to Ireland
> with her. She used to play a few bits herself. Anyway, she threw the
> fiddle into her trunk, and my father knew it was there. He said to

her one day, he said, "My son wants to play the fiddle." He went down to her house and brought the fiddle back with him, and I started on that.

My father said, "I'll have to get someone to get you going." He met Patrick O'Keefe. Patrick O'Keefe used to be a schoolteacher and then went teaching music to kids. He was a fierce popular man, teaching all the kids and brought them along nicely. He was a real drunk, too, but he never drank when he was teaching to kids.

I was in school, and Patrick O'Keefe come to the window of the school and told the teacher, "Leave out young Cronin. I'm going back to the house to teach him the fiddle. Let him out early." When I got home, he was there, playing for my father and mother.

He'd write down tunes for me. He'd line the copy with the back of the bow. One day I was out, and my mother said to me, she said, "Patrick O'Keefe was here. He left some tunes there for you." I counted, and there were thirteen tunes there he had written down. He was a mighty man for that stuff. He took good care of them and brought them along nicely.

When I made the first trip back to Ireland, he wrote down a jig for me called "Frahagh's." That was the last tune he wrote for me. And he wrote down "The Lanes of Scartaglen."

Cronin says he also learned from O'Keefe by performing with him in a local pub:

We sat inside Matthew Rinn's pub in a snug in the window Sunday after Sunday, and two fiddles. Patrick had no fiddle of his own, but there was one inside the counter that they used to keep for him. It was a session. You play whatever you want unless two or three girls and a fella come in and they want to dance a set. And then you play polkas. Every time we'd be there, that'd happen. There'd be always a session.

Some Irish and Irish-American musicians learned through a combination of formal teaching and self-education. Though self-education is a traditional style of learning, some Irish-Americans, such as Joe Derrane and Joe Joyce, used this traditional method to learn a nontraditional skill: they taught themselves to read music.

Self-Education

Written Notation

For better or worse, the ability to read music was to many the measure of one's musical proficiency, an attitude that fueled resentment between those who had been schooled and those who had learned in the traditional manner, by oral means, from a friend, neighbor, or family member. To make matters worse, the mechanics of many traditional instruments made it difficult for some musicians to adapt to playing American or popular music. Instruments such as the Irish flute and the D/C# accordion were designed to play only in the few keys used in Irish traditional music. They could not physically play in the keys used in so many modern tunes. Joe Joyce believes that this created resentment that sometimes came out disguised as ethnic pride:

> You'd never see a flute in the dance hall. There were guys playing flute, but they couldn't play a waltz; they couldn't adapt in the Americanization of the tune. That's what the music club was for, for their own enjoyment. They played mostly Irish music, and they were good players. Onstage, Billy Caples would play a waltz like "Charmaine." A lot of flute players wouldn't touch that: "That's not Irish at all." But Joe Derrane could play it. Both he and Billy could read and play.

Joe Derrane shares Joyce's assessment. He says:

> There were no flutes in the dance halls because most of the flute players were strictly into real pure traditional music. They followed the sessions. The old guys wouldn't play for dances. The thing is, it's folk music. It *is* dance music. But lots of guys were untrained. I am in constant amazement at how well the music was played by people who were self-taught. When it came to dance music—waltzes—they weren't into it. They found it boring. And, if they were going to play at the Intercolonial, they weren't interested at all.[3]

Derrane taught himself to read music when he changed from the Irish button accordion to the piano accordion at age fifteen. Joe Joyce learned a handful of basic note patterns when someone taught him the tune "The

Stack of Barley." Using these basic patterns as a guide, he taught himself other tunes using the hunt-and-peck system until he had memorized the fingering patterns. Over time, however, he used O'Neill's *Music of Ireland*, referred to colloquially as "the book," to teach himself to read musical notation. Joyce recalls:

> I'd go to Sully's house, and we'd sit in the kitchen playing while his mother was there doing the ironing. We'd sit there with O'Neill's *Music of Ireland* and try to read the jig "The Shandon Bells." It was the first jig in the book. We couldn't read music, but if you look at the tune long enough, you can make out the melody after a while. And if you hear it on a record, you can follow along with the music by watching the way the notes go. So I'd be over Sully's house in his kitchen till midnight sometimes, poring over O'Neill's. We'd prop it up and start trying to figure out how the tunes went. We had no formal education, but after a while through osmosis and reading the books, matching up what they're doing, and memorizing the scales, we'd figure it out.

Recordings

Musicians listened to records carefully in order to acquire new techniques and expand their repertoires. They would listen to their favorite recordings repeatedly and try to emulate the style and technique of the recorded performer. While this was not yet considered a traditional form of learning, both Irish and Irish-American musicians used recordings to learn.

Recordings became an important means to disseminate style. When musicians shared recordings with each other, they in effect were disseminating a preferred style and approach. For example, Joe Derrane recalls being particularly inspired by a John J. Kimmel recording lent to him by Tom Senier. Kimmel, a German-American nicknamed "the Irish Dutchman," made seminal recordings of early Irish accordion playing. Derrane was heavily influenced by Kimmel's crisp, ornamented style. He listened to Kimmel's records on his parents' Victrola, slowing the player down so that he could hear each of Kimmel's ornaments note for note. Says Derrane:

> I couldn't quite figure it out. I'd get the overall melody, no problem, but I couldn't figure out what Kimmel was doing. His approach was so different. He was with a wonderful accompanist.

The choice of chords, harmonic structure—it was simple, but the chords were very correct and proper and fit the music. What Kimmel did was, he took America-type things—marches like "I'm a Yankee Doodle Dandy," themes like "Swanee River"—and played them with all kinds of variations and ornamentation.

Prior to this, I had been thinking straight jigs, reels, hornpipes, nice tasty ornamentation, that was it. When I heard what this man was doing, he opened the door for me. It would never have dawned on me to play anything other than jigs, reels, or hornpipes, for the most part. The ten-key really was very limited. There were no accidentals. But what he did was, he compromised—he had these beautiful little triplets and things.

The way I finally discovered how he did it was I used the hand-crank control [on the gramophone], like you wind a spring, you let it slow down. You could sit there and say, "Aaaaaaaaaah! That's what he's doing!" Then you could sit down and apply that to whatever thing you were working on. His approach and the harmonic structures that were being used fascinated me. A very limited box though it was, this guy was using all of it. And it was his approach, too—his tendency to play tunes other than straight traditional Irish. That kind of turned on a light for me. That's the beginning.

Kimmel's liberal use of both Irish and American styles appealed to Derrane in ways that straight traditional Irish had not. And Kimmel's use of Irish ornamentation in American tunes was a revelation to Derrane.

Radio

The radio was the first place many musicians heard particular performers and tunes. Since the 1920s, Irish radio programs brought Irish communities together with music, news, and announcements of community events. Typical programming included live, in-studio performances as well as news and advertisements of interest to the Irish community.

One of the most popular programs in Boston was "The Irish Hour," hosted by Tommy Shields on WVOM 1600 AM radio, an independent station that took to the airwaves after World War II. Tommy Shields was a musician and tailor, and his shop was on the first floor of the Hibernian Hall building. His radio program, which started around 1948, aired nightly except Saturdays and was to become the longest-running Irish radio program in the United States.[4]

Larry Reynolds would listen to Tommy Shields's radio program almost every night during his early years in America to hear live Irish music as well as news of the Irish community.[5] Those radio broadcasts could be heard all over the East Coast. Skip Toomey recalls:

> My aunts would sit around in my grandmother's kitchen under a fifteen-watt bulb and listen to the music on "the Irish Hour" at night. I even played on the radio once—I played a polka, "The Galway Bells." I remember my class had no homework that night; the homework was to listen to us on the radio. It was a show by Tommy Shields, the oldest-running ethnic radio program in the country. It was on from eight to nine or so, only at night. My aunts listened to it every week. They would have their hot whiskeys, and my grandmother would make me a glass of hot water with sugar in it.

Musicians listened closely and learned the tunes played on these programs. Learning music from radio and recordings helped to expand both Irish and Irish-American musicians' repertoire, though many musicians report that their repertoires then were smaller than those of Irish musicians today. While musicians today may report that they know upward of five hundred melodies, the size of one's repertoire of Irish dance tunes in the 1940s and 1950s was apparently not as important as it is now, perhaps because of the demand for American waltzes and popular melodies. Derrane says that only a small repertoire was necessary: "You'd only do a couple of sets of reels during the night. You do a Siege of Ennis, basically all reels, and we'd pretty much play the same group of reels together. They'd play this group one night, then another one the next night. Then, they'd come back to it. They didn't have the huge repertoire of reels."

Another musician reports that his own repertoire in the 1950s was larger than that of his father. In his father's time, a large repertoire was deemed unnecessary, he explains.

> My father could play ten or so jigs, a few reels, lots of highland flings, a few hornpipes. That was all he needed to play. During those kitchen rackets, he'd play just a few tunes. I would learn tunes and bring them home, but he wasn't interested. He knew all he needed to know. The people dancing didn't notice anyway.

They might hear a tune they knew and say, "Oh, there's 'The Stack of Barley,'" and they'd want to get out on the floor.

Brendan Tonra found that when he arrived in America his repertoire was much larger than those of the Boston musicians he met. However, he says that, though small, American repertoires were up-to-date:

> The first night my sister Frances took me to Dudley Street, the Tara Céilí Band was playing "Cooley's Reel." It was new in comparison to other tunes. I was surprised to hear that music here, so when the dance was over, I went over to the band and said, "I never thought I'd hear music like that in this country." They asked me how long I'd been in this country, and I said, "A fortnight." They introduced themselves to me: Mickey Connolly, accordion, Larry Reynolds, fiddle, Frank Neylon, flute, Tom Garvey, piano, George Shanley, drums, and Terry Landers, accordion. They asked me to play a tune on the fiddle, and when I was finished, they asked me if I had a fiddle and a white shirt and black bow tie, and if so, to show up next Saturday night, and I could play with the band for $12 a night—not bad for those times, and that's how I started playing in this country.[6]

Playing Irish music was a natural choice for young men and women growing up in Irish Boston. For young Irish-American musicians such as Joe Derrane, Frank Storer, Jack Martin, Dick Senier, Gene Frain, and Joe Joyce, music was everywhere in their early lives—at kitchen parties, in the dining room after Sunday Mass, at weddings, and in the parochial schools. Their mothers and fathers before them had also gone to—and probably met at—the dance halls. There had been a huge influx of Irish immigrants from the 1920s up to the Depression, and those who played in the 1940s-to-1960s bands were molded by the experiences of their predecessors.

While many musicians in America did not learn Irish music exclusively by ear, they certainly were immersed in an Irish musical culture, and they would insist that they were traditional players. Irish-Americans learned through a variety of means: from their parents, with a teacher, and through self-education via written notation, recordings, and radio. The Irish, too, because of the introduction of radio and recorded music, had by this time also begun to broaden their musical tastes and the means by which they could learn music.

10

Copley Records: Boston's Irish Label

In 1926, Justus O'Byrne DeWitt opened the doors of the O'Byrne De-Witt House of Irish Music music store and travel agency in the heart of Dudley Square.[1] He had recently moved from New York, shaken by the sudden death of his mother, the enterprising Ellen O'Byrne DeWitt, who may be credited with single-handedly founding the Irish recording industry. The commercial recording of Irish instrumentalists in America began in full force in 1916, thanks to her efforts. Born around 1875 in county Leitrim in Ireland, Ellen O'Byrne emigrated to America at age fifteen. She settled in New York, where she met her husband-to-be, Justus DeWitt, a Dutch immigrant.

Ellen and her husband founded the O'Byrne DeWitt store on New York's Third Avenue, much to the dismay of their colleagues, shocked not only that a woman would own and manage a store but also that it would bear her name. The store sold musical instruments and also recordings of Irish music. Initially, she sold the few recordings of Irish music available at the time, cylinder recordings of the famed Irish tenor John McCormack and the piper Patsy Touhy.

Noting the large number of Irish people requesting recordings of music performed by Irish bands, she proposed to Columbia that they make authentic Irish records. With a provision that her store purchase five hundred copies, the company agreed. She sent her son Justus on a scouting mission to Celtic Park in Long Island, where musicians frequently gathered to play outdoors on Sunday afternoons.

Justus DeWitt Jr. identified the accordion player Eddie Herborn and the banjo player John Wheeler, and Ellen arranged to record the duo playing the popular reel "The Stack of Barley" on September 15, 1916. Aided by Ellen's door-to-door advance sales, the first five hundred copies of this 78 rpm sold quickly.[2] Eventually, both Columbia and Victor recognized the potential of the immigrant market, and both began to establish their ethnic catalogues. Soon, the O'Byrne DeWitt enterprise was celebrating its share of the profits. By the 1920s, the shop was calling itself the Sinn Fein Music House, having developed a healthy line of Irish records.

Justus O'Byrne DeWitt inherited the business around 1925. He closed the shop in New York and relocated it to Boston a year later, opening the new store under the O'Byrne DeWitt name in the heart of Dudley Square, in the Dudley Terminal Building at 51 Warren Street, Roxbury.[3] His mother had told him stories and sung him songs of Ireland throughout his childhood, and his adult involvement in Irish music, he felt, was an expression of that heritage.

Joe O'Leary, of Joe O'Leary's Irish Minstrels, helped him build his business in Boston. Very quickly, O'Byrne DeWitt established his reputation as a provider of quality Irish music. O'Leary's band was well known, playing frequently both in the Dudley Street dance halls and on a radio program that O'Leary hosted on WEEI, the only Irish radio program in Boston at that time.

With O'Leary's endorsement, word spread quickly: the best place to find Irish records in Boston was the O'Byrne DeWitt record store. O'Byrne DeWitt sold recordings from the Victor and Columbia labels by such popular bands as Dan Sullivan and his Shamrock Band, the Flanagan Brothers, and Paddy Killoran's Orchestra. At his shop, people could take music lessons or purchase record players, music books, and musical instruments—and book tickets to Ireland in the travel agency portion of his business.[4]

The store was hit hard by the market crash of 1929 and the Depression that followed. During the Depression, national record sales hit an all-time low, declining to only 25 percent of what they had been just five years before. Record prices dropped from seventy-five to thirty-five cents or even less. O'Leary offered DeWitt a space on his radio show for advertisement, and DeWitt took the opportunity by creating a commercial that urged listeners to buy accordions and records at the store, along with booking passages to Ireland through his travel business, O'Byrne DeWitt Travel, Ltd. Once diversified, the store was very successful for a decade, but things

Justus O'Byrne DeWitt en route to Ireland to organize a concert tour for Connie Foley. From the Boston Traveler, *May 5, 1953.* (Courtesy of the Boston Public Library, Print Department.)

changed at the outset of World War II. The rationing of shellac and vinylite for wartime applications meant that recording companies began to abandon the ethnic markets. With creativity and a smart head for business, De-Witt maintained traffic in the store throughout the war by supporting the record companies' exchange schemes, offering people a few pennies for returned albums that he would then return to the record companies to be recycled. He also maintained his presence and sustained his Irish-music-loving market in Boston by underwriting two Irish music radio programs each week on WMEX.

For musicians, O'Byrne DeWitt's store was an important landmark, a first stop for musicians when they arrived in Dudley Square to play. Mickey Connolly, who came in by bus from Dedham, a suburb of Boston, often arrived in Dudley Square with time to kill before taking the stage with Johnny Powell's band. He would stray into O'Byrne DeWitt. "I'd get off at the station and walk up," he says, "stop at O'Byrne DeWitt's, and kill some time there and listen to records in the booths at the back of the store. You could listen there, and if you liked the records, you could buy them." Even nonmusicians would stop into the shop on their way to the halls to listen to records in one of the ten listening booths.

After the war, Decca began to reissue prewar Irish recordings, and De-Witt had been promised sole distribution rights, but the promise was short-lived, for Decca soon stopped production of Irish records altogether. By the late 1940s, O'Byrne DeWitt had begun to release records on his own label—first called O'Byrne DeWitt in 1948, then the All Ireland label, and then, in 1953, its final name, Copley Records. He founded his label only after the large labels had abandoned the Irish market, for he saw a ready market in the influx of postwar immigrants.

Because O'Byrne DeWitt was centrally located in Dudley Square, he was plugged into the musical taste trends of the Boston audience, and he made decisions about whom to record accordingly. He selected musicians from Boston and New York with whom he was familiar or whom he had heard about from a reliable source, such as his in-house music teacher, Jerry O'Brien, who had performed with O'Leary's Irish Minstrels during the 1920s and 1930s.[5]

O'Brien had been hired at the O'Byrne DeWitt record shop first as a shipping clerk, but later he assisted in instrument sales and gave music lessons out of the shop. (The store published two accordion instruction books written by O'Brien with tunes written out according to his "press-and-draw" accordion tablature.) Upon the founding of the new label, O'Brien also served as a talent scout and record producer for the label.

Joe Derrane describes the founding of Copley Records, which he sees as a direct descendant of Tommy Shields's "Irish Hour" radio show:

> Tommy Shields was a very well-known figure in Boston. He played the accordion—a good player, not fantastic—a few polkas, a few waltzes, polkas, slides. He had immigrated from Galway and was . . . very active in the music circles in Boston. He got the bright idea that we didn't have a decent radio program that was the real McCoy: jigs and reels, Irish songs—not Irish-*American* songs. He went knocking on doors and found WVOM in Brookline Village, on the corner of Harvard and Kent. He started running the show on Sunday nights from eight to nine, then he went knocking on doors again for sponsors. He took out ads, and soon there were thousands of people listening to it. It was called "The Irish Hour."
>
> Tommy would get some local musicians, because he thought people wanted to hear the real thing. He'd have me come out to the studio on Sunday nights. Through my teacher, Jerry O'Brien, I had met Johnny Connors, and Tommy brought us in. We'd play for five minutes, then he'd have a singer, then maybe a fiddler, Paddy Cronin; then there would be interviews with the musicians.
>
> O'Byrne DeWitt was a sponsor for the show, and people were coming in to O'Byrne De Witt's shop on a Monday morning or on a Saturday on their way to the dance (he was open late on Saturdays, since that's when the crowds came into Dudley), looking for this Joe Derrane—"Do you have any records of him?" Well, he got enough inquiries that . . . he thought about it, and got himself a record label. First he recorded Jerry O'Brien, because Jerry worked in the store. Then he asked Jerry who else he should record. Jerry gave him my name. O'Byrne DeWitt called me to the store, and we talked. He said, "Why don't you make a record?" And I looked at Jerry, and he was nodding to me, so I said, "Okay, why not?"

This was in 1948. Joe Derrane was only eighteen, a senior at Mission High School in Roxbury. Derrane would go home from school and rush through his homework before taking the el to the studio that O'Byrne De-

Witt had booked for recording, Ace Studios on Boylston Street near the Boston Common, owned by Milton Yakis—the same studio in which Patti Page recorded the famous "Old Cape Cod." Derrane says:

> First I did just one record. You had three minutes on each side of the 78, and I played a medley of jigs or hornpipes. I thought that was going to be it, but the records started selling like hotcakes. Well, one led to another, and over a four-year, period from 1948 to 1952, I had recorded eight records, sixteen sides. That's how it got started.
>
> Then he recorded Paddy Cronin, then Connie Foley, the singer from Kerry. When Connie came out, Tommy Shields had heard about him and started putting together concerts at the John Hancock Hall and the Hibernian Hall. He had Connie Foley, myself, a backup player, another singer, the fabulous McNulty family, and he would broadcast those live. He was a prime mover. One thing sort of fed the other. It seemed like everywhere you turned, you were hearing Irish music.

Derrane performed on the recordings accompanied by the pianist Johnny Connors, who had been a regular with the Galway Bay Band on the "Irish Hour" radio broadcasts and at the Dudley Street Opera House. In addition to his sixteen sides with Connors, Derrane recorded ten duets with Jerry O'Brien and six sides with the Irish All-Stars. Derrane also performed on recordings by Connie Foley and Dorothy McManus.[6]

The unique reverberance that gives a live feel to Derrane's recordings was created by recording in a stairwell. During that time, artificial reverb would have sounded unnatural to most listeners, and to get a big-room reverberant sound, Derrane's producers got creative. The studios were in an office building, and they recorded after hours, when they could place a good speaker three flights down the concrete-and-steel stairway without worry of disturbing the other tenants. They would then play Derrane's recording through the speaker. A microphone suspended over the stairwell would capture the reverberation, creating a large-room sound. The resulting "reverb track" was fed back into the recording and mixed with the original "dry" track.

As one of only two companies in the world dedicated to recording Irish music during this era, Copley Records was in a good position to make a significant income. The only competition was a small record label called

Celtic, run by Francis Fallon of Providence, Rhode Island. Fallon produced twenty-four albums, many of which were of Boston musicians such as Billy Caples, Gene Frain, and Mickey Carton. Copley produced twenty-nine albums on their own label, featuring Scottish and Canadian as well as Irish artists.

Profit was one of O'Byrne DeWitt's prime motivations, though he also secured his place in recording history by recording artists who were representative of a unique musical style. He selected most musicians on the basis of their sales potential, recording primarily dance bands and vocalists. Very few of Copley's recordings were of solo instrumentalists, and according to Justus DeWitt, they were recorded solely for their artistry or their ability to preserve "stylistic nuances" of the time. For example, he told historian and musician Mick Moloney that he recorded Paddy Cronin not for his sales potential, but rather because "Cronin was the finest fiddler I've heard since Coleman."[7]

Along with Cronin, the singer and piccolo player Murty Rabbitte of Dan Sullivan's Shamrock Band, the accordionist Paddy Noonan, the flute player Frank Neylon, and Joe Derrane were featured solo artists in the Copley catalog.[8] Other featured artists included vocalists Connie Foley, Dorothy McManus, the McNulty family, Ruthie Morrissey, the tenors Jack Feeney and Thomas O'Brien, and Tommy Reilly.

Justus O'Byrne DeWitt was really the only one to profit from the record sales, however. He refused to pay royalties to musicians, offering them only a relatively small, fixed sum for their work, and claiming that sales were too uncertain—though some of the records sold up to ten thousand copies.[9] Paddy Cronin recorded on the Copley label but says he never relied on it as a source of income:

> They paid a small little bit, but it was hardly worth taking it home. If you went on a good drunk, you'd have nothing coming home! Paddy Noonan was the only musician I ever knew could live on it. Michael Coleman came out here, and Jim Morrison, all these great [recorded] fiddlers, had no money, and they were good musicians. I played for the love of the music. I never got a penny.

Sides by Joe Derrane's All-Star Céilí Band were a highlight of Copley's recordings. The band consisted of Joe and George Derrane, Johnny Connors, and Jerry O'Brien. Their first recording for Copley, titled *Traditional Irish Dance Music*, was an entire set dance with five figures—jigs, polkas,

COPLEY LP's & EP's IRISH RECORDS

ORDER FROM:

O'BYRNE DeWITT 51 WARREN STREET, ROXBURY, MASS. — Tel. Highlands 5-8616

COPLEY 33 1-3 LONG PLAYING RECORDS — 12" — $3.98

DWL 9-600
TRADITIONAL IRISH BALLADS
Sung by Connie Foley

Rose of Killarney
On the Banks of My Own Lovely Lee
'Neath Her Shawl of Galway Grey
Lovely Leitrim
Cottage by the Lee
My Beauty of Limerick
The Town of Coleraine
The Boys of Kilmichael
Eileen Oge, The Pride of Petravore
The Croppy Boy
Westering Home
The Mountains of Mourne

DWL 9-601
TRADITIONAL IRISH DANCE MUSIC
Played by The All Star Ceilidhe Band

Irish Dance Set—Figure 1: Haste to the Wedding and The Connaughtman's Rambles
Irish Dance Set—Figure 2: When the Kettle Boils Over & The Leg of the Duck. Jigs
Irish Dance Set—Figure 3: The Girl I Left Behind Me & The Rakes of Mallow Polkas
Irish Dance Set—Figure 4: Fire On the Mountain & The Cook In the Kitchen. Jigs.
Irish Dance Set—Figure 5: The Blackberry Blossom & Bonnie Kate Reels
The Londonderry Hornpipe
The Humors of Bandon
The Gie Gordons & The Canadian Barn Dance
The Liverpool & Off to California Hornpipes
The Job of Journeywork
The Keel Row — Green Grow The Rushes O. Highlands
The Red Haired Boy. Hornpipe

DWL 9-602
IRISH TENORS
Songs by
Jack Feeney and Thomas O'Brien

In the Valley Near Slievenamon
The Kerry Dance
A Shawl of Galway Grey
If There'd Never Been An Ireland
Galway Bay
The Fairy Tree
Thine Alone
The Hills of Donegal
The Harp That Once Through Tara's Halls
Danny Boy
Say A Little Prayer For Me
Minstrel Boy

DWL 9-603
IRISH BALLADS
Sung by Ruthie Morrissey

Home to Mayo
The Claddagh Ring
The Green On the Green
The Dying Rebel
The Whistling Gypsy
If You'll Only Come Across the Sea to Ireland
The Roving Journeyman
Pat O'Donnell From Donegal
Gramachree, I'd Like to See Old Ireland Free Once More
Sweet Are the Flowers That Bloom In Dear Kerry
Wrap the Green Flag Round Me, Boys
Songs We Love to Hear on St. Patrick's Day

DWL 9-604
THE McNULTY FAMILY ENTERTAINS WITH IRISH SONGS

When You're Winging Your Way to Old Ireland
Someone's Waiting For Me Back in Ireland
The Boys of the County Cork
NcNulty's Irish Showboat
There's A Sweetheart Waiting For You At the Close of an Irish Day
A Toast to the 32 Counties
The Star of Logy Bay
The Irish Rover
We'll Take You Back to Ireland
Likeable, Loveable Leitrim Lad
Hat My Father Wore on St. Patrick's Day

DWL 9-605
FOLK DANCE MUSIC OF IRELAND
By Johnny Powell and his Band

Medley of Jigs: Humors of Whiskey & The Prize Jig
Siege of Ennis: Scotch Mary & The Shaskeen Reels
Siege of Ennis: Green Groves of Erin—Four Hand Reel—Miss Thornton's Reel
Medley of Polkas: Connemara Fancy & Sweet Cork of Thee I Dream
Medley of Highlands: Billy's Tune & Macroom
Greencastles & Dunphy's Hornpipes
Two Steps: The Little Burnt Potato & The Bandon Blarney Stone
Medley of Polkas: My Love Is But A Lassie & Sweet Killaloe
Medley in 6/8 Time: The Maid of the Sweet Brown Knowe—Geese In the Bog —Trip to the Cottage
Highland Flings: Money Musk & If There Weren't Any Women in the World
Polkas: The Colleen Bawn & The Galway Rogue
If the Rest of the World Were Like Ireland—Irish Waltz with Vocal by Bill Ryan

DWL 9-606
IRISH BALLADS
Sung by Connie Foley

Irish Volunteer
Snowy Breasted Pearl
Doonaree
Connemara Shore
If We Only Had Old Ireland Over Here
Dingle Bay
Banks of Lough Corrib
Star of the County Down
Little Town in the Old County Down
This Place Called County Cavan
Down In the Glen
The Old House

DWL 9-607
DANCE MUSIC OF IRELAND
By Jerry O'Brien, Joe Derrane, & The Irish All Stars

The Irish Washerwoman. Jig
Miss McLeod's Reel
The Stack of Barley—Introducing Hennessey's Hornpipe
Medley of Highland Flings: The Primrose Lass & The Rakes of Mallow
Irish Marches: O'Donnell Abu—The Minstrel Boy—God Save Ireland
Medley of Highland Flings: The Orange and Blue & The Belle of the Ball
The Blackbird
The Varsouviana
Barn Dances: The Old Blackguard & The Nova Scotia
Sailor's Hornpipe
Two-Step Medley: Chase Me Charlie & The Hundred Pipers
Siege of Ennis: Mullingar Races & Sheehan's Reel

DWL 9-608
IRISH SONGS
Sung by
Connie Foley and Dorothy McManus

The Golden Jubilee
The Sailor's Sweetheart
The Stone Outside Dan Murphy's Door
In Old Ballymoe
O'Brien Has No Place to Go
Rose of Tralee
The Homes Around Ballinahone
The Little White Cross
Biddy Donahue
Good-Bye Johnny Dear
The Spinning Wheel
Come Back, Paddy Reilly, to Ballyjamesduff

The catalog of Copley Records, which included exclusively
Irish musicians. Copley shipped records worldwide.
(From the library of Mickey Connolly.)

reels, barn dances, highland flings, and hornpipes. *Dance Music of Ireland*, the All-Star Céilí Band's second complete album, featured the same style of dance music. Derrane did these recordings on a nineteen-key D/C# accordion, playing tunes either taught to him by Jerry O'Brien or learned from the *O'Neill's Irish Music* collection, or tunes specifically requested of him by Justus O'Byrne DeWitt.[10] For the most part, though, Derrane could pick his own material. "DeWitt gave me a lot of leeway," he says. "Some things he wanted us to do a certain way, because he'd had requests from customers for them to record."[11]

DeWitt's style was to approach a musician he had heard personally or whom someone had recommended. The artist would be taken to a studio, sometimes in Boston, but usually at the studios of the Decca or R.C.A. Victor label in New York. After the recording session, DeWitt would approve the master, and the record would move on to final cut and release. He would make the financial outlay to pay for the album covers and would secure the photos, often from the Irish tourist board. The initial pressing would be one thousand copies, and smaller lots of three or five hundred would be reissued if the first issue sold out. When Decca relocated their business to California, it became economically unfeasible for DeWitt to continue the arrangement he had with them, and that was the beginning of the end of his recording business.

Though the record production portion of the business closed in the late 1950s, the O'Byrne DeWitt store continued, as it published both sheet music and music books. Two prominent musicians of this era, Billy Caples and Jerry O'Brien, both gave lessons from the store. The store retained a large portion of its business through catalog sales, according to Joe Derrane:

> They were one of the largest record catalog dealers in the country. This guy was selling records to Australia, to England, to Ireland, you know.
>
> They sold commercial pop records at the time. You could buy records made by the McNulty family, or Joe O'Leary's, Irish records or Irish-American records—Dennis Day, that type of thing. Plus the Michael Colemans, and the Paddy Killorans, and you know, a lot of that stuff. But he also sold a very good line of classical records, operatic-type things. It was a rather complete record store at the time, and they also had the sheet music, anything that you would really expect to find in any good record stores today.

For years, the bulk of O'Byrne DeWitt's in-store customers had been the dance hall musicians and the dancers. But as the dance halls began to die away in the late 1960s, things began to change for DeWitt, too. With the record company closed and the neighborhood undergoing radical ethnic change, DeWitt eventually focused on the travel aspect of his business, opening O'Byrne DeWitt Travel Agency at 1576 Tremont Street, Roxbury, near Mission Church, which was located at 1545 Tremont. Dewitt stayed in business there until the late 1970s, when he moved again, this time six miles away, to 1751 Centre Street in West Roxbury, a more affluent suburb that had become a popular destination for many of the Irish who were moving out of the inner city.

Copley Records stopped producing albums in the 1950s. The old records were no longer profitable, and the record masters gathered dust in the travel agency's basement over the next three decades. In the early 1980s, an employee of the agencey, Ellie Logan, contacted the great New York Irish accordionist Paddy Noonan to ask if he was interested in purchasing the original master recordings from Copley Records. Noonan, who founded Rego Irish Records in 1969, had made two of his own records with O'Byrne DeWitt in the 1950s, *A Ramble in Eireann* and *The Delightful Music of Ireland and Scotland*. He also performed on seven records as the accompanying band for the wildly popular Irish singer Connie Foley, who recorded some forty albums for Copley Records in the 1950s.

Noonan was still building up Rego Records and was not prepared to make the investment at that time. But not long after, with the massive revival of Irish traditional music that occurred in the late 1980s, Rego Irish Records was starting to take off. Logan and Noonan spoke again, and this time around, he was ready.

Noonan settled a deal with Mrs. DeWitt to purchase the masters in 1990. He had a keen interest in rereleasing recordings made by the McNulty family, music he remembered fondly from his childhood. His dedication to Irish music and his lifelong association with Joe Derrane prompted him to also rerelease Derrane's pioneering recordings, which were influenced so heavily by the very early recordings of John Kimmel. The rerelease of these records sent a flutter through traditional music circles and in many ways sparked a revitalization of Joe Derrane's career, bringing him out of a thirty-year retirement that had been spurred in part by massive changes that occurred in the Irish music scene in the 1960s.

11

The Hucklebuck and Blue Suede Shoes

Showbands

A combination of events that began in the mid-1950s led to Dudley Street's demise. The Irish-born population in Boston began to come of age and move to the suburbs. A rising African-American population filled their place, resulting in a major demographic shift in the Dudley Square neighborhood. Meanwhile, in the late 1950s, the frenetic excitement of rock and roll began to seduce dancers away from the ballrooms. Over a ten-year period, crowds diminished, musicians left the scene, and the halls closed one by one. By the late 1950s, many of the Dudley Street dance halls had died. It was not until Ireland itself began to reconcile rock and roll with its own cultural identity in a new form of entertainment, the showband, that the scene began to change in America.

The gritty, urban sound of rock and roll diverted many young people's attention away from the smooth waltzes and cheerful highland flings that had defined the Dudley Street dance halls for more than a decade. As always, pop music spoke to the younger generation, while traditional music remained associated with the past. Brendan Tonra, who immigrated to America in 1959, describes the point of view of many Irish in America at the time: "The céilí music was considered a lower standard compared to modern music."

As rock and roll spread through Ireland, four- and five-piece "showbands" replaced the larger, more traditional-sounding céilí bands. Young people in Ireland were riveted. The unbridled, raw energy of showband singers generated the hysteria akin to what is normally associated with Elvis and the Beatles.

Brendan Bowyer and the Royal Showband, Dickie Rock and the Miami Showband, the Dixie Showband, the Rory Gallagher Showband, and individual singers such as Eileen Donaghy and Bridie Gallagher made a huge sensation playing the hit music of America and Britain, including country-and-western favorites, as well as skiffle, a form of popular music that had developed in England as a derivative of several American jazz forms. At the height of the showband era, there were some six hundred showbands in Ireland. The old céilí halls across Ireland, from rural villages to the heart of Dublin, were filled with the new sounds, and the large majority of Irish youth ignored traditional dance music in favor of the showbands, in which young men, smartly dressed in matching suits, swayed and gyrated onstage to just about anything the audience might request—"The Twist," the Siege of Ennis, "Unchained Melody," Brendan Bowyer's "The Hucklebuck," "I Left My Heart in San Francisco," or "Sean South from Garryowen."[1]

By the early 1960s, Irish showbands began to tour America, quickly becoming popular among Irish-American audiences—even more popular than the Irish dance hall bands. Bands on tour from Ireland would stop in Boston between New York and Chicago performances. The first showbands played at the Intercolonial, but most went to the New State Ballroom, which had opened at 217 Massachusetts Avenue in 1962, as the Dudley Street dance halls were on the verge of closing.

Long a performance space for swing bands of an earlier era, the New State Ballroom was leased and reopened by Kerry farmboy-turned-dance-hall-tycoon Bill Fuller and his wife, the Irish songbird and storyteller Carmel Quinn of Dublin. Quinn's debut as a winning talent contestant on *The Arthur Godfrey Show* made her a household name, and Bill Fuller was an internationally known entrepreneur who ran popular dance halls in London, the Keyman's Club in Chicago, the Carousel in San Francisco, and the popular City Center in New York City.[2] Fuller installed the well-known Irish personality Walter Norris as general manager, and after a time, Norris hired the Gaelic Athletic Association star and well-known dance instructor Mike Cummings as master of ceremonies. As emcee, Cummings, who may be credited with bringing many traditional céilí dances to Boston in the 1940s and 1950s, helped Norris run the show. Recalls Cummings:

I would announce songs and dances throughout the night, as well as make any special announcements. I would also announce the names of the band and musicians once a night, and also invite the dancers to line up for the Siege of Ennis. And you were constantly asking the crowds to move back off of the floor. People would crowd around the dance floor and sometimes impinge on the dancing area. There was one line of seats all around the sides of the hall. The hall was very elegant, with its mirrors and crystal ball—it was first-rate. You and your girlfriend could come there and meet and dance together, and there were no problems. Together with Billy Warren as the doorman and Mary O'Leary as ticket seller, we ran a tight ship. There was never a problem. No fights or drunkenness—there was none of that.

Within a short time of purchasing the New State Ballroom, Fuller acquired neighboring buildings as well: Mack's Bar and the Donnelly Memorial Theater. The New State Ballroom was similar in setup to the established dance halls: It could hold three to four hundred people; a large dance floor was outlined by seats around the sides; and upstairs was a soda bar.

Because tastes were in a rapid shift, Fuller ran through a litany of musicians and combos while he tried to determine the taste of the new young Irish crowds. He opened the hall with an American band, the Christopher Zaba Orchestra, but then tried to cater to Irish tastes by hiring a variety of Irish-run bands. One of those bands was run by Dick Senier, the son of Tom Senier of Dan Sullivan's Shamrock Band and Emerald Isle Orchestra fame. Dick had played the dance halls frequently as a young man in the 1940s, but he left the scene to attend the seminary and later Georgetown University in Washington, D.C. By the 1960s, he was back in town. He recalls the night he was invited to play at the State Ballroom:

Fuller had come in mad as hell, and had just fired the band-leader. Des O'Regan, whose brother-in-law Walter Norris managed the hall, asked me if I'd like to come in and play. So we put a band together. It didn't last long—maybe a couple of months—until we got fired. This was the 1960s, and the Irish kids themselves had lost interest in the Irish music. They were more into the country and western.

Finally, Bill Fuller hit it right. He discovered a recent arrival on the Boston scene, Terry Landers, and hired him to play the showband music that was popular in Ireland and England.

Terry Landers

Terry Landers arrived in America in 1959 at the age of thirty-eight. A Tralee native and married with nine children in Ireland, he came to Boston seeking opportunity and a better life for his young family. He had played saxophone and accordion with the famous Kingdom Band, an early showband in Ireland. He later formed his own orchestra, the Modern-Airs, which was rated as one of the top semi-professional combinations in the country. When he came to America, he saw that showband music was nowhere to be found, so he brought the music with him. He says:

> I had a brother here, my brother Joe. He worked in the State Ballroom running the cafeteria there. I had brought my accordion with me. Of course, I was involved in the music at home for years. My brother had said, "There are very nice bands in the States, but they don't play very much Irish music." I wasn't so much into traditional as I was into the ballroom music. That's all they danced in Ireland at that time. No céilí. But I brought in the accordion and I went up as a guest artist, and Joe Derrane was playing the accordion. That's the first time I met Joe. The State Ballroom on Mass. Ave. was a beautiful place, run by a man that came from not ten miles from me in Ireland, Bill Fuller, and his partner Carmel Quinn, the singer. Fantastic singer.
>
> I met Joe Derrane there for the first time, and I thought he was brilliant. Dermot O'Brien was here at that time, too, and he played accordion for the PTAA—the Pioneer Total Abstinence Association, run by Joe Gaffney and Mrs. O'Sullivan. I was a total abstainer at the time, a Pioneer. There was a strong branch of the PTAA in Boston. There was a floor manager there named Joe Finnegan, and Joe told me that Dermot O'Brien was leaving to go back to Ireland. The last night he was there, I went down and joined him with my accordion. We played a session and the PTAA

crowd would go dancing. And that time, you had to play fox-trots and slow waltzes and old-time waltzes. We played together that night, and Dermot left the next weekend. So I fell in to play for the Pioneers; that's how I got to meet a lot of the Irish crowd. I hadn't met many up to that.

I played alone in Boston for a few nights, and then I met George Shanley. George was a drummer with the Tara Céilí band. George played with me then for the Pioneers, and then asked me to come in and sit in with the Tara Céilí Band. That's where I met a terrific bunch of guys: Larry Reynolds, Mickey Connolly, Frank Neylon, Desie Regan, Tommy Garvey. Desie Regan left to go to California, and I more or less settled in his place. The crowd coming over that time were at the early stages of the showband scene, and I was there more or less to play for the pop tunes, the fox-trots and waltzes, while the lads played all céilí. I played for the waltzes and fox-trots, and I guess the word got out. At that time, it was all American-born musicians that were playing for the Irish crowds, with few exceptions.

I had the three-row accordion that you could play the chromatic scales on. See, the two-row accordions that they had were made specially for the traditional music. Mickey was very good at it. But you couldn't play any pop music on them. They were big for G and D, the two keys of Irish traditional music, and occasionally the key of A. But I could get the flats and everything on my three-row B/C/D-flat accordion, which you couldn't get on the two-row accordions. That's where the guys were caught. They couldn't play any of the modern tunes. So then we could play some of the modern stuff, George and the piano player Tommy Garvey—lovely man, great sense of humor.

Mickey Connolly recalls meeting Landers for the first time:

Terry came out here all alone. He was an accordionist, and he was a good musician. We were playing up on Dudley Street, in the Intercolonial Hall. Johnny Cronin came and said, "Mickey, come in here for a minute." We went into the bathroom. I had finished playing for the night. "I want you to hear this man." Landers, he had the big accordion, and auditioned for the band with the three-row accordion in the bathroom! That's where I first heard Terry.

The Terry Landers Orchestra at the Intercolonial in 1962. Front row, left to right: Fred O'Connor, piano; Bob Connors, bass; Dick Mulholland, guitar; Steve O'Callaghan, drums; Terry Landers, alto sax; Bob Iovanelli, tenor sax; Mike Landers, tenor sax; John Foley, trumpet; Al Birtwall, trumpet; Tony McDonnell, trombone.
(From the library of Terry Landers.)

After about a year in America, Landers went back to Ireland and, helped along by money raised by benefit concerts held by his new friends in the PTAA and the Tara Céilí band, brought his family over in 1960. Not long after he stepped off the plane in Boston with his wife and nine airsick children, Landers started a band of his own with his nephew Mike Landers on tenor saxophone, Corkman John Foley on guitar, Steve O'Callaghan on drums, and Dick Mulholland on guitar. The band caught on straightaway. They performed for all the Irish weddings, sometimes booking two and three years ahead. The band appealed to the young immigrants who had left the dance scene at home and wanted to hear something like what they had left. Landers's band fit in perfectly. The other bands were still playing the céilí music of the 1940s. Landers's band took off.

Terry Landers also formed an eleven-piece group called the Terry Landers Orchestra. Pete Lee and Timmy Walsh were running the Intercolonial. In the main ballroom upstairs, Billy Caples and his orchestra played, while the Boston Céilí Band, formerly the Tara Céilí Band, were downstairs. The crowd that enjoyed the céilí danced downstairs, and the crowd that wanted to dance to the modern music of the Billy Caples Orchestra or another modern group called Four Provinces were upstairs. One night, Maurice O'Toole of the Four Provinces invited Landers to sit in with the band, and not long after, Landers started the Terry Landers Orchestra. The orchestra graduated from the Intercolonial to the State Ballroom. According to Landers:

> In the big orchestra, we had four saxes, two trumpets, trombone, and then we had a rhythm section—piano, bass, guitar, and drums. Smashing band. All ballroom stuff, but we had the quartet incorporated into it. And we had a Dixieland section incorporated in. Plus we had a skiffle group in there. Different times, the four would step out. We had a great Dixieland section. It was fantastic. It could do anything. And we could play the traditional music then again. We played all the Glenn Miller stuff, big band music. We got the music from London, Braun's was the name of the place. The orchestrations were all ready-made, just to send for them. I used to write some of the stuff myself.
>
> I had very strict rules in the band. We always got there an hour before to set up the stuff, tune the instruments, leave them on the stage, and do whatever we had to do—get dressed. Then we'd come back on the stage straightaway and start playing. No fussing around. No drink on the stage, absolutely not. No food. No smoking, strictly professional, and tuxedos with the dickey bows. I was very strict.
>
> That band was a big hit because it was the only band with a bunch of Irish guys in it and an Irish guy that formed it, you know.

For a while, showbands and traditional music coexisted on the dance hall stage, as Frank Storer's memories of Boston at the time corroborate. Storer says:

> The times were changing. The traditional music in itself was starting to turn to showband-type of music. This is moving into the sixties. You started to get more of a country-western, jive-dancing presentation. The newer crowds that were immigrating were of a different generation, where we were still maintaining the thirties and forties mode of operation because we were playing for the people who had been here since the twenties, thirties, and forties—they were getting older. The younger crowd coming, they were evolving to the point where they never knew what Irish mu-

sic was until they came to America. I mean, traditional dancing. A lot of them did know, don't get me wrong, but a lot of them did not. They wouldn't dance to that stuff.

Fuller started to bring showbands from Ireland, which made a sensation with young Irish crowds who were willing to pay a bit extra to get the new sounds. Because Fuller owned halls in several U.S. cities, he could offer a series of dates to visiting Irish showbands. It wouldn't pay to bring a showband to Dudley Street—the crowds were too small, and according to Mike Cummings, "the old-timers wouldn't like it." Between the visiting bands from Ireland and New York, Boston bands were the mainstay. During the transition years in Boston, bands such as the Joe Fahey, the Four Provinces, and John Foley and the Diplomats held ground at the Intercolonial on Thursday nights, playing Irish music as well as such popular American songs like "My Boy Lollipop" and Patsy Cline's "I Fall to Pieces."

Meanwhile, the Terry Landers Orchestra began to cater to the young Irish crowd at the State Ballroom. Following Terry Landers's lead, other showbands soon began to form in Boston: the Shannonaires, the Desie Regan Showband, the Jimmy Kelly Showband, and the Professionals. Showbands had a completely different performance format from that employed by the old dance hall bands, according to Frank Storer:

> When the showbands came in, they were doing things like "Little Arrow" and things like that: Irish compositions with a country-western type of beat. For a while they both existed, the traditional type of bands and the showband style, where you did a lot of vocalizing, singing, and a lot of more country-western.
>
> At one time, you just played music, and nobody sang songs. You heard a band, and no one sang vocal unless they were a guest artist coming in. When the Terry Landers Band came in, you had three or four of them that sang. They'd have numbers where they'd sing, they'd do choreography, and they'd sway left and right, so you see, that was changing.
>
> We were all a little older, but we were pretty well schooled in the Irish traditional jigs and reels and hornpipes. That's what we presented, with a little flair for American music.

Showbands provided the feel of rock and roll through their instrumentation, while appealing to the Irish taste for narrative song. They also retained some traditional Irish dance repertoire. Storer said that showbands would play dances such as the Siege of Ennis, though not nearly as often as the dance hall bands that preceded them. Terry Landers describes his band's repertoire and showmanship as being closely related to the approaches of showbands in Ireland:

> We all had moves, the band swaying. We all did that because that's what they had at home. The showbands at home were brilliant. They had an instrumentation that was totally different. They had a drummer, three guitars—a bass, rhythm, and lead guitar—and you could imagine what three amplified guitars could do at that time. The sound was so new. They'd have brass—a sax and trumpet. The sound was fabulous. Rock and roll—"the Hucklebuck." That's a tune. You wiggle like a duck and waddle like a—whatever, and the crowd would do it on the floor. That was Brendan Bowyer [who popularized that song]. And D. J. Curtin was with him, a beautiful singer.
>
> Most of the [music] they copied was from here [the U.S.]. Then they started writing a lot of their own stuff, which was pretty good. Fabulous era. We did some Irish songs as well. We had to, of course. "Wild Colonial Boy" and "Galway Bay." Then a highland fling, a polka. They wanted a lot of stuff they were hearing at home. They were still coming out at this stage. That's what they had at home; that's what they wanted to hear. And we gave it to them. We were flying at that stage, going great, and I was working full-time, as well.

Showbands were so popular that the only choice for professional musicians who wished to continue performing was to adapt. Technological advances in sound amplification meant that it was possible for almost every dance hall band to have a vocalist, as well as electric instruments. In addition to a singer, typical instrumentation in the showbands was electric guitar, electric bass, drums, piano, and often brass instruments or saxophones, depending on the size of the band. Says Frank Storer, "From that point on, every band had to sing songs, or you didn't play much." He responded to the change by forming the Shannonaires, which became extremely successful in Boston. He says:

> Showband music . . . we made the switch. We could play the traditional music, too, but we were still young enough—I was maybe

in my thirties. About that time, the band that I mainly played in for the next twenty years with my brother, we formed the Shannonaires, which was a four-piece group made up of myself on accordion and piano, my brother on saxophone, a fellow from county Mayo, Frank Lavelle, on guitar. The drummer was Art Poirier, he was from Foxborough, and also George Bearse, also a drummer with us. We formed the Shannonaires and played mostly weddings, parties, dance halls, but no steady hall.

Many of the showbands in Boston played the newer music but also catered to their local audience by including some of the Irish-American repertoire of decades past. The newly arrived Irish in the late 1950s and early 1960s saw a difference between what some of the showbands were doing in America and what they had left behind in Ireland. Young Irish audiences in America didn't necessarily think the American bands were as good as those in Ireland, but they went anyway. Liam Keyes, an immigrant from Dublin, reflects this attitude when he says:

> The showbands! The music didn't measure up here, of course. They played a lot of what I called the old Irish-American songs: They weren't Irish. You know, like "Too-ra-loo-ra-loo-ra," "When Irish Eyes Are Smiling," "Did Your Mother Come from Ireland?" "Who Threw the Overalls in Mrs. Murphy's Chowder." But things were changing with the folk boom in Ireland, too. You see, what they were doing now with the Jet Age, they were able to bring the big-name showbands over from Ireland. And they would charge twice the price in the State Ballroom.
>
> As you went back further, the bands just had the old squeeze box and fiddle. . . . But the showbands were brought over from Ireland, and they were doing the tour of the big cities: New York, Boston, Chicago, San Francisco. And there was big money in it. The showbands did everything. They had all the great modern songs—Elvis.

By the early 1960s, the crowds of decades past had dwindled. The Dudley Street dance halls were dead in comparison with the late 1940s. Promoters Pete Lee and Timmy Walsh picked up management of dances in the Intercolonial from 1957 through the 1960s, while Tommy Geraghty and Johnny Kelly promoted dances at the Hibernian Hall. By the 1960s, a new cast of musicians had come on the scene, including Larry Reynolds, Brendan Tonra, Des Regan, George Shanley, and Terry Landers, and they were playing under the name of the Tara Céilí Band at the Intercolonial. Mickey Connolly recalls:

> Pete Lee heard me playing down in Cambridge, down in Prospect Hall in Cambridge. Pete says, "Are you playing steady anywhere?" I says, "No." I didn't know him and Timmy Walsh. . . . He said, "Why don't you come in next Friday night? I have a band up there, they're like a house without a father, and one of them don't know what the other guy is going to play, and they need someone," and I said, "All right." And that's why I came in, met Larry Reynolds, drummer George Shanley, and a bunch of them. I went up playing, and Larry says, "You're running the thing from now on." Almost sixteen years we were together, Larry and myself.

The Intercolonial's biggest night now was Thursday, when the State Ballroom was closed, but the young crowd had moved on from Dudley Street. Many Irish-born young people who went to the Dudley Street dance halls in the early 1960s were disappointed. Many had come to America by way of London, and they found that music in expatriate dance halls in London was more in step with the rock and roll that was all the rage with American youth. In London, young men dressed in Teddy Boy suits, DA haircuts, stovepipe-tapered pants cut short to display patterned socks, and pointy-toed boots known as winklepickers. The girls, for their part, were following the lead of First Lady Jackie Kennedy. Mame O' Shaughnessy, who arrived in Boston from London in 1963, thought the Boston dance halls felt provincial. In London, she says,

> you'd go to so many places and meet so many people, you really didn't get to know the people like you did here in Boston. When I came here, it was very hard. I had to step back and say, "Oh my, you can't go do much around here without everyone knowing about it." Small town was the feeling I had. When I came out in 1963, there was really only two places in town to go to, [the Intercolonial and the State Ballroom], and it was the same crowd going there all the time. Everyone knew everyone.

Jana Louise

With the increasing popularity of singers, there was a new place on the dance hall stage for women. The darling of Dudley Street, Janice ("Jana Louise") Hansen, was from a well-known Irish family in Boston. Her mother had always been good to the Irish in Boston, having people back to her house in Jamaica Plain for tea and sandwiches after the dances

Janice and her two sisters were raised to perform; they appeared frequently at church benefits and field days, and they tap-danced live on the weekly "Irish Hour" radio program. Boston's Irish-American social clubs were the very heart and soul of the Columban Fathers' fund-raising efforts, and there were ample opportunities for the girls to perform at county club dinners and dances held in honor of the fathers' missions. Janice's older sister Chris tells a story of their mother Mary Ann's encouragement of their performance skills:

> Most of us played instruments. We'd think nothing of sitting around playing instruments. Every Sunday morning at our house, after Mass, they'd come to our house, my cousins and my uncle. We would practice because we used to go out doing a lot of singing and dancing. We'd have to go out into the hall, and my mother would be sitting on the couch, and I can see her now. We'd walk in, like we were going to walk onstage. And she'd say, "Go back. Go back. You're walking out too slow! Stand up straight, walk out fast, and put a smile on your face." Well, she'd have us walking out twenty times before we ever sang a note. And Maureen's at the piano, playing away.
>
> This would go on every single Sunday. Then we'd have dinner, and up to benediction at quarter of three at the church. We would perform mostly at Columban Fathers' benefits. There were some nights we went five nights in a week. There'd be little projects they'd do, too, and they'd probably only make fifty or seventy-five dollars a night, but at that time it was a lot of money. They'd pass the hat. They'd show a movie like *Wings over Ireland*, and we'd dance and sing a bit.
>
> Now, our mother couldn't carry a tune, but she knew when we were out of tune. My father was the singer. A beautiful singer and

a gorgeous dancer. Oh, you would love to waltz with my father. My mother could dance okay; she knew the basic little steps that she had in school in Ireland, the little baby steps, the slip, jig, and the reel. But she knew to correct us. She was great.

Janice is grateful for her mother's encouragement, attributing her own performance skills to her early training. "God forbid when I used to practice and I used to bow, if I ever turned my back on the audience to leave the living room to go back to the hallway! I had to back out! She was awesome," recalls Janice.

Janice had her Dudley Street debut at age fifteen, in 1959, as a two-week fill-in for Anne Marie McNally, who was getting married. Pete Lee and Timmy Walsh had seen Janice perform at local events and asked her sister Maureen if Janice was up to the task. Says Janice, "Boy, it was scary stuff. I had never done that before. But I knew all the songs. I knew every single Irish song. So I got out the petticoats and went down, and I started with the Four Provinces Orchestra." When McNally came back, Janice stayed with the orchestra to cover the pop song area. "I did the pop and [McNally] did the Irish, the waltzes," she says. "She was so nice, such a nice girl. Then she just left. I ended up staying, and I was there Thursdays and Saturdays until the Intercolonial closed down. It was the best time of my life."

From the Intercolonial, Hansen moved on to the State Ballroom, at the invitation of Bill Fuller. Fuller quickly recognized her potential and assumed the role of agent, sending her to New York to work in his ballroom there, City Center. Soon after, Fuller was booking performances for her in venues all over the world, including his own ballrooms in Chicago, San Francisco, and New York. Says Hansen:

> After high school, I had to make a decision. I was going to broadcasting school; that's what I wanted to do. I had to decide between that or moving to New York. I decided on going to New York. So I lived there, and I worked for Mr. Fuller at the City Center with Paddy Noonan. We worked on the weekends together in the ballrooms. My stage name became Jana Louise. My middle name is Louise, and Mr. Fuller's publicity agent gave me the name Jana.
>
> When I was living in New York, I lived right across from City Center. Every so often, I'd go to Chicago for a weekend, and eventually [Fuller] asked me, "Do you want to move to Chicago for a while?" I did that, and then he was opening up a new ball-

room in San Francisco, so I moved in with a family. He always had me living with a family, which was kind of nice. I stayed out there for quite a while. Sometimes I'd come back to New York and sing for a week and go back to San Francisco. I moved around a lot.

Fuller also sent Hansen on tour to England and Ireland as a solo act. She says:

> Everywhere we went, they would get me a band and then I would rehearse with the band. It was not easy. I was doing Irish and popular with those groups—Teresa Brewer numbers, Patsy Cline— just a good mix. But my heart was really in the Irish.
>
> When I traveled England and Ireland singing, I did all popular music. I didn't do Irish at all. All the songs that were popular here, that's what I did. That's what they wanted. They didn't want to hear Irish; they just weren't interested. Audiences were only interested in that music here in America.

As showbands rose in popularity, the Dudley Street dance hall venues began to slow down significantly in favor of other newer venues in the Boston area. The Intercolonial was now seen as welcoming and familiar but a little too cozy and the music played there a bit backward. Joan Gannon says, "It was a big, real old-fashioned place, from another era, but it was nice." She continues:

> You really could not believe how much Irish music there was in the halls in America, because coming from Ireland, we never heard that music in the dance hall. There, it was showbands, modern music, sort of rock and roll, you know . . . more modern music in sixty-one. Then you came here, and you went right into the Intercolonial, and I couldn't believe it. It was Billy Caples or Terry Landers playing the accordion. I had never danced a highland fling until I came here. But I always enjoyed the dances at the Intercolonial. You just couldn't wait to check in your coat and start dancing.

By the late 1950s, Irish immigration had declined significantly. When the New State Ballroom opened across town, on Massachusetts Avenue in Boston, Dudley Street dance crowds nearly disappeared. Connie McEleney, who arrived in America in 1957, recalls only three halls remaining on Dudley Street. Dudley Street was no longer the mecca that Joe Derrane de-

John Foley and the Diplomats pictured at the New State Ballroom. Front row,
left to right: Jana Louise, vocals; John Foley, trumpet. Back: Joe O'Callaghan,
Jimmy Kelly, trombone; Bob Iovanelli, tenor sax; Rudy Ruhrig, tenor sax;
Phil Garufi, guitar; Dick Mulholland, guitar; Maurice O'Toole, bass.
(From the library of Janice Hansen Kleinbauer.)

scribed, but, rather, one musical destination among many. McEleney's recollection of leaving Dudley Street to hear a band elsewhere indicates a
change in Dudley Street's appeal:

> We used to leave there some nights and go out to the Knights of
> Columbus hall in Mattapan, right in the middle of Mattapan. You'd
> leave Dudley Street and go out there by bus. You'd leave maybe at
> ten-thirty, if it was supposed to be a good night. You went out to this
> other place if there was a popular band out there. But you thought
> nothing of going around at night from one place to another.

Joe Derrane, who had seen the heyday, when all five dance halls were
booming, says it was over by 1960 or 1961:

It just died overnight. There was major change in the demographics. They built a whole system of those housing projects right behind where the ballrooms were. A lot of the Irish girls were quite
uncomfortable walking down the street, looking at all these different kinds of people. In addition to that, there were a number of
pubs that were just starting. Prior to this, we had just your old typical bar, serious business. They went in for drinking, and that was it.
But then the pubs started to open up, and they brought that culture
with them from Ireland, and they were bringing over the showbands with all the newer tunes and a lot of country-and-western
flavor. And now the immigrants that were coming out in that time
were much younger than the other generation that had come before them. And they brought with them a taste for this music.

The crowd at the Dudley Street halls, like the music, was getting older.
The showbands coming over from Ireland and England attracted the
younger crowd, charged more money than local bands, and also started to expand the venues at which Irish music was being played. Liam Keyes recalls:

When I was first coming to the dances, it was a lot of the older
people that had been out here forty years at the time. They all met
their husbands and their wives down at the Intercolonial, and
Roxbury was predominantly Irish at that time. They would come
for a night out, and a lot of them would head in to the old Irish
dance halls.

But that was the beginning of the end. The black population
was moving in. You could see it at that time. We could go to the
Dublin House bar, which is still there in Upham's Corner, and
Dudley Square was only a half mile down. Even down on Dudley
Street itself there was a few Irish clubs and Irish bars, but they
were on the way out.

The State Ballroom was beginning to become the favorite place.
It was in its own neighborhood. And the Donnelly Memorial The-
atre was a few doors down from the State Ballroom. There'd be a
big crowd there in the State Ballroom. In fact, there was a ballroom
there for years and years. Glenn Miller and all played there, going
back to the war years. The Royal Showband played in the Tremont
Hotel, which had a big ballroom—any place you got a big ballroom, a big stage, they'd have the showbands. It was big money.

With the showbands from Boston, it was about two and a half dollars to get in. That was quite a lot of money at that time. But when the showbands would come over [from Ireland], you're maybe talking eight, nine, or ten dollars. But you've got to realize that you're getting a beer for a buck, and a coffee and a donut was ten cents, and a paper was five cents. A new car then was about twenty-two hundred dollars.

In the winter of 1965, the young Boston Irish discovered the intoxicating combination of alcohol and music, and there was no turning back. Terry Landers recounts the transition period and traces the end of the ballrooms to a single night, not long before the State Ballroom was to close its doors:

I was playing with the Terry Landers Orchestra at the State Ballroom when Fuller informed me that he had sold the property. The Christian Science was across the way from Symphony Hall, and they bought all that block next to Symphony Hall. Fuller sold it, and got an immense amount of money. This would be about sixty-three or sixty-four. He said, "I'm telling you this in confidence. The building is sold, and depending on how soon the developers want to take the property, this hall will be no longer here." That's when I formed the quartet in the meantime. John Foley and the Diplomats stayed in the State Ballroom with Dick Mulholland, and they built a band around themselves. It didn't last long.

There was a guy approached me then that there was an opening in Roslindale for a club. The club that was there was called Ker-Mac's, it was Kerrigan and McDonough. The two of them owned it as partners, but it was reopening with the name of Ireland's 32. I knew the State Ballroom was being sold, so I left it.

Ireland's 32 was located at 4161 Washington Street, in Roslindale. Owner Pat McDonough's Irish friends had suggested that he make it an Irish club because there were no other established Irish clubs in Boston. He hired the Terry Landers Orchestra and opened the doors for business on January 16, 1965, during one of Boston's biggest snowstorms. According to McDonough, "The weather didn't seem to matter. Not only was the club filled to capacity of over four hundred people, but there were another three hundred outside the doors standing in line, waiting to get in."[3] Terry Landers recalls that the timing of the opening night was perfect:

The night Ireland's 32 opened, the State Ballroom happened to be closed because there was a snowstorm. The crowd came holus-bolus over to Roslindale, and it was an instant hit. It was the first time a lot of the Irish guys and most of the Irish girls were ever in a nightclub where there was a bar. There was never a bar where the Irish crowd went dancing—there was no bar there in the State Ballroom.

The Irish girls went over, and they were all soft drinkers. And the guy said, "Hell, I'm not going to make any money with them sitting there. There's no profit in this." I said to him, "Hey, you don't have the girls, you don't have the guys. It doesn't matter if they never drink anything. You should treat them to the drink. . . ."

Once they got a taste of the nightclub atmosphere, that was it. In the dance hall, there was just seating at both sides and the huge floor cleared for the dancing. When the music started, you'd see the guys going across the floor to the girls in a wave. But in the nightclubs, they were sitting at tables. It was like something they had seen in the movies. . . .

They had never been in a place in Ireland where there was liquor sold where they danced. It wouldn't be allowed, and it was never here, either. The nearest bar to the State Ballroom was Mack's, outside and around the corner. The guys would go in and out and have a drink. But imagine them going to a place where they could sit at their own table and come back, and the seat would be there for them, and their drink would be there. Totally new experience altogether. . . . That was the end of the State Ballroom.

The new playing environment was a novel experience for musicians, as well, according to Landers. It took a little getting used to, though he never forsook his Pioneer pledge of total abstinence from alcohol. He says:

The band was over in the corner, out of the way. There was a nice big dance space about . . . thirty by twenty, and then there were tables all around. Shaded lighting and all of this business. We'd take an intermission every three quarters of an hour for ten minutes to give time for the waitress to get through the crowd to serve the tables. Then we went back up straightaway again, and they'd be dancing. It was a totally new experience for them. For us, too. . . . We had never played where there was a bar, either. Not in Ireland, not here.

Turning Point: The Kennedy Years

The Irish had come a long, long way since the first famine ships arrived in the 1840s. The years following World War II through the early 1960s were the American Dream years: high salaries, strong unions, and upward mobility. The 1950s had marked a turning point for Irish-Americans. The number of second-generation Irish outnumbered the Irish-born in the United States by four to one.[4] John F. Kennedy provided a role model for Irish-Americans, placing the American dream within the reach of the Boston Irish and demonstrating just how far an Irish immigrant family could come in the United States. Joanne McDermott says she felt a very personal connection to Kennedy:

> Jack Kennedy, we all loved him. He was one of our own. His mother was from Dorchester. He was *my* president. Every time I bring someone to the Kennedy library, I start to cry. Steve and I got married in 1960, and we went on our honeymoon, and we had a big black Pontiac convertible. We had Kennedy stickers all over our car, and people in Canada, no matter where we went, they were beeping their horns, and waving to us, and getting all excited because we had Mass. plates, so they knew we were from Massachusetts if not Boston. It was a very exciting time.

Irish pride ran high with Kennedy's rise. The shame once attached to being Irish in Boston was gone forever.

Instead of Digging Praties, I'll Be Digging Lumps of Gold

The Irish had made significant gains in their economic position in American society by the 1950s. A single generation made a huge difference in economic position, as many a father-and-son story attests. Owen Frain, a flute player who came to America in the 1920s, had run away from home in Ireland when he was just fourteen years old to work in the coal mines of England. Eventually, Frain joined the English navy and eventually immigrated to the United States, bringing his music with him. His son Gene, in contrast, born and raised in America, worked steadily for more than forty years as a machinist at a rubber mill in Watertown, Massachusetts.

Likewise, not long after he was married, Mickey Connolly took a job in a mill running a forklift for $2.63 an hour. His first check was fifty-three dollars. Knowing he'd never see Ireland again on that salary, he gave his notice and joined the carpenters' union, where he quickly rose to foreman and then sponsored many of his musician friends, including Martin McDonough, Larry Reynolds, and dance promoter Timmy Walsh.

Still, white-collar positions were rare for Irish Bostonians, and held mostly by first-generation Irish-Americans. Many worked hard for a living. But, says Éamon Connolly of South Boston, you sometimes had to be creative to make a good living in Boston. While Mickey Connolly was working as a foreman, building homes in a Boston suburb, Éamon (no relation) was selling fish that "fell off" the back of freight trains in South Boston. Éamon speaks of

> the days when you might have hooked school to longshore two days a week, and you could make more than your father was making. We'd be shining shoes at twelve or thirteen in South Station, peddling papers, and stealing fish or watermelons from the freight cars and selling them door to door all through Southie. They'd be putting them on one side, we're taking them out the other side, bringing them back to Southie like regular hucksters: "We got some great fish for you today, Mrs. O'Malley!"

Other first-generation Irish-Americans, such as Mike Powell, the mastermind behind the Intercolonial dance hall, had begun to rise up the ranks to white-collar positions—but in the civil service world. In banking, however, there were still few Irish born, even in the 1960s. Seamus Mulligan recounts how few Irish there were in the executive positions:

> I came in 1959. I had a pretty good job by Irish standards. I was a clerk with the largest worsted spinners in Ireland. But I think every second child in Ireland had a stamp on his bum that said, "For export." I mean, there were nine of us, and five came to

America. And I don't think there's a family in Ireland today that doesn't have some blood relative in the United States.

When I came out here, I came first of all to New York, and worked with Chase Manhattan Bank for eight or nine months. I wasn't really that crazy about the social life there. The weekend was heavy-duty drinking, and that was about all that you did. They would all get together at Gaelic Park for the games and they would just get polluted. I really wasn't into that.

So I wrote to Bank of Boston here, got myself up for an interview, and gave in my notice. I was in banking here for about twenty years. I recall very vividly that during that period, say the fifties . . . a Roman Catholic—now, I'm not talking just Irish now—would not be an official or officer in any one of Boston's banks. None. Period. And into the sixties. None. Matter of fact, when Joe Kennedy [JFK's father] set about originally founding a bank, they wouldn't let him. They said, "You're not getting it," and it was as simple as that. They really did keep the Irish at blue collar.

Dick Senier was from the first generation to attend college in his family, the only son of eleven to earn a college degree, while his father had played music at night but worked a wide variety of jobs during the day. In his working life, Tom Senier did just about anything he could to get along. He worked for O'Byrne DeWitt installing radios that DeWitt had sold in his shop. During World War II, he was a pipe fitter at the Fore River Shipyard in Quincy, and he also worked at carpentry and paperhanging—and all that time, he was running dances at night. Says Dick Senier:

> You had various strata within the Irish immigrant community, just as with many other immigrant communities. The first generation comes out and then has children, who advance a bit further. Lots of Irish people encouraged their children to go to college, so the next generation gets involved in law and politics. A lot worked hard to get their kids into college, but still others didn't want to go on to college. My father didn't push us to get into the academic life. My brother went to one semester of college; then he went to the war. I was the only one who went and finished.
>
> I must say that the Second World War changed everything for many Irish families. My brother Bill was in military service a mere eleven years after he had emigrated from Ireland. Frank, too.

When they came home, they were mid-twenties, a bit late for a lot of guys to start college. In fact, the accepted wisdom in my father's house was that you got a job with the Boston Elevated Railway, the Boston Gas Company, Edison Light, the telephone company, or General Motors. Those jobs were good, steady, offered advancement, and led to pensions. Once you were hired, you could think about getting married.

For the Irish-born, it wasn't hard to get work as a laborer because as long as you were sponsored, you could eventually get citizenship. Liam Keyes got a job with the city's electric utility, Boston Edison, and spent more than thirty years working there:

> When I came over, they were still mourning Jack Kennedy here in Boston. The door had been kicked open. There were no more "No Irish Need Apply" signs in Boston. I would go look for a job, and it was, "What part of the old country are you from?" "My mother was from Donegal, and my mother was Cork," and they didn't even interview you. They just gave you the job.

Get Me to the Church on Time

From the 1940s through the 1960s, Cardinal Richard Cushing (1895–1970) emerged as a strong spiritual leader, for Catholics not only in Boston but also nationwide. Born in South Boston to Irish immigrant parents, Cushing was ordained a bishop in 1939 and became archbishop of the Boston Archdiocese in 1944. During his twenty-five-year tenure in Boston, he was a prolific fund-raiser in the community, holding innumerable charitable events and building schools, homes for the disabled, hospitals, and homes for the elderly.

Until the 1960s, Irish and Irish-American social life in Boston was closely connected to the church. The special novena masses on Wednesday nights at Mission Church were a great gathering place for hundreds of both Irish and Irish-Americans. According to Larry Reynolds:

> All the Irish went there. There were two novenas, at seven and nine, and they all went, just like in Ireland. It was helped by Father

Cardinal Cushing does the highland fling with two parishioners.
His fun-loving ways won the hearts of all of his Irish parishioners.
(Photo courtesy of the Archdiocese of Boston.)

Manton. Oh, he was an awesome man to give a sermon. He'd keep your attention all the time. Then at nine, everyone one stood around outside, like you did in Ireland, and met people. Most times a céilí would take place after church.

Father Joseph Manton was a very popular priest, and people were as religious about him as they were about the church. Frank Devin, like Reynolds, remembers Manton as a good talker. He had a raspy voice, but you could hear him. [Attending church] was just the thing to do in those days. Faith in those days wasn't a faith of convenience; it was a faith of centuries of beliefs. I mean, people went to church because they *believed*, not because they thought it was right or they wore their clothes or that kind of stuff. It has lost a lot of that these days.

There were often dances on Dudley Street after the novena, and a good part of the congregation would rush from the novena to the dances. According to Dick Senier, "Those of us teenagers who wanted to get out for the night would tell our parents we were going to the novena. It worked every time." Across from Mission Church was Fontaine's coffee shop, which seemed to be as big a draw as the church. According to Joan Gannon, "The only reason you went to the novena was to meet the guys after, across in the coffee shop. It was a big gathering place for the Irish." And according to Mary Murphy, born in Mission Hill in Roxbury, the men were there faithfully to meet the women:

> Wednesday night novenas, thousands of them would come to it and stand outside. And the Irish guys were so loyal. If a guy said to you he'd meet you up the novena, he'd be there. Thousands of guys were there, and they all got together there. It was hard for them coming out!

Sundays were important for the Irish. Joan Gannon, who came to America in 1961, describes Sunday as a much-awaited day: "Sunday really was what kept the Irish really together, where you'd see people from home. The Intercolonial was a great place to meet everyone. You'd really look forward to going there to see a familiar face."

Sunday after Mass was also a busy time for the coffee shops near Mission Church. Peg Reidy of Mission Hill in Roxbury recalls Ellie's Donut Shop, which, like Fontaine's, was across the street from the church:

> Sunday after Mass . . . it would be jammed, shoulder to shoulder. Then, the station wagons would pull up out front: "Do you want sweaters, do you want records, jackets?" These local hoods'd pop open the trunks, and they'd have camel-hair coats. They used to steal off the ships that came into the harbor. So after Mass, you had your coffee and donuts, and you went outside and got your Sinatra records and Elvis and your sweaters—cashmere sweaters—

the camel-hair coats, leather jackets. And these were two brothers, dressed to the nines. Movie-star pretty. Thieves. Absolute thieves. They'd go to church, then they'd hit Ellie's after. That's what Sunday was, in the early sixties. All this would go on in a two-hour window.

By the 1960s, Sunday had also become a dance hall day. However, because of the blue laws that required shops, dance halls, and liquor stores to be closed, Sunday events were "unofficial" at first. According to Chris Hansen:

> There was no dances on Sunday night, but the opera house some-times would have them. We'd all wait outside the opera house to see if there was going to be a dance. I remember standing down-stairs outside the opera house, hoping to God they'd open the door for a dance. You know, it'd be getting late, and then a couple of guys would come in with their violins, and they'd just go up-stairs. They'd leave the door open, and they'd be playing, and we'd be dancing in the dark. It was pitch-dark in the hall, and the musicians would be playing until the cops would find out and they'd come and we'd all have to leave.

Later, because of the enterprising efforts of Monsignor George Kerr in Roxbury, Sunday dances became regular and, if not fully legal, at least condoned by Cardinal Cushing—so the police turned a blind eye. Larry Reynolds has vivid memories of helping Monsignor Kerr organize Sunday dances:

> How the Sunday night dancing came about was Monsignor George Valentine Kerr. He was a great football player in his col-lege days. An All-American, and a handsome man, striking, big, strong man. Cardinal Cushing gave him a parish in Roxbury, St. Francis de Salles. It was a very poor parish, it was attended by very low-income people, and of course, the area was starting to go down a little bit at that time. Some of the Irish were leaving the area. The cardinal had said, "The archdiocese doesn't have that much money to keep that and all the other parishes that needed money, so do whatever you can to raise money for the parish." So Monsignor Kerr, he got an idea, knowing how much the Irish loved to dance. So a bunch of us, we had a meeting. Before I came out here, the big thing on a Sunday [in Ireland] was dancing. We

talked about this, and he thought we'd try and get around the blue laws, and get permission from the police to dance on Sunday nights. Needless to say, it was an instant success.

It's funny, I'll tell you, the clout that Cardinal Cushing had. I remember one night we went in and the sergeant came down, and he stopped the dancing and cleared the hall: "Everybody out, you're not supposed to be dancing." And the following day, he got a telephone call, I think—well, it was through the cardinal's urging: "Mind your business, or you'll be walking the beat in Oshkosh someplace." That tells you. I think the sergeant either wasn't getting enough in the envelope or he *wanted* an envelope or something. But he was soon told to mind his business. It was the captain, I think; it was the top man. So they continued for several years and did extremely well, and of course it brought the parish right up. It was a great parish.

The 1960s, however, brought an abrupt end to an age of innocence and postwar optimism. Many young Irish-Americans in the 1960s identified less with Catholicism ever so slightly. As America became increasingly secular, discrimination on the basis of religious belief became a much less common feature of daily life for the Irish in Boston. At the same time, the Irish had become virtually indistinguishable from the Boston population at large. By the 1960s, as Seamus Mulligan puts it:

> The Irish weren't in your face. They figured out that they were able to be assimilated. The only way that you could tell an Irish person was by their name, because a lot of them had now been born in America. As a consequence, they were speaking with an American accent, from whatever area they came. Then with the advent of Kennedy, and then with the increased number of Irish-American kids having an opportunity to go to college, a sense of Irish pride began to emerge.

Able to blend in easily once the inherited brogues gave way to "bettah" ways of sounding like a Bostonian, the second and third generations began to climb high up the social ladder.

12

The Exodus

There were new players on the cultural stage on Dudley Street in the 1960s. During World War II, African-Americans from all parts of the rural United States migrated in large numbers to New England to work in its industrial plants, army posts, armories, and shipyards. Boston's black population rose from 23,000 in 1940 to more than 40,000 in 1950.[1] The traditionally small black community in the South End–Roxbury area began to expand into areas that had been exclusively white and, for the most part, Irish. This was met with much resistance in Irish neighborhoods in Dorchester, Jamaica Plain, Roslindale, and Hyde Park. A large black community also began to take root on Dudley Street.

Though the Irish had historically been discriminated against, they had never been exempt from their own strains of prejudice. Despite the efforts of a few liberal Irish social and political leaders, there had always been ample racial tension in Boston between the working Irish, Italians, Jews, and African Americans, for it seemed that every new ethnic group to arrive in Boston was moving into the low-rent areas that were already overflowing with Irish.[2]

Throughout the 1940s, Boston had been a segregated city, and Roxbury a multicultural (but primarily Caucasian) area where things were peaceful but only so long as ethnic and racial group lines were not crossed. Frank Devin recalls: "The Italians were down in one section. The Jewish people were about seven blocks up Blue Hill Ave. The Irish/Jewish line was at

Quincy Street, right off from Blue Hill Ave. There was a lot of animosity; there was not a lot of love between the areas in those days. But there were very few blacks in Roxbury in those days, just on two or three streets."

The cultural lines were observed and obeyed by young and old alike. The Irish steered clear of the fruit stands, fish markets, pharmacies, and delicatessens along Blue Hill Avenue, which cut through the city's ninety thousand-strong Jewish neighborhoods in Dorchester, Mattapan, and Roxbury. Throughout the 1940s, there were frequent skirmishes in Franklin Park between gangs of knife-wielding Irish and Jewish youths, and the Irish hatred of "Christ-killers" was condoned if not encouraged by the nationally syndicated anti-Semitic radio broadcasts of Father Charles Coughlin.[3]

Likewise, though Italians and Irish were both white, they did not mix either. Joanne McDermott explains:

> They were a different culture, mostly. In their area, down near the area we called the Prairie, down near Massachusetts Avenue in Roxbury, was a baseball field. My brother was allowed to go down there to play baseball and sports. I, on the other hand, and all my girlfriends were not allowed to go to the Prairie. Our parents didn't want us down there, because that was territory that they weren't sure of. The gang we called the Red Raiders lived down there, and they had a football team—but they were a different culture. For the most part, they were Italian.
>
> And, yes, they were at the dance halls, Hibernian and Intercolonial, and, yes, they did dance with us. In fact . . . it wasn't just Irish going to the dance halls. . . . A lot of times, they taught us how to dance, because they were very good dancers, unlike our Irish friends, who were kind of klutzy. The Italians could dance, and that was one of their things, and they knew that we were the nice girls, so they would dance with us, and that was it. They never tried to socialize, they never asked us out, or anything like that.

Through the 1940s and early 1950s, there had been only a small black population in the area, and blacks and whites appear to have lived with relative tolerance. Frank Storer remembers a friendly atmosphere, saying, "There was no problems all of the decades as I understand it; I never had problems. In fact, it was not uncommon to be on the street corner after the dance, two o'clock in the morning, and discuss music with black musicians. A very casual place, a congenial place, no problems whatsoever."

Musicians remember seeing families in homes near Dudley Street in the 1940s and early 1950s—black and white alike—dancing on their balconies to the music that poured out of the dance hall windows. The small black population moved quietly among the Irish, and there was little perception of threat on the busy streets of Dudley Square. Instead, there seemed to be a measured camaraderie in shops and restaurants. Slade's, a popular barbecue restaurant owned by a man named Renner Slade—a runaway slave, according to local legend—was frequented more by a white than a black crowd, according to Mr. Cappadona, a Roxbury resident.[4] Says Frank Storer:

> I remember one night down in Slade's, this black fella was our waiter. "I know a good Irish song," he said, "but you have to stand." We didn't know what he was talking about. But we said, okay, and we all stood up. He sang the Irish national anthem, and he sang it word for word, straight through. That's how commingled he was with the Irish crowd that used to go in there. He was privy to this stuff.

But urban renewal efforts sparked by the Housing Act of 1949 and led by the Boston Redevelopment Agency (BRA) evicted many blacks from their homes in the South End and demolished the properties to build fashionable housing for the middle class and wealthy. Instead of resettling these people into clean, decent homes, the city moved black families into hastily built public housing projects, notably the projects built by BRA contractors in Dudley Square.[5]

As the racial mix changed in the Dudley Square neighborhood, many Irish and Irish-American people felt that the area was no longer safe. The neighborhood had started to "change over," as they said, and many Irish began to steer clear of the neighborhood. According to Mickey Connolly:

> They were scared to go into the pubs. The Irish were coming in, but the Windsor Tap was the only place they would come in. Pete Lee bought it from Joe McPherson, and renamed it the Irish House. There was a couple of bars down the street, but there was no music or entertainment, and they were afraid to go there. But they come in, because, well, they had two big cops there. They had Frank McEiver there, who's six-foot-eight, and they had Joe Griffin, who was about six-six. They were on duty there every night. They had to be.

The perception of danger in Dudley Square may have differed from reality, however. Jack White, an Irish-American social worker and musician
who went to Dudley Street often in the late 1950s and 1960s, suspects that
the Irish-Americans' fears of blacks were unfounded. "In all the years I
went down there, I never saw a fight between blacks and whites. It was the
Irish who were fighting with each other," says White.[6]

However, not too far away, in Roxbury Crossing, where whites and
blacks lived in side-by-side projects, racial incidents were becoming com-
monplace in the early 1960s. Recalling one such incident, Dan Reidy, a
Roxbury native, says:

> This kid, one night, he was a roofer by trade, he got pushed one
> night, outside the door of a neighborhood bar. The extension
> project to our project was basically the black project. A guy came
> by and pushed Red—and Red had been drinking. Red turned
> around and saw it was a black kid. I guess the kid had said some-
> thing to him. Then you hear, bang, bang, bang, bang! The kid's
> running up the street. Red walks in, and he says, "I missed him."
> Everything was in real life, and everything was right at the mo-
> ment. Nobody said, "Geez, why did I do that?" People didn't care.
> They just did what they wanted to do, or *had* to do. It was just a
> tough group of people. This was on Station Street, which is down
> by Roxbury Crossing, at the junction of Columbus Avenue and
> Tremont Street. There was a set of unspoken rules, and you didn't
> cross them—illegal, but you didn't cross them.

The increasingly mixed racial scene in the Dudley Street area was to
many a sign that things were going downhill and Roxbury no longer belonged to the Irish—and was no longer as "pleasant" as it had once been.
The Irish generally agreed that the place had declined. A typical statement
from an anonymous speaker epitomizes it: "Roxbury was a lovely place in
its time, in its heyday. When I got here, it had gotten very mixed."

By the 1960s, the false promises of urban renewal gave way to the realization that the effort had been what the scholar Reebee Garofalo calls
"little more than neighborhood removal."[7] This realization sparked anger
and frustration in the city's black population. In the mid-1960s, race riots
in Roxbury permanently changed the perception of the area. Where once
people could and would stay on the streets all night without incident, now

the area was considered unsafe. Frank Storer describes the fear many felt as civil rights–era tensions soared:

> You wouldn't get a good dance down there because nobody would dare go down there. It was kind of dangerous there now. Maybe it wasn't as dangerous as we thought, but there were incidents that weren't there back in the fifties, in the early sixties. But now it was pretty well commonplace that they stopped having details in the dance hall. The cops weren't there anymore.

By 1963 and 1964, many said, "You wouldn't take the bus to Dudley Street anymore." The fact was that the population *had* changed, and many Irish people were uncomfortable being in places not only where the population was mixed but where they were a racial minority. The Irish were moving out, and as racial tension approached the snapping point, it was no longer as safe a neighborhood as it had been for the Irish.

The Beginning of White Flight

Discrimination and growing competition from new immigrant arrivals in Boston had historically forced the Irish to stick together in tight communities. One expression of this cultural cohesion was a vital musical life, and its most public platform, the Dudley Street dance halls. But as job opportunities increased and new ethnic groups arrived and took the entry-level jobs, the Irish were no longer at the base of the social ladder. The compulsion to stick together began to wane. The Irish community had "arrived," so to speak, and no sooner did it arrive than it completely scattered.

As new faces moved into the Dudley Street area—mostly African Americans from other parts of Boston and from the southern United States, as well as Cape Verdeans, West Indians, and Puerto Ricans—the Irish moved out. Recalls Joanne McDermott:

> I loved Roxbury. I stayed there till I was twenty-one, and then it was changing. I left around 1954. I often ask myself, why did South Boston stay an Irish community, as it has until very re-

cently? Why did Roxbury change so fast? Not everyone there owned their own house, that's part of it. And people who didn't own a house lived in an apartment, and when the houses started being bought out and they saw things changing, then they moved.

It was an exodus. My street, my neighbors, my friends—it seemed that they all moved out very rapidly. My mother was one of the last ones to go, because she didn't want to leave. I knew that we had to move, so I had to get my family to persuade her to move. It wasn't because things were happening. It was just because things felt so different. People were moving in who didn't speak English. They were coming in from various places, and it felt very strange to us because we had been such a close-knit community.

In Roxbury, the people coming in were the new immigrants, really. They were coming from the islands, and they would sit outside and play their Spanish music. For us, it was culture shock. And it wasn't crime. It was just culture shock. It was not the culture that we grew up with; [it was] so different for those of us who had been there all our lives. . . .

We moved to Dorchester first. A lot of people moved in to Dorchester. But we didn't go as a group. We were scattered around the Dorchester neighborhoods, so we never again had that close feeling. The next succession for most of the Irish people that I knew moved to Milton. That was the ultimate goal, to buy a house in Milton.

I didn't leave Roxbury because I hated it. I left Roxbury because we *had* to leave. It was *necessary*. No. I loved it. I still do. I'm totally emotionally attached to the people I grew up with. When we had our reunion two years ago, our high school reunion, it was incredible. We just felt so close.

The Irish who had served in World War II or the Korean War were helped along in their exodus by the GI Bill, which was signed into law by President Roosevelt in 1944 to provide education, training, and home loan guarantees for veterans. Many Irish hit the high road for suburban locales, where mass-produced houses were springing up like popcorn. Jobs in freshly built suburban industrial parks were easily accessible by new highways, and from 1950 to 1960, Boston's population dropped from 801,000 to 697,000, as many young people married and left the city for suburbs like Braintree, Quincy, Scituate, and Weymouth.[8]

There was yet another factor reducing attendance at the dances. The young people who had come to America after the war were coming of age. Many of them had married, and as Connie McEleney says, "Once people married, you'd never see them [in the dance halls] again." Jack Martin confirms this view, saying:

> In the late forties, early fifties, all these kids coming out from Ireland that were going to all these different dance halls, now they're here to stay. In the early days, it had been a group of singles, so the place was just bombing with people. But now what happens, they get married. They start having families. Well, you have families, and that's the end of the old dance hall. You know, you've made your scoop.

Despite the loving words that Roxbury natives have for their old neighborhood, moving out of Roxbury was a distinct status change. Frank Devin calls Roxbury

> kind of a landing spot. If you made a little bit more money, you went to Dorchester. It was the home of the lace-curtain Irish. The two-toilet Irish, as they were called. Southie was also a step up, and it kept its Irishness much longer. Jamaica Plain was a little bit of a step, and West Roxbury was a big step up. If you moved to West Roxbury, you were in Fat City. But I don't want to run down Roxbury because Roxbury was a great place to live. Absolutely the best. Everybody that got married in Roxbury, Dorchester, or Southie moved to Randolph, Canton, Plymouth, or something like that. Everybody. A few people moved west, like we did. If you could get there by the Boston el, you moved.

It was the inevitable "white flight" scenario. A Roxbury native, Frank Devin, sees the population outflow as merely a repeat of history:

> Obviously people move where they can afford. When my parents moved into Roxbury, Roxbury was where they could afford. And as long as Roxbury stayed the same way it was, it stayed at the same price. When any new minority moves in, *they* in turn moved

where they could afford. At that time, the minorities were down in Ruggles Street, down around where Northeastern [University] is. But all of Boston was rebuilding in the 1950s, and they were being forced to move. They saw affordable places up the street in Dudley, and they moved there, while the Irish who had been there were moving out.

Competition Increases

As crowds on Dudley Street began to decline in the late 1950s and early 1960s, promoters, who relied on admission fees for their survival, began to get intensely competitive. By this time, says Frank Storer:

> There was more talent than there were halls to play in, and more promoters, where in the early days there were only a few people who would take the chance to invest in halls and leases and bands. I think the whole scene was becoming more affluent, and there were people around who were taking more chances, saying, "Oh, I can do this; there's money to be made there."
>
> In the early 1960s, there was a good four-year period there where all kinds of bands were playing here, and all sorts of factions breaking up, one band going there, one guy going over here; competition was brewing. It just fractured the whole thing. What was once a big comradeship, now there was different bands competing all over the place—and all good in their own right.

Early descriptions of Dudley Street paint a picture of a happily thriving scene, but later descriptions show signs of Dudley Street in decline, with tension brewing among both musicians and dance hall promoters. With fewer jobs to go around, increased competition, and decreased camaraderie, Gene Frain and other musicians saw the need for a musicians' union. He says:

> Among the accordion players, there was an awful race to try and undercut each other. Me and Caples, for a long time we tried to get a union going; that way we could hold the prices at all one thing. The only thing is, this was going on for a long time, and

the guys that were in the union were all undercutting each other. Then we decided we were going to elect officers. There was a little money in the kitty. Not much, but a little.

Everyone wanted to run! Me and Billy said to ourselves, "We'll take the money out to the bar, a little Polish club not too far from Dudley Street, and we'll drink up the whole kitty. No one wanted to run after all the money was gone. We gave up on the union. They were going to cut each other's throats.

Dance hall promoters began to go to great lengths to build their crowds, sometimes at the expense of other halls. Storer describes one such tactic:

Occasionally, the dirty fighting was going. They'd have people out in the street. To get to the Intercolonial, you'd have to walk right by the front door of the Hibernian Hall. You had people saying, "Oh, did you hear about down the street? They lost electricity, there's no dance down there tonight." And they'd say, "Oh, let's go up here, then," you know. You'd have a barker up further, saying, "Don't believe what they tell you down there! There *is* a dance down here!" It got like that.

The story from this point gets convoluted—or lost to a conspiracy of silence. Few who were there will discuss specific details of what was perhaps the most frightening story of the Dudley Street era, an incident of vandalism in which someone attempted to bring in a hired gun to torch a hall. Frank Storer tells the story this way:

See, there was a scare here in the hall; there was gasoline; they tried to torch it. I remember one night, some men in plain clothes came in with a flashlight and started looking around in the piano. I found out later, they were looking for a bomb. I had to play that thing, and they're looking for a bomb in there! It was a result of rivalry and competition between the Intercolonial and Hibernian. Different factions were running the halls, and it got hot and heavy, so we don't know who did what.

Gene Frain was also familiar with this story. Frain says:

That happened near the end. . . . I think they found the bomb in Intercolonial. They claim they found it. No one ever got nabbed for it; there was all kinds of suspicion. I heard that if it had gone off, a lot of people would've got killed. Anyway, no one ever found out which of the halls did it. It had to do with someone running the dances. It was the competition. The hall was getting too many people; the guys that ran the other hall figured they were getting cheated. At that time, there were so many of them over there, competition was kind of stiff.

Joe Derrane had returned from living away from Boston for a time to find a completely changed atmosphere on Dudley Street. He had been hired to run the band at the time, and describes the way the incident affected him:

> I worked in New York for two years—when I came back, this guy wanted me to open up Hibernian. I put a ten- or eleven-piece band in there, and man, it was crazy; the thing only lasted four weeks.
>
> He took off for California owing everybody and his brother, and I got stuck with four weeks' pay I owed the band. The guys were very good to me, saying, "Don't worry about it." But nobody's seen the guy since. However, that's neither here nor there.

In this case, competition—and greed—exceeded the strength of multi-generational kinship ties from the homeland. Though the identity of the culprit was never proven, everyone believed it was Christy O'Brien.[9] A relative of O'Brien's recalls the day he heard about the bombing attempt:

> Christy O'Brien came out here [from Ireland], and he was going to seminary, in college to be a priest. As a matter of fact, he had gotten to that point of having received the round collar. Then he started a business, travel and televisions, in Somerville, on Elm Street. He was doing quite well in that; then he rented the Intercolonial. At the same time, Tom Gallagher had been here, another entrepreneur, since forty-eight or forty-nine. He came here when he was about sixteen—maybe even forty-seven. He had rented the Hibernian.
>
> They were both vying for the patrons. They were doing various things to bring the people. And of course, the people would swing. Every six months, there'd be a swing. They'd get tired of going to the Intercolonial, and they'd choose to go to the Hibernian, and so on and so forth.
>
> But it's interesting to note that Christy O'Brien's brother, or his

father, and Tom Gallagher's father, they lived side by side; they came from the same village at home in Ireland. They worked in "co.," meaning each of them had a horse, so when you needed to double up, they both worked together. And the sad part about it, O'Brien got the idea that if the other hall wasn't there, he would do well. And he hired somebody from New York to come down and do away with it. It didn't work. The guy, of course, was caught, and of course, he implicated O'Brien.

So he's now in California, O'Brien is. And he's a car salesman out there. When he left Boston, he had the wrath of the people who enjoyed going dancing, and the families that were intertwined.[10]

After that, efforts were made to resurrect the Dudley Street crowds, and a new owner bought the Intercolonial and tried to modernize it, refurbishing the bar and, by all accounts, doing a beautiful job—but the crowds weren't coming into Dudley Street, and someone stood to lose an awful lot of money. The bar was reopened by the McGary family, the patriarch of which, Buster McGary, controlled most of the liquor flow in South Boston. According to one account:

Somebody decided to revitalize Dudley Street, and he was half crooked, anyway. He tried everything, but there was no way [the crowds] were coming back. It was gone for good. He got the liquor license for the place down on Dudley Street—his father was kind of a crook, but he was in with one of the politicians, and they arranged for him to get the license. That would have been early 1960s. He thought they were going to make a comeback but it just never did happen. He stayed till about sixty-five, sixty-six, in a very anemic fashion. He lost a fortune. You see, it was a transformation. Dudley Street went all urban. The projects came in, and people were scared for their lives of the projects. The projects were a very, very bad experiment in America.[11]

Whatever happened in what hall, and whoever may have done it, the incident represents a desperate attempt to eke some profit from what was already a dying scene. However, no fire or bomb could have caused the lasting damage produced by a much bigger time bomb: the racial tension that erupted on Dudley Street in the late 1960s.

Winds of Change: Civil Rights Comes Home

The year 1965 was pivotal in American history. Several events of the civil rights movement triggered unrest in black communities nationwide: Malcolm X was assassinated; Martin Luther King Jr. led activists on a march from Selma to Montgomery, Alabama; race riots broke out in the Watts neighborhood of Los Angeles; and the phrase "black power," coined by the writer Stokely Carmichael and laden with meaning for the Black Panther Party, entered the political lexicon.[12]

On June 3, 1967, rioting reached Boston. The riot began after protesters were violently removed by police from the Grove Hall welfare office, which touched off two nights of rioting, looting, and burning in Roxbury. Ten months later, Martin Luther King Jr.'s murder, on April 4, 1968, set off another wave of anger. At 1:00 P.M. the following day, two hundred black youths left the YMCA on Dudley Street and marched to Blue Hill Avenue. The crowd quickly grew to nearly eight hundred as it reached Dudley Station. Smaller groups broke off from the march and stormed into white-owned businesses, ordering store owners to close in honor of King. Forty businesses were looted and burned in Roxbury that day. The following day, an activist group known as the Black United Front issued a long list of demands in front of a crowd of almost five thousand black people in Franklin Park. Among the demands was that all white-owned businesses within the black community be closed until further notice.[13]

Mickey Connolly was playing in the lounge on the first floor of the Intercolonial during the riots. The lounge had been bought and renovated, and the new owner had spent thousands of dollars bringing it up to date and converting it into more of a restaurant setup, with booths and live music. Though the bar was attractive, very few Irish would venture into Dudley Square anymore, and there was nothing any bar owner could do to change that. The forces of change were simply too powerful for any single man's marketing. The night of the riots was to be the last night of the new Intercolonial's short last hurrah. Says Connolly:

> They had rioted at Grove Hall in Dorchester, the blacks, and they
> marched down the street to Dudley Street, which is about five
> miles. And they burned everything as far as Dudley, tipped over
> buses and set fire to them, burned police cars and chased all the

cops out of there. That night we were playing on Dudley Street. At about ten-thirty, there were five of us on the stage, and a guy came in with a big revolver, and he says, "Who's the leader?" I said, "I am." I was going to tell him Larry. [Laughs] He says, "I'll give you fifteen minutes to get your equipment out of here. Because we're going to rip this place apart, and in the meantime, let's throw three of these boxes in from the bar," and they're packing all the booze. I got away with one bottle and we drank out in my car. [Laughs.] They even took a television out of the lounge where we were.

That was the one night my wife, Cathy, and my cousin from New York came in to Dudley Street, and they went out and they hid in my station wagon, locked the doors. One cop got shot, but it didn't kill him. Brendan Tonra and I carried him into the Irish House, and waited for an ambulance. He lived, though. He was a Scotchman.

We never went back to Dudley Street. A week after, there were bars on the doors. That was the end of Roxbury. The night they rioted there, that was the last night that we played there. Of course, that didn't make me leave the music. We played for years after that.

The social change brought on by the black population's rightful and aggressive demands for social justice—culminating in the Roxbury riots—coincided with the beginning of the unraveling of the tightly knit Boston Irish community. The two occurrences were not necessarily connected, but many do believe they were—that it was the increasing strength of the African American population in Dudley Square that led to the Irish move to the suburbs. One thing is certain: the Irish community's economic gains made the move possible—this was one of the first times in Boston Irish history that they could *afford* to move. The question remains: Would they have moved, were there no influx of black people in Roxbury?

The consensus seems to be: no. The following anonymous comments indicate a reserved acceptance of the change in Roxbury. Made more than thirty years after the fact, they hint at the long-term resentment that the civil rights movement was to bring about between the Irish and black communities in Boston:

> Yeah, it stirred the pot up. Whether it was good or bad, I suppose it was good. In the long run, I suppose it was good. It was prob-

ably due. How it was presented, maybe it wasn't right. But I think, I'm looking because I'm on the short end of the stick here, I just lost a job, reliability, in an area that I used to carouse around in, all night long if you wanted to. Now all of a sudden you can't even go near the place.

The Final Blow: Immigration Restriction

The same year that civil rights activities reached their peak, a 1965 amendment to the Immigration and Nationality Act began to take effect. The new amendment did away with immigration quotas by nation, and gave preference to immigrants with skills needed in the United States. The amendment, signed by Lyndon B. Johnson in 1965, had gotten its momentum during the Kennedy years, thanks to the close relationship of Ireland's Taoiseach (President) Éamon de Valera, Boston's Cardinal Richard J. Cushing, and John F. Kennedy. Ireland seemed to be educating its youth only to see them emigrate, leaving the old people to take care of the country. There was a massive brain drain of youth who could have helped the country make a successful transition from a rural to a modern economy. A strong Irish and Catholic lobby encouraged Kennedy to support the legislation in its early stages.

Once passed, the legislation took three years to take full effect. By 1968, it had put an end to Irish immigration and, in effect, to the Irish dance halls. Rebecca Miller asserts that the end of immigration was the final nail in the coffin for dance halls: "With no new audiences of young, unattached immigrants in search of a night life, the dance halls closed, one by one, and the showband era ended."[14] As if on cue, on January 26, 1968, the last direct successor to the Dudley Street dance halls, the New State Ballroom, closed its doors.

When the dance halls closed, musicians went their separate ways. The music world had changed radically. The youth who had patronized the dance halls in the 1960s had other things on their minds now. Of that time, Liam Keyes says:

> Everything was changing: out in San Francisco, the flower children and all that. I came over to an America that was everybody

had a crew cut, a war orphan's haircut. Then the Beatles came along with what they said was tremendously long hair. It went on and on, all the rebels and the Vietnam protests and the hair and the beards—all the social changes.

Terry Landers also sees the Beatles as having changed the tastes of dance hall patrons. "The 1960s were new, young crowds," he says. "The Beatles changed the whole trend of the music scene. I went in with the Tara Céilí Band, and they'd be all crazy around the floor for the popular songs. It was all modern they were into—no traditional music whatsoever. Just the Siege of Ennis, that's all."

Joanne McDermott says that the dispersion of the Irish community in Roxbury was just a symptom of the disintegration of American society as a whole: "The sixties changed Americans' way of looking at things. People got more isolated. Innocence and trust disappeared. By the seventies, it was kind of gone. I don't see community happening today the way it did for us then, that same closeness, that same trust."

By 1960, the wave of immigration that filled Boston and other East Coast cities with young Irish immigrants had washed ashore and receded, and an economic boom in Ireland in the 1960s kept many at home who otherwise might have left. Immigration slowed significantly, not picking up again until the 1980s. Dance hall crowds diminished, musicians left the scene, and the halls closed, one by one. By the early 1960s, Dudley Street had all but died out, and the cohesive Irish community that had defined Roxbury for more than a century was gone. The closing of the last dance halls in the mid-1960s was the end of a golden era for Irish dance music in America.

13

And the Band Played On

The radical social change of the 1960s set the secular age into motion, and it began to undermine the strength of the cohesive parish-based Irish community that had defined Roxbury for almost a century. With it went the colorful cultural expressions of the Boston Irish—including the Dudley Street dance halls. Still, some of the dance hall musicians remained active in traditional music, though the scene grew smaller. Some musicians sold their instruments. Still others followed the showband circuit, while others found new musical styles altogether.

With the demise of the dance halls and the rise of smaller showbands, fans of Irish music searched out other spots. While new venues such as Ireland's 32 in West Roxbury, Kilgarriff's Café in Jamaica Plain, the Roxbury Grill, and the Arbida Club in Jamaica Plain attracted young Irish, the rest of American youth were tuned to the folk revival of the 1960s. As always, it wasn't long before the Irish adopted the new sounds, as well, says Liam Keyes.

> You had these folksingers, they'd be down at the pubs singing, and the people would be singing all these new—well, old—ballads that had been rehashed. The old Irish tunes were almost dead till the Clancy Brothers brought them back. Then in Ireland you had the Dubliners, the Chieftains, and the Wolftones, all these—the Fureys. The standard became so high that you just didn't get some guy going in with a guitar and banging out a song anymore.

Spurred by the growing folk revival in the United States, the Irish balladeers the Clancy Brothers touched off a new era in Irish pride and a huge
revival in folk-style performance of Irish music that lasted for some forty
years. When the Clancy Brothers were invited to be on the *Ed Sullivan
Show* in 1961, they took Irish music from showband to folk on a national
scale. Seamus Mulligan recalls:

> All of a sudden, the Irish came out of the closet. That's when the
> Kingston Trio and Bob Dylan were doing the folk. The Clancy
> Brothers were looking for an acting job, so they were down in
> New York and were hanging around the theater district, and got
> jamming with these guys, and remembered all the songs that their
> mothers had taught them. And then Tommy Makem joined them,
> who brought with him a huge portfolio of the Irish songs.
>
> It became popular to be Irish. Ed Sullivan invited them to the
> *Ed Sullivan Show*, and they walked in, and they had little cases
> with them with their tuxedos and asked, "Where are our dressing
> rooms to change into our tuxedos?" These guys were wearing
> Aran hand-knits—and someone said, "Oh, no, no," and puts them
> onstage. At the time, they were one of the first acts going onstage
> without a tuxedo. Hand-knit sweaters just proliferated, you
> wouldn't believe it! And everybody began to sing the songs.
>
> Next thing, they're the hottest thing in Carnegie Hall. All of a
> sudden, we have the Wolftones, the Dublin City Ramblers, we
> have the Dubliners, we have Christy Moore, we have the Fureys—
> I mean, they all just locked in and grew in leaps and bounds. And
> we came up with a kind of Irish folk pop, which took the country
> over and swept the decks of all of the traditional music, and there
> was a complete transformation in the lives of everybody who was
> making a living in this kind of music.

As dance hall gigs disappeared, musicians were forced to change their
musical mastery to other genres. Others gave up playing altogether. Gene
Frain indicates that the latter was the case for the jazz musicians who had
made their way to Dudley Street after the swing ballrooms shut down:
"They were all more into jazz than anything else. They all sold their instruments, as far as I knew, after the dance halls shut down. Many of them
weren't too interested in the Irish music, anyway; they were there for the
bucks for a couple of nights a week." Many other musicians kept playing,

but the venues changed. Where once it had been strictly dance halls, now it was social clubs, weddings, and parties.

Frank Storer's band, the Shannonaires, which had been founded during the showband era, continued to perform regularly until 1993. Storer updated his instrument—from a piano to a keyboard—but otherwise the repertoire remained more or less the same. Storer tells of the day he decided it was time to pull the plug on his keyboard at last:

> I got called on the phone one night from this girl who said, "Will you play for my wedding?" I said, "Sure," and got out the book, and booked it. Now, my brother had passed away at this point, so we no longer had a saxophone in the band. So I said, "Okay, have you heard the band?" She said, "No, I haven't, but my mother has." I said, "Your mother has. Well, I'd like you to come hear the band. What your mother likes, you may not like." So I figure I'm talking to at least a twenty-two-year-old, anyway, and her mother has to be at least forty or fifty. And she says, "Oh, no, I don't have to; my mother says you're very good." I said, "That's all well and good, but your mother's probably from a different era." Well, the girl said, "No, it's okay. She heard you recently, and she still likes you." She *still* likes you! That was the key. I said, "What do you mean she *still* likes us?" "Oh," she said, "you played for her wedding."
>
> I turned to myself, and I said, "My God, have I been around that long? I'm playing for the children's weddings?" Maybe it's time for me to step aside. It was the first time I realized I was getting old. I said, "Wow, that means I've been out here for well over thirty-five years, and now I'm playing for the *children's* weddings. Next thing it'll be the *grandchildren's* weddings. I've got to get outta here." So I got a funny streak this time. I said, "Even though I played for your mother's wedding, I'd still like you to come and hear the band. Next Saturday evening at the McKeon Post in Dorchester. Come over around ten o'clock, and we'll be in full swing playing the dance music, and out of the formalities." She said, "Well, how will I know you?" I said, "I'll be the one with the walker!"

Mickey Connolly's band also continued to perform for years after the dance halls closed, but he had to expand its scope far beyond Boston:

We played right through the 1960s, but not in the Intercolonial. Weddings, we did everything. Field days. I busted my rear end playing for step dancers, myself and Larry. And that's an unthankful job, I'll tell you. They want you there at ten o'clock in the morning, feises, out in fields. Out in the hot sun. It'd do a number on you, sitting out in the hot sun. Paddy Cronin and myself, Larry, we used to play a lot of them. Brendan Tonra, flute and accordion, fiddle and accordion. But oh, God, come five or six o'clock in the evening, they'd be still going. I often packed up and left.

We used to go out of town, Hartford, Springfield, Windsor, Connecticut, Holyoke, Mass., Cape Cod, and a couple more, for the dances. Five- or six-piece, you know. We used to come home, five of us, at two o'clock. I'd say, come on, have a drink. They'd come in, sit here with me. And the next thing, Martin McDonough would have the accordion, and Larry with the fiddle. Cathy would get up out of bed and come up with sandwiches and tea. And the next thing you know, you see three little white heads looking over the top of the partition. My three kids would sneak around to see—not a sound out of them, though. They'd get the word from Cathy, then: Upstairs! We had a beautiful time. A lot of memories, you know.

One particular snowy night after a performance in Hartford, the band was standing outside in the parking lot discussing music. This night, Bobby Gardiner, an accordion player from county Clare, and Frank Storer had come along with Mickey and the band. The discussion began to get heated, and Bobby got upset, so he pulled out his accordion and began to play a reel. Perhaps anger suited him, for he sounded so good that Mickey Connolly asked him to play another and another. Meanwhile, stragglers from the dance had joined them and started to do a Siege of Ennis in the snowy parking lot. Bobby was excited now, and he got up on top of the roof of a car and continued to play, while a pyramid of snow began to accumulate on his head.

Next thing the band knew, a crowd of people staying in the hotel next door began to come out into the parking lot in their tuxes and fur coats, and scuffed along with the dance until the police finally came along and put an end to the late-night merriment, and the musicians packed up and drove back to Boston.

Larry Reynolds and Billy Caples, with John Curran and Pat and Mary Barry of Kerry, went on to found the Boston chapter of Comhaltas Ceoltóirí Éireann (Irish Musicians Association) in 1975, to promote traditional Irish music, dance, and song in New England. The Comhaltas Ceoltóirí Éireann, founded in Ireland in 1951, had started bringing tours of young musicians to American cities and had notified Paddy Cronin of the first tour, in 1972. The following year Cronin, Reynolds, and others lobbied to bring the Comhaltas concert to Boston. Reynolds notes that

> the music was becoming purer again. There was such a revival in Ireland, it was infectious. It was spreading here, because there were great musicians coming out from Ireland. Seamus Connolly, Paddy O'Brien, Joe Burke were on the first Comhaltas tours in America. They had a tremendous lineup. There were tremendous musicians coming out, the cream of the musicians. You were getting a very pure strain of traditional music.

With his partners, Reynolds petitioned to start a branch of the organization in Boston, and soon Chairman Diarmuid Ó Cathain of Ireland and Bill McEvoy of New York arrived in Boston to install Pat Barry as chairman of the branch and Reynolds as vice chairman. Billy Caples took the role of secretary and music director. After a couple of years, Reynolds took over the chairmanship and has maintained the role ever since.

An active member of Comhaltas was the flute player Gene Preston—affectionately referred to as "the boss" by its members. Born in 1902 to a musical family in Ballymote, county Sligo, he emigrated to America in 1928 and joined Dan Sullivan's Shamrock Band. He returned to Ireland in 1932 but in 1958 came back to Boston where he was one of the founding members of the Connaught Céilí Band. He remained active in Comhaltas Ceoiltóirí Éireann until his death, in 1988.

It is widely acknowledged that Comhaltas musicians have been critical in keeping Irish music alive in Boston and beyond; the Boston branch of Comhaltas boasts the largest membership of any branch in North America. The organization produced its own record in 1982, titled *We're Irish Still*. According to Skip Toomey:

> Billy Caples, Larry Reynolds, and Seamus Connolly ignited a renaissance in Irish music with founding the Comhaltas. It is incalculable how much time and energy these guys put into the music.

They were amazing to start the Comhaltas. They knew they had a
mission. It was a spiritual kind of thing, to whet the appetites of
these kids to propagate the culture.

Along with his brother Johnny, Billy Caples was ever-present in the Boston music scene, making frequent appearances not only at dance halls but
also in the music clubs, church-sponsored events, pubs, and kitchen rackets until his death, in 1986. Even at his own funeral, his legacy continued
to bring good humor to all who knew him. Toomey says:

> When Billy died, we were at his house in Arlington after the
> funeral. He had a little room to the side where he would give
> lessons. I was in there with Larry Reynolds and Jimmy Kelly.
> The bell rang, or someone knocked, and I answered. This great
> big fair-haired guy, about six-two and two hundred twenty
> pounds, was standing there with an instrument box hanging
> from his left hand. He looked like a cop, but he was very meek.
> He was probably about fifty or something—I was young, and he
> seemed old to me at the time. He looked absolutely puzzled.
> But my antenna went up: that's when people get robbed, during
> funerals. He said, "'Tis a weddin'?" I said, "No, it's a funeral,"
> and he whispered, "Who died?" And I told him Bill. And he
> said, "Oh, Jaysus! I'm just here for me lesson!" So Jimmy took a
> swig of his beer and said, "Well, why don't you come in and
> muck it up for us?" because that's what Billy used to say to his
> students all the time. It was like his trademark line: "Sit down and
> muck up the tune for me." Billy would have gotten a big kick out
> of that.

Mickey Connolly and Larry Reynolds have remained fast friends, and
Irish music has been a soundtrack for their friendship. After some forty
years, neither has lost his sense of humor. According to Connolly:

> I had a stroke a while back, and I was under for thirty days. Larry
> and his wife, Phyllis, used to come out here to see me when I was
> in the hospital. He said, "Jeez, you were thirty days gone! How
> did it feel?" I said, "I was up above there. There was a fella playing
> the clarinet." Larry asked me, "What was his name?" I said,
> "That's the archangel." Larry said to me, "What did he say?" I
> said, "He told me, 'Go down, and come back the next day and

Joe "The People's Choice" Joyce (right) still plays with his gloves on, as proven by this photo from the South Boston St. Patrick's Day parade, 2003. Howie Winrow, left. (From the library of Joe and Karin Joyce.)

bring the accordion.'" Well, they laughed. Larry said, "You'll make it because you've got the sense of humor."

Today arthritis interferes with Connolly's ability to play the accordion, but Reynolds is still the anchor of regular weekly sessions in the Boston area, and he appears leading the Comhaltas musicians at dances, festivals, and special concerts year-round.

Connolly and Reynolds's bandmate, Brendan Tonra, has continued to perform and to compose. He is widely recognized as a living legend in traditional Irish music, and his tunes are widely known and played in traditional Irish sessions worldwide. He is best known for his original jig "Tonra's," which was made famous when recorded by Séan Maguire in the 1960s. The recording was played all over Ireland—and in its travels the jig has acquired numerous aliases, including (but surely not limited to) "Tone Row's," "Tone Roe," "Toner's," and "Tundra's."

Tonra was inducted into the Comhaltas Ceoltóirí Éireann Northeast Regional Hall of Fame in 2000. In 2002 he was recognized by Ireland's Irish-language television station TG4 with a National Traditional Music Award and as composer of the year; his contributions to Irish traditional music were thereby set alongside those of such past honorees as the uillean piper Paddy Keenan, the whistle player Mary Bergin, the flute player Matt Molloy, and the fiddler Tommy Peoples. Tonra's original compositions are published in two volumes, *A Musical Voyage with Brendan Tonra* and *The Music of Brendan Tonra*. His music has been recorded by Séan Maguire, Siona, Liverpool Céilí Band, Catherine McEvoy, Paddy Canny, Seamus and Martin Connolly, Marcas O'Murchu, Desie Donnelly, and Seamus Tansey.

As for Joe Derrane, he changed his musical direction completely when Dudley Street began to die out. He says he felt that there was a two-year period in which it was as if the scene were being "slowly bled to death." Shortly thereafter, Derrane started studying harmony and arranging with a teacher at Schillinger House (later to become the Berklee College of Music) in order to broaden his musical repertoire in preparation for a change of venue and musical style. "When the Dudley Street demise happened, I really had to jump on this," Derrane says. He adds that the barrooms held no attraction for him as a performance venue. "I got married in fifty-five," he says, "and didn't want to play in the bars as the ballroom scene died out. I didn't want to be playing for some drunk in the corner."[1]

At that time, Derrane's journey veered away from Irish music altogether.

The Irish and American flags emblazoned on Joe Derrane's accordion in this publicity photo from the early 1990s show that Derrane identifies with his mixed ethnic heritage. (From the library of Frank Storer.)

In an interview with Seamus Mulligan, he said that he felt that his livelihood had been ripped away when the dance halls ended. Derrane talked about the halls' demise and the years that followed to Mulligan, host of the radio program "A Feast of Irish Music," on 95.9 WATD:

> It upset my whole life at the time, really. This was a major part of my income. By that time—I got married in 1955, and then there were the children, and then there was the house, so I had this economic responsibility that I had to meet, and there were no places left for us to play. Oh, you'd get an odd gig here or there, but that was not sufficient. I couldn't get by on that.
>
> So I had to do something, and music was the thing that I loved the most and the thing that I did the best. I thought about it long and hard, and Ann, my wife, and I, we talked about it and talked about it and turned it upside down and sideways, examining everything, and the only thing that made sense for me was to say, "Well, I've got to play music, but I'll have to do something else." So I sold my button box, and I bought a new piano accordion. I had been dabbling in piano accordion for a while, but nothing serious, but at that point, I had to get deadly serious. I committed myself to a very, very rigid course of study. Then I went into the pop field, then I was doing jazz, and swing, and Dixieland stuff, Latin, a lot of ethnic stuff, Polish, Jewish, and Italian. Even though I tried desperately to get that piano accordion going in the Irish circles, there was a kind of reluctance on the part of the people to accept it. They just didn't like it. They wanted the button box if they were going to listen to Irish accordion.
>
> A lot of people back then, and even some that are still left today, seem to feel that I left Irish music. Actually, it would be more accurate to say that Irish music left us—myself and the other people that played down there. It seems like I was driven further and deeper into the pop field, and the pop field became quite successful for me. I was very, very busy, so I stayed with that for a long, long time. [But] by the middle to late seventies, you couldn't sell a piano accordion. Brides didn't want it for their weddings, and it just was given an awful bad reputation. I had to go synthesizer and electronic piano keyboard. I did that until the late eighties, but then I said, "That's it. I've had enough"—I enjoyed it, but my first

love was and always will be the button box and traditional Irish music. So I just packed the whole thing in. . . .

But then, something happened that changed my life. Paddy Noonan, the then-owner of Rego Records, was on a nostalgia kick. He wanted to reissue some of the old records and the old music material that had been recorded in the forties. He bought the rights to just about everything that the old Copley label had. He felt that my music would be perfect for a CD.

Well, my God, those recordings just took off. They created a whole wave of interest. Earle Hitchner, who writes for the *Irish Echo* in New York, came across this, and it intrigued him. I guess he just loved it. (Hitchner later discovered, through fiddler Seamus Connolly of Boston College, that Derrane was still alive and living outside Boston, but not playing—and apparently had no interest in reviving his performing career. This piqued Hitchner's interest, and he telephoned Joe and conducted a very long interview.)

He was amazed at that time to find out that not only was I not playing at all, but I didn't even have a button accordion. He was saying, "Well, when are you going to come back?" This was in 1993. I said, "My God, I'm sixty-three years old, I don't see myself coming back! I'd never play like that again." But he spoke to me for three hours on the telephone—a man I had never met. He told me he could hear a change in my voice when we talked about traditional Irish music and the accordion. He felt that the fire still burned brightly and that if I wanted to bad enough, I could do this if anybody could.

That stuck with me, and I started practicing then, and a little more, and a little more. In the meantime, my friend Jack Martin had given me his old button accordion. Finally I got a call to do the Wolf Trap Arts Festival, the traditional festival down in Washington the following year, 1994. (Earle Hitchner had encouraged festival organizer Mike Denney to invite Derrane to appear at the festival.) They wanted me to come down and talk about my life, where I had been, what I had done, and what I was doing now, that type of thing. I said, "Well, I'm not all that good at talking. Usually I prefer to play." And before I knew it, he said, "You're on. Somebody will call you in a couple weeks."

At that point, all I had was this man's name. I didn't have a telephone number or anything. What I saw was one last performance on the button box, you know, to put a final cap on everything and what a way to go out. I committed myself to a very, very rigid schedule of practicing. Six, seven hours a day, seven days a week. I had set aside certain tunes that I figured I could get a handle on, and I worked out enough material to do about an hour and a half of playing.

I took the stage down there, and they got the great Felix Dolan to play piano for me. I had put stuff on tape, with an awful lot of mistakes and flaws in it, but sent it down to him, and he worked on it at that end in New York. I met him on the stage at Wolf Trap National Park for the Performing Arts in Vienna, Virginia. We did a full, one-hour, full-bore concert set. And when it was finished, people were standing and crying, I was crying, my wife was crying. My son and my daughter were there. They had never heard me play button box, and they were crying, and my God, it was the most emotional day. When it was all done, I thought that was it.

But when I went to leave the stage, standing there at the exit was this woman named Wendy Newton. It turns out that she's the owner of Green Linnet Records, and she identified herself and asked me to record for her label. Instinctively, I said, "Yeah, sure." "Fine, we'll be in touch. We'll talk about a contract, and you'll have to build a budget," and so forth, and that was it. Well, that album led to a second album. Then I became a free agent. Shanachie wanted me to do an album for them, and I did. That's *The Tie That Binds*. Then finally, this most recent one, which just came out the end of this March or April [2002], *Ireland's Harvest*, with Frankie Gavin and Brian McGrath. We did that one on the Maple Shade label down in Upper Marlborough.

Roxbury's Fall and Rise

When the Irish left Roxbury, businesses, jobs, opportunity, and government interest and resources went with them. It seemed that the city had completely abandoned the new residents of Dudley Square. What happened over the next forty years is a critical chapter in the history of a changing city.

The neighborhood's racial demographics had changed from 90 percent white in 1950 to 40 percent in 1970 and 7 percent in 1990. As the Dudley Street area became home to a large community of African American, Latino, and Cape Verdean people over thirty years beginning in the late 1950s, systematic disinvestment, abandonment, and arson turned the area into a wasteland of empty lots full of illegally dumped toxic chemicals, abandoned cars, rusting appliances, household and construction debris, and other garbage. Residents struggled with the consequences of discrimination: unemployment, extreme poverty, and unsafe living conditions. In their introduction to the book *Streets of Hope*, Peter Medoff and Holly Sklar describe the city's treatment of Roxbury: "This inner-city neighborhood, like so many around the country, was treated like an outsider city: separate, unequal, and disposable."[2]

Widespread arson in the 1960s and 1970s, under arson-for-profit schemes that "allowed the city to receive insurance and tax deductions on rebuilding in the interest of 'urban redevelopment'"[3] left an estimated 840 lots vacant and earned Roxbury the tragic title of "arson capital of the nation." By the 1980s and 1990s, the poverty rate in the Dudley Street area was double Boston's average, and income was half that of the city as a whole. In 1984 frustrated yet hopeful Dudley residents stood up to resist the complete decline of the neighborhood by forming the Dudley Street Neighborhood Initiative (DSNI), a resident-driven movement to revitalize the Dudley Street area and put the power to create a thriving, vital community neighborhood in the hands of residents.

Residents gained control over a significant portion of the 1,300 parcels of abandoned land in the neighborhood by convincing Boston city government authorities to grant the community the power of eminent domain. In addition, the Neighborhood Initiative's 1986 community-wide "Don't Dump on Us" campaign was victorious in getting the city of Boston to clean up vacant lots and tow abandoned cars. Since the formation of the DSNI in 1984, 600 of the 1,300 vacant lots have been transformed into sites for nearly three hundred new homes, a town common, gardens, urban agriculture, parks, and playgrounds; three hundred older housing units have been rehabbed, business continues to grow, and rebuilding continues.

Conclusion

There was this story of two pipers, Brown and Murphy. One of them was a pipe maker. They played a concert together, and one of them squeaked a few times during the concert. After the concert, he said to the other one, "I'm just not the man I used to be." And the other replied, "You never were."

— Gene Frain

From the Truman era through Korea until Kennedy and up through the days of the civil rights movement, the Dudley Street dance hall floors were the platform on which old and new thrived together. There, Boston's Irish community established its identity, welcomed its new, fell in love, nurtured its cultural leaders, and revived and then redefined traditional music and dance. Dudley Street dance halls connected Boston's resident Irish nationals and Irish-Americans to the motherland while fully absorbing them in their new American home.

Though immigrants from Ireland arrived and felt that they had stepped back in musical time, in reality the dance hall bands combined musical innovation and tradition in a way that had widespread appeal among the immigrant population and helped to preserve a musical tradition that was temporarily out of vogue in Ireland.

The musical tastes of Irish people have expanded in countries the world over, wherever the Irish have gone during four centuries of constant emigration. The continually evolving forms of Irish traditional music reflect the ways in which the Irish at home and abroad have synthesized outside influences into the Irish experience. The dance halls show that the Irish, in the words of the scholar Gearóid Ó hAllmhuráin, "have ways to keep the best of the new, and discard the rest."[1]

The nontraditional elements of dance hall music were palatable to the Irish in America precisely because the bands offered just the right balance of old and new styles. American Irish dance hall music contained enough familiar elements to be Irish yet also offered the modern popular sounds favored by the increasingly cosmopolitan Irish on both sides of the Atlantic. Though the bands might play only a few Irish jigs or reels each night, traditional instruments such as the accordion, fiddle, and flute had a strong presence, giving the ballroom sound a distinctly traditional Irish lilt.

What is widely known as "traditional Irish music" today is different than what it was even fifty years ago. Today's Irish music seems to fit as naturally in Symphony Hall as yesterday's Irish music fit in the kitchen. Today's Irish music also thrives in Boston's small theaters and in nightclubs across the Charles River, where young Irish bands perform tight, sophisticated, and often fiery arrangements of traditional tunes for a mostly college-educated, middle-class audience. The repertoire is much the same as always, but the approach to performing Irish music is vastly different.

What is really meant by the term "traditional," then? It certainly does not mean static and unchanging; a tradition that does not evolve will quickly become extinct. To survive, musical traditions must adapt and transform while remaining rooted in a historical continuum. Certain elements of Irish music have remained constant, no matter what the venue: repertoire, ornamentation, primary instruments, and tune form. But within Irish music, there is also room for great variety. Regions of Ireland, for example, have always had prominent and distinct musical accents, and embracing this sort of diversity has helped to keep the tradition vital.

Thus, there is room within the bounds of "tradition" for musicians such as Finbar Storer, George Derrane, and Clary Walsh to play Irish hornpipes on their saxophones. Indeed, many of the Irish session instruments that no one blinks an eye at today—including the bouzouki, mandolin, banjo, guitar, and bodhran—would have been unthinkable fifty years ago. Likewise, the music of Joe Derrane—with its American-style trills tucked neatly into Irish tunes beside strictly Irish ornamentation such as cuts and rolls—is traditional. The family tree of Irish traditional music has many limbs, but it also has far-reaching roots that drink from diverse streams. As an expression of Irish cultural life, whether on the pavement in Roxbury or the spongy grass of Tipperary, the music is part of the tradition still.

In America, the Irish musical tradition may have adopted traces of an American accent, yet it remained the same, a tradition at once stable and on the move. Surrounded by their music and dance traditions, the Boston Irish could proudly sing, "We're Irish still." In the dance halls on Dudley Street, the Irish could express a newfound Boston Irish identity without having to assimilate completely.

The dance hall social environment bore many of the trappings of Irish cultural life, as well as those of an emerging ethnic identity in America. Thus, the dance halls were not so much a symbol of assimilation as a place for the Irish to meet and to celebrate Irishness within America. What mattered was not so much what was played at the halls, but rather that music was a part of social life—both for new immigrants and for their children—just as it had been in Ireland.

Irish traditional music has seen a major revival on a global scale since the last Dudley Street dance hall closed its doors. The revival was inspired by the 1960s folk revivals in both Ireland and the United States; it was later rejuvenated by the resounding successes of ensembles such as the Chieftains, as well as the Broadway gala *Riverdance*. Such commercial triumphs have had a trickle-down effect on countless musicians who play Irish music. In Boston today, accomplished musicians have little trouble finding ample venues—and often, adequate compensation—for their efforts.

Because the Dudley Street musicians have continued to play traditional music as it has come into and out of vogue, they have helped to preserve the lively music scene that has drawn generations of new Irish musicians to Boston. Joe Derrane, in his return to Irish music after nearly forty years away from the scene, says he sees a whole new market:

> Traditional Irish music has come ahead by leaps and bounds. Now, it doesn't have as widespread a market as, say, rock or country-western, but compared to what it used to be, it's a major market today. When I was doing it back in the forties, it was mostly immigrant Irish. That was pretty much your market. But today, the Irish-American segment of that market is enormous. My God, I'm doing concerts in places like Denmark, Switzerland, the Netherlands, all over Germany, France, England, Canada, Alaska, Cali-

fornia. It's unbelievable, and I'm just thrilled. It's become a very, very viable and a great market today. And I hope it continues!

While most of the musicians who kept dancers on the floor in Roxbury forty or fifty years ago keep well out of the fray of Boston's most crowded Irish pubs today—where amplified traditional music tears out of corner speakers over the din of exuberant college students—their continued presence is a part of why the younger musicians came here in the first place. From their corner spot at Boston Irish pub sessions, at monthly céilís, at family christenings, wedding anniversaries, and eightieth-birthday parties, the older generation of musicians continues to play Irish music. They remain the stalwarts of Boston's Irish music scene. One of them, Frank Storer, says:

> I have a brick from the facade of the Intercolonial Hall. It was given to me by an accordion player named Tommy Barton. It's a relic of an era. If you played or danced there, you'd know what that is. If that brick could talk. . . . If that brick could talk, it would abound in stories and fables, of stardom and people, situations, all sorts of things stored in that brick. If I walked into any of the Irish pubs in Boston and said, "Hey, would you like this piece of Dudley Street?" most would say, "Where was that?" The new young Irish musicians probably wouldn't know what Dudley Street was. But if I said that to anybody who frequented the halls of Dudley Street during its heyday, they would say, "Oh, my God, that brings back memories." They would look at it and say, "My God, the end of an era. That was an era."

Discography

Derrane, Joe. *Joe Derrane: Irish Accordion*. Copley Irish Records compact disc COP 5008, 1993.

Derrane, Joe, Frankie Gavin, and Brian McGrath. *Ireland's Harvest: A Tribute to the Golden Years of Music in Irish America*. Mapleshade Productions compact disc 09232, 2002.

Derrane, Joe, and Jerry O'Brien. *Joe Derrane and Jerry O'Brien: Irish Accordion Masters*. Copley Irish Records compact disc COP 5009, 1995.

Lamey, Bill. *From Cape Breton to Boston and Back: Classic House Sessions of Traditional Cape Breton Music 1956–1977*. Rounder Records 82161-7032-2-2000, 2000.

Landers, Terry. *At Ireland's 32*. Brandon Records, c. 1965.

Sullivan, Dan. *Dan Sullivan's Shamrock Band*. Topic sound recording 12T366, 1979.

Interviews

List of Interviews

Anonymous	Untaped interview with Susan Gedutis, Watertown, Mass., October 2, 1999.
Connolly, Éamon	Untaped interview with Susan Gedutis, Duxbury, Mass., September 2002.
Connolly, Éamon	Taped interview with Susan Gedutis, Duxbury, Mass., April 24, 2003.
Connolly, Mickey	Taped interview with Susan Gedutis, Norwood, Mass., August 9, 2002.
Cronin, Paddy	Taped interview with Susan Gedutis, Needham, Mass, November 15, 2002.
Cummings, Michael	Untaped interview with Susan Gedutis, Milton, Mass, April 24, 2003.
Derrane, Joe	Taped interview with Susan Gedutis, Randolph, Mass., November 5, 1999.
Derrane, Joe	Taped radio interview with Seamus Mulligan on "A Feast of Irish Music," WATD 95.9, October 2002.
Derrane, Joe	Untaped informal phone interview with Susan Gedutis, Plymouth and Randolph, Mass., December 19, 2002.
Derrane, Joe	Untaped formal phone interview with Susan Gedutis, Boston and Randolph, Mass., January 9, 2003.

Derrane, Joe, and Seamus Connolly   Taped interview with Brian Lawler, Boston College Interviews, Connolly House, Chestnut Hill, Mass., April 25, 2002.

Devin, Frank and Ann   Taped interview with Susan Gedutis, Framingham, Mass., October 15, 2002.

DuBeau, Ernie   Informal untaped conversation with Susan Gedutis, Plymouth and Mashpee, Mass., September 2002

Ferrel, Frank   Untaped interview and discussion, Ipswich, Mass., November 1999.

Frain, Gene   Taped interview with Susan Gedutis, Watertown, Mass., November 11, 1999.

Gannon, Joan, Patsy Hurley, and Mame O'Shaughnessy
Taped interview with Susan Gedutis, East Bridgewater, Mass., September 19, 2002.

Garvey, Thomas   Untaped phone conversation with Susan Gedutis, Waltham, Mass., July 30, 2002.

Groff, Paul   Taped interview with Susan Gedutis, Watertown, Mass., October 28, 1999.

Joyce, Joe   Taped interview with Susan Gedutis, Watertown, Mass., October 28, 1999.

Keyes, Joanne   Untaped conversation with Susan Gedutis, Winthrop, Mass., September 5, 2002.

Keyes, Liam   Taped interview with Susan Gedutis, Winthrop, Mass., September 5, 2002.

Keyes, Liam   Untaped phone conversation with Susan Gedutis, Boston and Winthrop, Mass., August 2003.

Kleinbauer, Janice (Hansen), Maureen Hansen Keohane, and Chris Hansen Knopp
Taped interview with Susan Gedutis, Canton, Mass., January 16, 2003.

Landers, Terry   Taped interview with Susan Gedutis, Melrose, Mass., January 3, 2003.

Martin, Jack   Taped interview with Jack Martin, Norwell, Mass., August 7, 2002.

McDermott, Joanne   Taped interview with Susan Gedutis, Scituate, Mass., September 3, 2002.

McDermott, Joanne   Untaped phone conversation with Susan Gedutis, Scituate, Mass., October 4, 2002.

McEleney, Connie and Mary   Taped interview with Susan Gedutis, Medford, Mass., November 2, 1999.

McGillicuddy, Nora   Untaped informal conversation with Susan Gedutis, Quincy, Mass., August 22, 2002.

McGillicuddy, Nora   Taped interview with Susan Gedutis, Roslindale, Mass., September 1, 2002.

Mulligan, Seamus   Taped interview with Susan Gedutis, Randolph, Mass., October 24, 2002.

Murphy, Mary   Untaped phone conversation with Susan Gedutis, Plymouth and Rockland, Mass., January 9, 2003.

Noonan, Paddy   Untaped phone interview with Susan Gedutis, Plymouth, Mass., and Garden City, N.J., April 28, 2003.

O'Brien, Thomas   Untaped informal conversation with Susan Gedutis on Plymouth and Brockton bus lines, from Plymouth to Boston, October 2002.

O'Connell, Anne Powell   Untaped phone conversation with Susan Gedutis, October 14, 2002.

O'Malley, Myles   Taped interview with Mick Moloney, Melrose, Mass., August 26, 1984.

Reidy, Dan and Peg   Taped interview with Susan Gedutis, Plymouth, Mass., November 17, 2002.

Reynolds, Larry   Taped interview with Susan Gedutis, Waltham, Mass., March 6, 2000.

Reynolds, Larry   Untaped interview with Susan Gedutis, Waltham, Mass., July 30. 2002.

Senier, Richard   Untaped interview with Susan Gedutis, Orange and Plymouth, Mass., April 25, 2003.

Storer, Evelyn   Part of interview with Frank Storer, Quincy, Mass., November 16, 1999.

Storer, Frank   Taped interview with Susan Gedutis, Quincy, Mass., November 16, 1999.

Tonra, Brendan   Untaped interview with Susan Gedutis, Watertown, Mass., November 18, 1999.

Toomey, Skip   Untaped phone interview with Susan Gedutis, Plymouth and Hingham, Mass., October 30, 2002.

White, Jack   Untaped conversation, Brighton, Mass., March 2000.

Lectures

Derrane, Joe

Untaped lecture, Canadian American Hall, Watertown, Mass., October 2, 1999.

Ó hAllmhuráin, Gearóid

Taped lecture, Boston College, October 6, 1999.

Savage, Robert

Untaped lecture, Boston College, February 22, 1999.

Catalog of Musicians
and Their Instruments

So many musicians define the dance hall era—whether they played at a ballroom, a music club, or at home with family and friends—that it would have taken another full volume to do their contributions justice. Many are still playing away; some have passed on. Here is a tribute to the musical contributions of many of those who lived and played in Boston from the 1930s to the 1960s—and the list is certainly incomplete:

Barton, Tommy. *Accordion.*

Bates, Carlton. *Piano and musical arranging.*

Bearse, George. *Drums.*

Birtwall, Al. *Trumpet.*

Boyle, Neilidh. *Fiddle.*

Bresnahan, Johnny ("Jackie"). *Accordion.*

Brooks, Joe. Known as "The Duke of Leinster." *Accordion.*

Caples, Billy and Johnny. *Accordion.*

Carey, Pat. *Fiddle.*

Carr, Frank. *Accordion.*

Casey, Pat. *Fiddle.*

Cavanaugh, Paddy. *Drums and accordion.*

Coakley, Sonny. *Accordion.*

Colletti, Dan. *Piano.*

Collins, Timmy. *Accordion.*

Concannon, Jackie. *Accordion.*

Connolly, John ("Tut"). *Drums.*

Connolly, Mickey. *Accordion.*

Connolly, Pat. *Fiddle.*

Connors, Bob. *Bass.*

Connors, Eva. *Accordion.*

Connors, Johnny, a.k.a. Peter Feeney, Melvin Baylis. *Piano.*

Conroy, Jack. *Accordion, and, later, flute.*

Cooley, Joe. *Accordion.*

Cooper, Charlie. *Accordion.*

Corbett, Dan. *Accordion and tin whistle.*

Coriam, Danny. *Accordion.*

Cronin, Mike. *Flute and whistle.*

Cronin, Paddy. *Fiddle.*

Curran, Paddy. *Piano.*

Daly, Leo. *Whistle and accordion.*

Deiss, Al. *Saxophone.*

Deiss, Billy. *Drums.*

Deiss, Dutchie. *Drums.*

Deiss, Walter. *Trumpet, and, later, saxophone.*

Derrane, George. *Banjo, guitar, and saxophone.*

Derrane, Joe. *Accordion.*

Diamond, Jack. *Accordion.*

Doherty, Jack. *Spoons and stomping.*

Doherty, Veronica. *Accordion.*

Doyle, Joe and Jack. Musicians from 1930s Boston.

Duffy, Eddie. *Drums.*

Elwood, Joe. *Saxophone.*

Faherty, Mike and Jim. *Accordion.*

Fahey, Martin. *Piano.*

Fahey, Mikey and Joe. *Banjo.*

Fitzgerald, Johnny. *Fiddle.*

Fitzmaurice Sisters. Step dancers who performed with O'Leary's Irish Minstrels and Emerald Isle Orchestra.

Flaherty, Martin. *Accordion.*

Flynn, Éamon. *Accordion, fiddle, whistle; composer.*

Flynn, Jim. *Accordion.*

Foley, Connie. Solo vocalist. Well known for singing Irish favorites, especially "The Wild Colonial Boy."

Foley, John. *Trumpet.*

Ford, Pat. *Accordion.*

Frain, Gene. *Piano, flute, and saxophone.*

Frain, Owen. *Flute and pipes.*

Garvey, Thomas. *Piano.*

Gildea, Frank. *Fiddle and piano.*

Glennon, Joe. *Piano.*

Hanafin, Billy. *Fiddle, pipes.*

Hanafin, Connie. *Accordion.*

Hanafin, Frankie. *Accordion.*

Hanafin, Mike. *Tin whistle and fiddle.*

Hanbury, Harry. *Fiddle.*

Hannon, Frank. *Fiddle.*

Hansen, Janice (later Kleinbauer). Stage name ("Jana Louise"). *Vocals.*

Harte, Tom. *Fiddle.*

Healy, Andy. *Piano.*

Henry, Noel. *Guitar, vocals.*

Higgins, Billy. *Piano.*

Hogan, Jimmy. *Flute and whistle.*

Irwin, Eddie, Jackie, and Richie. A musical family; children of Mary Irwin.

Irwin, Mary. *Piano.*

Joyce, Joe. *Accordion.*

Joyce, Peter. *Accordion.*

Joyce, Tommy. *Accordion.*

Jyllka, Duke. *Saxophone.*

Kavanaugh, Éamon. *Accordion.*

Kelly, Frank. *Flute.*

Kelly, Jimmy. *Piano and banjo.*

Kelly, Jimmy. *Trombone.*

Kelly, Sally (MacEachern). *Piano.*

Kelly, Tom. *Flute.*

Keough, Frank. *Accordion and spoons.*

Lamey, Bill. *Fiddle.*

Landers, George. *Tenor saxophone, guitar, vocals.*

Landers, Mike. *Tenor saxophone.*

Landers, Terry. *Accordion, saxophone.*

Lavelle, Frank. *Guitar.*

Lavelle, Vinnie. *Bass guitar and vocals.*

Leavey, Joe. *Piano.*

MacDonald, John. *Vocals.*

Maloney, Alan ("Red"). *Drums.*

Maloney, Joe. *Piano.*

Maloney, Johnny. *Banjo.*

Martin, Jack. *Accordion.*

Martin, John. *Accordion.*

Martin, Pat. *Flute.*

Martin, Tom. *Flute.*

Martus, Bob. *Bass.*

McCormick, Mickey. *Accordion.*

McDermott, Josie. *Flute, whistle, and saxophone.*

McDonnell, Tony. *Trombone.*

McDonough, Martin and Mike. *Accordion.*

McGlynn, Sean. *Accordion.*

McHale, Mike. *Flute.*

McManus, Dorothy. *Vocals.*

McNaught, Joe and Dick. *Drums.*

McSharry, Tom. *Piano.*

Mellett, Tommy. *Accordion.*

Meyers, Frankie. *Drums.*

Montgomery, Tommy. *Accordion.*

Mulholland, Dick. *Guitar.*

Murphy, Chris. *Guitar, vocals.*

Murphy, Frank. *Saxophone.*

Murphy, Johnny. *Accordion.*

Murray, Eddie. *Fiddle.*

Neylon, Frank. *Flute.*

Nolan, Niall. *Banjo (left-handed).*

O'Brien, Dermot. *Accordion.*

O'Brien, Jerry. *Accordion.*

O'Callaghan, Steve. *Drums.*

O'Connor, Fred. *Piano.*

O'Leary, Dan and Nell. *Accordion.*

O'Leary, Joe. *Fiddle.*
O'Leary, Ken. *Accordion.*
O'Malley, Joe and Pat. *Accordion.*
O'Malley, Myles ("The Whistle King").
   Saxophone and whistle.
O'Toole, Maurice. *Bass.*
Pimental, Cookie. *Drums.*
Poirier, Art. *Drums.*
Portenova, Mike. *Clarinet.*
Powell, Johnny. *Accordion.*
Preston, Gene. *Flute.*
Preston, John. *Accordion.*
Quinn, Larry. *Fiddle.*
Rabbitte, Murty. *Flute, tin whistle, and
   piccolo.*
Regan, Des. *Accordion.*
Reynolds, Larry. *Fiddle.*
Ridlon, Terry. *Guitar, vocals.*
Ryan, Tom. *Fiddle.*
Senier, Jackie. *Piano (jazz and Irish).*

Senier, Gerry. *Vocals.*
Senier, Richie ("Dick"). *Piano, flute.*
Senier, Tom. *Accordion.*
Shanley, George. *Drums.*
Shannon, Babe. *Whistle.*
Shields, Tommy. *Accordion.*
Storer, Finbar. *Soprano saxophone.*
Storer, Frank. *Piano.*
Storer, Jack. *Accordion.*
Sullen, Henry. *Piano.*
Sullivan, John. *Fiddle.*
Sullivan, Johnny. *Fiddle.*
Sullivan, Martin. *Fiddle.*
Tansey, John. *Pipe.*
Tonra, Brendan. *Fiddle, flute; composer.*
Toohy, Matty. *Accordion.*
Walsh, Clary. *Saxophone.*
Wilson, Frankie. *Banjo.*
Wynn, Joe. *Flute.*
Young, Jim. *Accordion.*

Notes

Chapter 1

1. Patrick Blessing, "Irish," in *Harvard Encyclopedia of American Ethnic Groups* (Cambridge: Harvard University Press, 1980), 526–527.

2. O'Connor, Thomas, *The Boston Irish: A Political History* (Boston: Northeastern University Press, 1995), 69.

3. Ibid., 5, 47–48; Dennis Ryan, *Beyond the Ballot Box: A Social History of the Boston Irish, 1845–1917* (Amherst: University of Massachusetts Press, 1983), 21.

4. Blessing, "Irish," 528.

5. Ibid.

6. See http://www.bostonfamilyhistory.com/neigh_roxb.html.

7. Dick Senier, personal correspondence with Susan Gedutis, May 1, 2003.

8. See the Massachusetts Bay Transportation Authority Web site, www.mbta.com/insidethet/taag_history9.asp.

Chapter 2

1. Robert Savage, notes from untaped lecture, Boston College, Newton, Mass., February 22, 1999; Blessing, "Irish," 540; Dermot Keogh, *Twentieth-Century Ireland: Nation and State* (Dublin: Gill and Macmillan, 1974), 37.

2. Blessing, "Irish," 540.

3. Mick Moloney, "Irish Music in America" (Ph.D. diss., University of Pennsylvania, 1992), 249; Mick Moloney, "Irish Ethnic Recordings and the Irish-American Imagination," in *Ethnic Recordings in America: A Neglected Heritage*, ed. Pekka Gronow (Washington, D.C.: American Folklife Center, Library of Congress, 1982), 93.

4. Moloney, "Irish Music in America," 241.

5. Francis O'Neill, *Irish Minstrels and Musicians: The Story of Irish Music* (1913; rept., Cork and Dublin: Mercier Press, 1987), 370.

6. Méabh Ní Fhuartháin, "O'Byrne DeWitt and Copley Records: A Window on Irish Music Recording in the U.S.A., 1900–1965" (M.A. diss., University College Cork, 1993), 60; Philippe Varlet, liner notes to Joe Derrane and Jerry O'Brien, *Joe Derrane and Jerry O'Brien: Irish Accordion Masters*, Copley Irish Records COP-5009, 1995.

7. Information on Jerry O'Brien's life comes courtesy of Philippe Varlet, who interviewed O'Brien's daughter for liner notes when O'Brien's original recordings were reissued on CD in 1995.

Chapter 3

1. Joe Derrane, untaped lecture, Canadian American Hall, Watertown, Mass., October 2, 1999.

2. Ibid.

3. Gearóid Ó hAllmhuráin, *A Pocket History of Irish Traditional Music* (Dublin: O'Brien Press, 1998), 37

4. Ibid., 46.

5. Ibid., 111. Ó hAllmhuráin's book includes no indication of the actual document in which this statement appeared.

6. John O. Cullinane, "Céilí Dance," and Sean E. Quinn, "Céilí Bands," and "Céilí," all in *The Companion to Irish Traditional Music*, ed. Fintan Vallely (New York: New York University Press, 1999), 60.

7. Richard ("Dick") Senier, private correspondence with the author, May 4, 2003.

8. Derrane, lecture.

9. Reebee Garofalo, *Rockin' Out: Popular Music in the USA*, (Boston: Allyn and Bacon, 1997), 73–74.

Chapter 4

1. Keogh, *Twentieth Century Ireland*, 108.

2. Ibid., 164.

3. U.S. Immigration and Naturalization Service, *Annual Report, 1975* (Washington, D.C., 1976), 62–64.

4. See http://www.historicboston.org/99cb/hibernian.htm.

5. John Boyle O'Reilly was a poet, novelist, and editor, born in Drogheda, Ireland, in 1844. As a young man he became an active supporter of Irish emancipation from British rule, but he was betrayed to the authorities, court-martialed, and sentenced to twenty years' penal servitude in Australia. In 1869 O'Reilly escaped from Australia aboard a whaling ship from New Bedford, Massachusetts. In 1870 he became editor, and later part owner, of Boston's Catholic newspaper, the *Pilot*. He was an outspoken supporter of brotherhood and tolerance for others.

6. "Ask the Globe," *Boston Globe*, May 18, 1999, A16.

7. Edwin Bacon, *King's Dictionary of Boston* (Cambridge, Mass.: Moses King, 1883), 160.

8. Derrane, lecture.

9. Buddy Stuart, "Dance Music," *Boston Sunday Post*, February 7, 1953, 5.

10. From liner notes to Bill Lamey, *From Cape Breton to Boston and Back: Classic House Sessions of Traditional Cape Breton Music 1956–1977*, Rounder Records 82161-7032-2-2000, 2000.

11. Frank Ferrel, "Introduction," in *Boston Fiddle: The Dudley Street Tradition* (Pacific, Mo.: Mel Bay Publications, 1999), 3–8.

12. Derrane, lecture.

13. Ibid.

14. Ibid.

15. Michael Quinlin, "Friends Rally for Big Martin," *Irish Echo*, December 3, 1988, 17.

Chapter 5

1. *Bog men* is a derogatory term used to describe people from rural Ireland.

2. Derrane, lecture.

3. Rebecca Miller, "Irish Traditional and Popular Music in New York City: Identity and Social Change, 1930–1975," in *The New York Irish*, ed. Ronald H. Bayor and Timothy J. Meagher (Baltimore: Johns Hopkins University Press, 1996), 494; Fintan Vallely, "Céilí Dancing," and Pat Murphy, "Set Dancing," in *The Companion to Irish Traditional Music*, ed. Fintan Vallely (New York: New York University Press, 1999), 64, 346.

4. The term *set dance* describes a set of quadrilles, extended multipart group dances taught in eighteenth-century Ireland by traveling dance masters. Sets, which tended to be more regionally known, did not flourish in America. In Boston, when people danced sets, they were abbreviated versions of the ones performed in Ireland.

5. Vallely, *Companion to Irish Traditional Music*, 433.

6. TG4, http://www.tg4.ie/english/eolas/bton.htm.

7. Ó hAllmhuráin, *Pocket History*, 122–123.

8. Miller, "Irish Traditional and Popular Music," 488.

9. Ní Fhuartháin, "O'Byrne DeWitt," 101–102.

10. Eva Connors wrote the regular "Irish Rambler" column in the *Irish World and American Industrial Liberator*.

Chapter 6

1. Blessing, "Irish," 541.

2. Dick Senier, personal correspondence with the author, May 1, 2003.

3. Derrane, lecture.

4. Paul Feeney, "Irish Memories of the Street We Loved So Well" *Boston City Paper*, April 5–11, 1997, 1–8.

Chapter 7

1. Thomas Garvey, "Dudley Street Has Fond Memories for Many of Us." *Boston Irish Reporter*, October 1976, 8–9.

2. Frank Storer, informal discussion with Susan Gedutis, Quincy, Mass., April 11, 2000.

3. Ibid.

4. Ibid.

5. Paul McDonald in liner notes to Joe Derrane, Frankie Gavin, and Brian McGrath, *Ireland's Harvest: A Tribute to the Golden Years of Music in Irish America*, Mapleshade Records 09232, 2002.

6. Michael Quinlin, "The Life and Legacy of Billy Caples," *Boston Irish Echo*, August 2, 1986, 12.

7. For musical analysis of dance hall band recordings, refer also to Ní Fhuartháin, "O'Byrne DeWitt," chap. 4, "Musicians and Their Material."

8. *Joe Derrane and Jerry O'Brien: Irish Accordion Masters*, Copley Irish Records, COP 5009, 1995. The recording features Joe Derrane and Jerry O'Brien on accordion, Joe's brother George on banjo, and Johnny Connors on piano.

Chapter 8

1. Hillel Levine and Lawrence Harmon, *The Death of an American Jewish Community: A Tragedy of Good Intentions* (New York: Free Press, 1992), 28–29.

2. Derrane, lecture.

3. Dick Senier, personal correspondence with the author, May 5, 2003.

4. Fintan Vallely, "Irish Music," in *Arguing at the Crossroads: Essays on a Changing Ireland* (Dublin: New Island Books, 1997), 156.

Chapter 9

1. Frank Ferrel and Joel Cowan, "Joe Derrane," with an introduction by Earl Hitchner, *Concertina & Squeezebox* 32 (Winter 1995), 15.

2. Helen Kisiel, "Introduction," in *The Music of Brendan Tonra* (Boston: Quinlin Campbell, 1988), vii–viii.

3. Joe Derrane, untaped phone conversation with Susan Gedutis, November 1999.

4. According to the Boston Radio Archives, WVOM debuted in Boston in 1948. In 1955 WVOM was sold to Herbert Hoffman's Champion Broadcasting and became WBOS. From that time until the present, the station has broadcast mostly foreign-language programming directed at Boston's many ethnic communities. WBOS added FM service on 92.9 MHz in the late 1950s, and as the FM station began breaking away with its own programming, Hoffman changed the AM call letters to WUNR in 1976. The new letters were meant to identify the station as a "United Nations of Radio" for Greater Boston.

5. Larry Reynolds, who has since become one of the most important figures in maintaining the strength of the Irish cultural community in Boston, now runs his own Irish music program every Saturday on behalf of Comhaltas Ceoltóirí Éireann. The program has run for more than fifteen years.

6. Brendan Tonra and Helen Kisiel, *A Musical Voyage with Brendan Tonra* (Watertown, Mass.: Mac an Rí Publishing, 2000), ii–iii.

Chapter 10

1. Philippe Varlet, liner notes to Joe Derrane, *Joe Derrane: Irish Accordion*, Copley Irish Records COP-5008, 1993.

2. Moloney, "Irish Ethnic Recordings," 90. Much of the information in this chapter comes from an interview of Justus O'Byrne DeWitt conducted by Mick Moloney on March 3, 1977. Moloney's interview is recounted in Ní Fhuartháin, "O'Byrne DeWitt."

3. Varlet, liner notes to Derrane, *Joe Derrane.*

4. Ní Fhuartháin, "O'Byrne DeWitt," 63.

5. Ibid., 70, 79.

6. Varlet, liner notes to Derrane, *Joe Derrane.*

7. Moloney, "Irish Music in America," 92.

8. Moloney, "Irish Ethnic Recordings," 94; Varlet, liner notes to Derrane and O'Brien, *Irish Accordion Masters.*

9. Ní Fhuartháin, "O'Byrne DeWitt," 69, 82.

10. Varlet, liner notes to Derrane, *Joe Derrane.*

11. Ferrel, *Boston Fiddle*, 4.

Chapter 11

1. Miller, "Irish Traditional and Popular Music," 496, 481.

2. Boston legend has it that not only was Fuller a tycoon but he also fancied himself a bit of a playboy. He is remembered to have once said, "If anybody should ask you who I am, tell them I'm the fella with all the wives."

3. Pat McDonough, liner notes to Terry Landers, *Terry Landers at Ireland's 32*, Brandon Records, c. 1965

4. Blessing, "Irish," 543.

Chapter 12

1. Thomas O'Connor, *South Boston: My Home Town* (1988; rept., Boston: Northeastern University Press, 1994), 208.

2. Ryan, *Beyond the Ballot Box*, 137.

3. Levine and Harmon, *The Death of an American Jewish Community*, 12, 22. According to Levine and Harmon, the appointment of Cardinal Richard J. Cushing changed the anti-Semitic atmosphere in Roxbury. He encouraged interdenominational understanding and took a personal interest in putting an end to the anti-Semitism that had plagued Roxbury's neighborhoods.

4. Ronald Bailey et al., *Lower Roxbury: A Community of Treasures in the City of Boston* (Roxbury, Mass.: Lower Roxbury Community Corporation and Afro Scholar Press, 1993), 15.

5. O'Connor, *Boston Irish*, 240–241.

6. Jack White, untaped conversation with Susan Gedutis, Watertown, Mass., March 5, 2000.

7. Garofalo, *Rockin' Out*, 183.

8. Levine and Harmon, *The Death of an American Jewish Community*, 71. So many Irish people went to Scituate, a small town on the coast south of Boston, that it adopted the nickname "the Irish Riviera."

9. Not his real name.

10. Anonymous.

11. Anonymous.

12. Garofalo, *Rockin' Out*, 213.

13. Levine and Harmon, *The Death of an American Jewish Community*, 142.

14. Miller, "Irish Traditional and Popular Music," 497.

Chapter 13

1. Derrane, lecture.

2. Peter Medoff and Holly Sklar, "Introduction," in Peter Medoff, *Streets of Hope: The Fall and Rise of an Urban Neighborhood* (Boston: South End Press, 1994), 1–6.

3. See http://clinton3.nara.gov/Initiatives/OneAmerica/Practices/pp_19980804.2778.html.

Conclusion

1. Gearóid Ó hAllmhuráin, taped lecture, October 6, 1999, Boston College, Chestnut Hill, Mass.

Bibliography

Abramson, Harold J. "Assimilation and Pluralism." In *Harvard Encyclopedia of American Ethnic Groups.* Cambridge: Harvard University Press, 1980.

Alarik, Scott. "An Irish Master Returns." *Boston Globe*, March 13, 1998, D18.

———. "To His Surprise, He's an Irish Music Legend." *Boston Globe*, March 12, 2000, 4.

"Ask the Globe," *Boston Globe*, May 18, 1999, A16.

Bacon, Edwin M. *King's Dictionary of Boston.* Cambridge: Moses King, 1883.

Bailey, Ronald, with Diane Turner and Robert Hayden. *Lower Roxbury: A Community of Treasures in the City of Boston.* Roxbury, Mass.: Lower Roxbury Corporation and Afro Scholar Press, 1993.

Blessing, Patrick J. "Irish." In *Harvard Encyclopedia of American Ethnic Groups.* Cambridge: Harvard University Press, 1980.

Bradshaw, Harry. "New York's Golden Age." *Irish Music Magazine* 1, no. 6 (February 1996): 18–19.

———. "New York's Golden Age, Part II." *Irish Music Magazine* 1, no. 7 (March 1996): 18–19.

Breathnach, Breandán. *Folk Music and Dances of Ireland.* 1971; rept., Cork: Ossian Publications, 1996.

Breathnach, Breandán, and Seóirse Bodley. "Ireland." In *The New Grove Dictionary of Music and Musicians.* Washington, D.C.: Grove's Dictionaries of Music, 1980.

Carolan, Nicholas. *A Harvest Saved: Francis O'Neill and Irish Music in Chicago.* Cork: Ossian Publications, 1997.

Carson, Ciaran. *Irish Traditional Music.* Belfast, Ireland: Appletree Press, 1986.

Cobb Murphy, Maureen (Hanafin), and John Latchford. "The Irish Dance Halls: Dudley Street Roxbury 1906–1963." *Mission Hill News*, March 10, 1997, 3–6.

———. "Memories of Irish Dance Halls." *The Weymouth Journal*, March 27, 1997: 12.

Conway, Katherine E. "John Boyle O'Reilly." In *The Catholic Encyclopedia, Volume XI.* New York: Robert Appleton, 1911.

Cowdery, Jim. "A Fresh Look at the Concept of Tune Family." *Ethnomusicology* 28, no.1 (1984): 495–504.

Dowling, Martin W. "Communities, Place, and the Traditions of Irish Dance Music." In *Crosbhealach an Cheiol 1996 (The Crossroads Conference): Tradition and Change in Irish Traditional Music*, edited by Fintan Vallely, Hammy Hamilton, Eithne Vallely, and Liz Doherty. Dublin: Whinstone Music, 1999.

Epstein, Dena. *Sinful Tunes and Spirituals: Black Folk Music to the Civil War*. Urbana: University of Illinios Press, 1981.

"Eugene Preston: The Dean of Music." *Treior* 20 (1998): 2, 32–33.

Feeney, Paul. "Boston's Finest Bid Farewell to the Hibernian Hall in Roxbury." *Boston City Paper*, April 12–18, 1997, 5–6.

———. "Irish Memories of the Street We Loved So Well." *Boston City Paper*, April 5–11, 1997, 1–8.

Ferrel, Frank, producer. *As Played by Joe Derrane*. 25:30 min, 1996. Videocassette.

———. "Introduction." In *Boston Fiddle: The Dudley Street Tradition*. Pacific, Mo.: Mel Bay Publications, 1999.

Ferrel, Frank, and Joel Cowan. "Joe Derrane." With an introduction by Earl Hitchner. *Concertina & Squeezebox* 32 (Winter 1995): 12–28.

Garofalo, Reebee. *Rockin' Out: Popular Music in the USA*. Boston: Allyn and Bacon, 1997.

Garvey, Thomas. "Comhaltas: Boston Chapter Includes Many Talented Musicians." *Boston Irish News*, July 1976, 2.

———. "Comhaltas Ceoltoiri Eirann: Boston Group Preserves Irish Music." *Boston Irish News*, June 1976, 3.

———. "Dudley St. Has Fond Memories for Many of Us." *Boston Irish News*, October 1976, 8–9.

———. "Irish Community Mourns Loss of Musician Johnny Caples." *Boston Irish News*, June 1976, 8.

Gertzen, Chris. "Mrs. Joe Person's *Popular Airs:* Early Blackface Minstrel Tunes in Oral Traditions." *Ethnomusicology* 35, no.1 (1991): 31–53.

Handlin, Oscar. *Boston's Immigrants 1790–1865: A Study in Acculturation*. Cambridge: Harvard University Press, 1941.

Harris, Craig. "Joe Derrane." All-Music Guide, www.allmusic.com (September 3, 2003).

Hitchner, Earl. "Boston's Booming with Irish Music." *Treior* 23 (1991): 4, 49.

Horgan, Dan. "News from Boston." *Irish World and American Industrial Liberator*, May 18, June 1, July 13, 1946, 5.

Katz, Larry. "Joe Derrane May Be the Best on Button Box, but He Had to be Coaxed Out of Retirement." *Boston Herald*, March 13, 1998, S15.

Kennedy, Frank. "Brendan Tonra at the Cultúrlann." *Treoir* 34 (Winter 2002): 20.

Keogh, Dermot. *Twentieth-Century Ireland: Nation and State*. Dublin: Gill and Macmillan, 1974.

Keohane, Kieran, "Traditionalism and Homelessness in Contemporary Irish Music." In *Location and Dislocation in Contemporary Irish Society: Emigration and Irish Identities*, edited by Jim MacGlaughlin. Cork: Cork University Press, 1997.

Kisiel, Helen Rosemary, and Brendan Tonra. *The Music of Brendan Tonra*. Boston: Quinlin Campbell, 1988.

Levine, Hillel, and Lawrence Harmon. *The Death of an American Jewish Community: A Tragedy of Good Intentions*. New York: Free Press, 1992.

Lummis, Trevor. "Structure and Validity in Oral Evidence." In *The Oral History Reader*, edited by Robert Perks and Alistair Thomson. New York: Routledge, 1998.

MacShimu, Gavin. "O'Byrne DeWitt: From Irish Music to Travel Agency." *Boston Irish Reporter*, October 1991, 27, 35.

McCullough, Lawrence E. "An Historical Sketch of Irish Traditional Music in the U.S." *Folklore Forum* 7 (1974).

———. "Irish." Part 4 of "European-American Music." In *The New Grove Dictionary of American Music*. New York: Grove's Dictionaries of Music, 1986.

———. "Irish Music in Chicago." Ph.D. diss., University of Pittsburgh, 1978.

McMahon, Sean A. *A Little Bit of Heaven: An Irish American Anthology*. Dublin: Mercier Press, 1999.

Medoff, Peter, and Holly Sklar. *Streets of Hope: The Fall and Rise of an Urban Neighborhood*. Boston: South End Press, 1994.

Meek, Bill. "Irish Instrumental Music in America." In *Songs of the Irish in America*. Dublin: Gilbert Dalton, 1978.

Miller, Rebecca. "Irish Traditional and Popular Music in New York City: Identity and Social Change, 1930–1975." In *The New York Irish*, edited by Ronald H. Bayor and Timothy J. Meagher. Baltimore: Johns Hopkins University Press, 1996: 481–507.

Moloney, Mick. "Irish Ethnic Recordings and the Irish-American Imagination." In *Ethnic Recordings in America: A Neglected Heritage*," edited by Pekka Gronow. Washington, D.C.: American Folklife Center, Library of Congress, 1982.

———. "Irish Music in America: Continuity and Change." Ph.D. diss., University of Pennsylvania, 1992.

Moloney, Mick, and Leo Sullivan. Liner notes to *Dan Sullivan's Shamrock Band*. Topic sound recording 12T366, 1979.

"Myles O'Malley, 80, Known as the 'Tin Whistle King'" (obituary). *Boston Globe*, June 28, 2000, B7.

Ní Fhuartháin, Méabh. "O'Byrne DeWitt and Copley Records: A Window on Irish Music Recording in the U.S.A., 1900–1965." M.A. thesis, University College Cork, 1993.

Ó Canainn, Tomás. *Traditional Music in Ireland*. Boston: Routledge & Kegan Paul, 1978.

O'Connor, Thomas. *The Boston Irish: A Political History*. Boston: Northeastern University Press, 1995.

———. *South Boston: My Home Town*. 1988; rept., Boston: Northeastern University Press, 1994.

Ó hAllmhuráin, Gearóid. *A Pocket History of Irish Traditional Music*. Dublin: O'Brien Press, 1998.

O'Neill, Francis. *Irish Folk Music: A Fascinating Hobby, with Some Account of Allied Subjects Including O'Farrell's Treatise on the Irish or Union Pipes and Touhey's Hints to Amateur Pipers*. Chicago: Regan Printing House, 1910.

———. *Irish Minstrels and Musicians: The Story of Irish Music*. 1913; rept., Dublin and Cork: Mercier Press, 1987.

O'Sullivan, Patricia. "The Irish Dance Halls in Dudley Square 1906–1963." *Mission Hill News*, March 10, 1997, 8.

———. "Memories of the Great Times Will Go On Forever: Boston's Irish Dance Halls, 1906–1963." *Boston City Paper*, April 5–11, 1997, 4–5.

Oliver, Paul. *Songsters and Saints: Vocal Traditions on Race Records*. New York: Cambridge University Press, 1984.

Petrie, George. "Dr. Petrie's Introduction." In *The Complete Collection of Irish Music as Noted by George Petrie (1778–1866) from the Original Manuscripts, Part One*. Edited by Charles Villiers Stanford. 1903: rept., Felinfach, Ireland: Lanerch Publishers, 1994.

Quinlin, Michael P. "An Appreciation: The Life and Legacy of Billy Caples." *Boston Irish Echo*, August 2, 1986, 12.
———. "Friends Rally for Big Martin." *Irish Echo*, December 3, 1988, 17.
———. "From Ballinasloe to Boston: Fiddle Player Larry Reynolds, a Study in Finesse." *Irish Echo*, November 24–30, 1993, 17.
———. "Irish Traditional Music in Boston." In program book from Gaelic Roots Festival 1997, Boston College, Chestnut Hill, Mass., 4.
———. "Remembering a Time at Hibernian Hall: When You and I Were Young, Maggie. . . ." *Boston Irish Reporter*, May 1997, 1, 6.
Rosenthal, Robert, Bernard Bruce, Faith Dunne, and Florence Ladd. *Different Strokes: Pathways to Maturity in the Boston Ghetto* (A Report to the Ford Foundation). Boulder, Colo.: Westview Press, 1976.
Ryan, Dennis P. *Beyond the Ballot Box: A Social History of the Boston Irish, 1845–1917.* Amherst, Mass.: University of Massachusetts Press, 1983.
———. *A Journey through Boston Irish History.* Charleston, S.C.: Arcadia Publishing, 1999, 2000.
Schramm, Adelaida Reyes. "Ethnic Music, the Urban Area, and Ethnomusicology." In *History, Definitions, and Scope of Ethnomusicology.* Edited by Kay Kaufman Shelemay. New York: Garland, 1990.
———. "Explorations in Urban Ethnomusicology: Hard Lessons from the Spectacularly Ordinary." In *International Yearbook for Traditional Music* 14 (1982): 1–14.
———. "Tradition in the Guise of Innovation: Music among a Refugee Population." In *International Yearbook for Traditional Music* 18 (1986): 91–102.
Schuller, Gunther. *The Swing Era.* New York: Oxford University Press, 1989.
Shannon, William V. *The American Irish.* New York: Macmillan, 1963.
Senier, Richard. Personal correspondence with author, May 1, 2002, and May 3, 2003.
Slobin, Mark. *Subcultural Sounds: Micromusics of the West.* Hanover, N.H.: Wesleyan University Press, 1993.
Smith, Graeme. "Modern-Style Irish Accordion Playing: History, Biography, and Class." *Ethnomusicology* 41, no. 3 (1997): 433–463.
Spradley, James P. *Participant Observation.* New York: Harcourt Brace, 1980.
Stuart, Buddy. "Dance Music." *Boston Sunday Post*, February 7, 1953.
Tonra, Brendan, and Helen Kisiel. *A Musical Voyage with Brendan Tonra, Sligo Fiddler and Composer.* Watertown, Mass.: Mac an Ri Publishing, 2000.
"Tommy Cummings Succeeds Shields on WUNR Irish Hour." *Boston Irish News*, September 1976, 2.
U.S. Immigration and Naturalization Service. *Annual Report, 1975.* Washington, D.C., 1976.
Vallely, Fintan. *The Companion to Irish Traditional Music.* New York: New York University Press, 1999.
———. "Irish Music." In *Arguing at the Crossroads: Essays on a Changing Ireland.* Dublin: New Island Books, 1997.
"William Caples, 58." (obituary). *Boston Globe*, July 12, 1986, 20.

Web Sources

Boston History Collaborative. "Roxbury." *Boston Family History*. http://www. bostonfamilyhistory.com/neigh_roxb.html (accessed September 3, 2003).

The Dudley Street Neighborhood Initiative, *One America: The President's Initiative on Race*. http://clinton3.nara.gov/Initiatives/OneAmerica/Practices/pp _19980804.2778.html (August 1998) (accessed September 3, 2003).

Halper, Donna. "Some John Shepard History." http://www.bostonradio.org/radio/ shepard.html (accessed September 3, 2003).

Historic Boston. "Hibernian Hall, Roxbury." In *Historic Boston Incorporated 1999 Preservation Revolving Fund Casebook: Property Entries Online*. http://www.historicboston. org/99cb/hibernian.htm (May 1999) (accessed September 3, 2003).

Massachusetts Bay Transportation Authority. "The Chronicle of the Boston Transit System." http://www.mbta.com/insidethet/taag_history9.asp (2003) (accessed September 3, 2003).

TG4 (Ireland's Irish language television channel). "Brendan Tonra: TG4 National Traditional Music Awards 2002—Cumadóir Ceoil TG4." http://www.tg4.ie/english/ eolas/bton.htm (September 2002) (accessed September 3, 2003).

Index

Page numbers in *italics* indicate an illustration or caption.